Between Two Rivers

I0120499

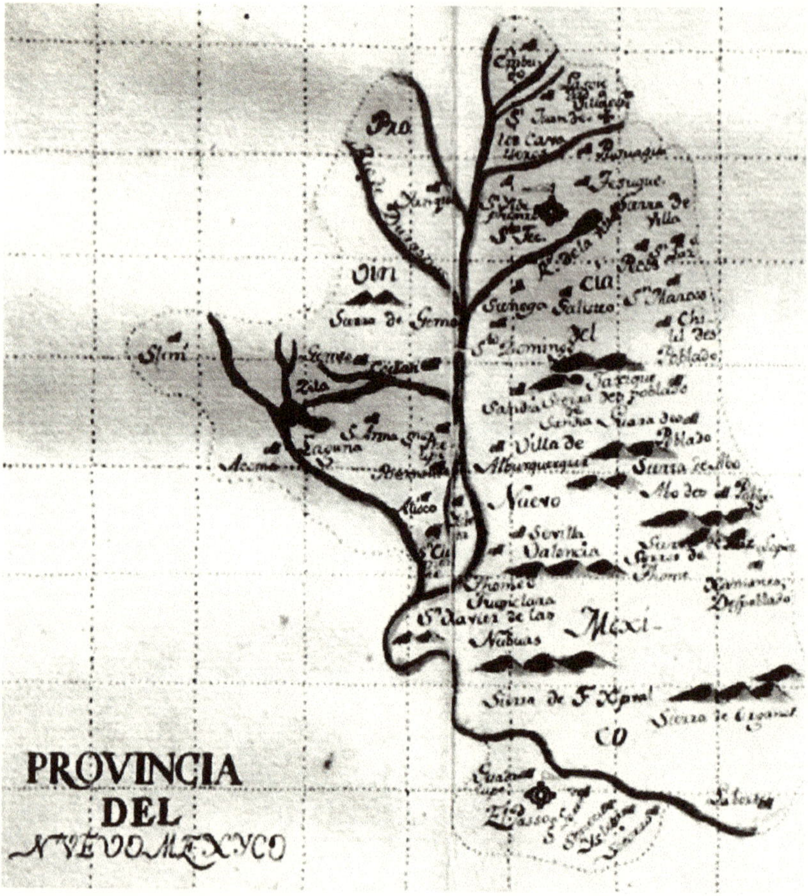

Map 1. Detail of original eighteenth-century map of New Mexico.
Atrisco is located at the center of the map.
Archivo General de Indias, Sevilla, Spain

Between Two Rivers

The Atrisco Land Grant
in Albuquerque History,
1692–1968

Joseph P. Sánchez

University of Oklahoma Press: Norman

Also by Joseph P. Sánchez
The Río Abajo Frontier, 1540–1692: A History of Early
Colonial New Mexico (Albuquerque, 1987)
(coedited with John V. Bezy) *Pecos, Gateway to Pueblos*
and Plains: The Anthology (Tucson, 1988)
Spanish Black Legend: Origins of Anti-Hispanic Stereotypes (Albuquerque, 1990)
Spanish Bluecoats: The Catalonian Volunteers in Northwestern
New Spain, 1767–1810 (Albuquerque, 1990)
(by Gaspar Pérez de Villagrá, translated and edited with Miguel Encinias
and Alfred Rodríguez) *Historia de la Nueva México, 1610: A Critical*
and Annotated Spanish/English edition (Albuquerque, 1992)
The Aztec Chronicles: The True History of Christopher Columbus, as
Narrated by Quilaztli of Texcoco: A Novella (Berkeley, 1995)
Explorers, Traders, and Slavers: Forging the Old Spanish
Trail, 1678–1850 (Salt Lake City, 1997)
(with Bruce A. Erickson and Jerry L. Gurule) *Between Two Countries: A History of*
Coronado National Memorial, 1939–1990 (Los Ranchos de Albuquerque, N.Mex.,
2007)

Library of Congress Cataloging-in-Publication Data

Sánchez, Joseph P.
Between two rivers : the Atrisco land grant in Albuquerque
history, 1692-1968 / Joseph P. Sánchez.

p. cm.

Includes bibliographical references and index.
ISBN 978-0-8061-3902-9 (hardcover) 978-0-8061- 9408-0 (paper) 1. Atrisco
(Albuquerque, N.M.)—History. 2. Albuquerque (N.M.)—History. 3. Land grants—New
Mexico—Albuquerque—History. 4. Hispanic Americans—New Mexico—Albuquerque—
History. 5. Hispanic American families—New Mexico—Albuquerque—History. 6.
Hispanic Americans—Land tenure—New Mexico—Albuquerque—History. 7. Pioneers—
New Mexico—Albuquerque—History. 8. Frontier and pioneer life—New Mexico—
Albuquerque. I. Title.

F804.A3S255 2008   978.9'61—dc22

2007049617

The paper in this book meets the guidelines for permanence and
durability of the Committee on Production Guidelines for Book
Longevity of the Council on Library Resources. ∞

Copyright © 2008 by the University of Oklahoma Press, Norman, Publishing
Division of the University. Paperback published 2024. Manufactured in the U.S.A.

All rights reserved. No part of this publication may be reproduced, stored in a retrieval
system, or transmitted, in any form or by any means, electronic, mechanical,
photocopying, recording, or otherwise—except as permitted under Section 107 or 108 of
the United States Copyright Act—without the prior written permission of the University
of Oklahoma Press.

In Memoriam

For my parents
José Patricio Sánchez and Bertha M. Sánchez

[Atrisco grant boundaries]: On the north, by the Barranca de Juan de Perea; on the east, by the Río Grande; on the south, by the lands of Antonio Baca; and on the west, by the *ceja* of the Río Puerco.

[Río Puerco grant boundaries]: On the north, by the Cerro Colorado which is located two leagues south of the San Francisco del Río Puerco; on the east, by the *ceja* of the Río Puerco Mountain; on the south, by a point three leagues south of the Cerro Colorado; and on the west, by the Río Puerco.

TOWN OF ATRISCO GRANT, OFFICE OF THE
SURVEYOR GENERAL, 1881

Now Know Ye, That the United States of America . . . have given and granted and by these presents do give and grant unto the Town of Atrisco and to their successors in interest and assigns the tract above described:

To Have and To Hold the same together with all the rights, privileges, immunities and appurtenances of whatsoever nature thereunto belonging unto the said Town of Atrisco in trust for the use and benefit of the inhabitants of said original and additional grants as their respective interests may appear, and to their successors in interest and assigns forever.

PATENT TO THE TOWN OF ATRISCO, 1905

Contents

Maps

Preface

The said plaintiff and petitioner is the lawful successor
in title and interest of the original grantees and owners
of that . . . grant made . . . in the year one thousand six
hundred and ninety-two . . . and also to that other . . .
made to the . . . settlers of said town, community and
settlement of Atrisco . . . in . . . one thousand seven
hundred and sixty-eight.

CHIEF JUSTICE JOSEPH R. REED, 1894

The said land so confirmed as aforesaid in width from north
to south, three leagues, more or less, for the entire length,
thereof from the Rio Grande to the said Rio Puerco.

CHIEF JUSTICE JOSEPH R. REED, 1894

Few places in the United States have retained the influence of Spain
and its successor government, Mexico, as strongly as the land grants in
New Mexico. The history of Atrisco offers a unique view of the role of
the land grant in a historical process shaping New Mexico's social and
cultural fabric.

My purpose in researching and compiling this account is to offer an
overview of the Atrisco land grant and the participation of its early
settlers and their descendants in the development of ranching, farming, and settlement in the area. This study considers Atrisco's part in
the evolution of Albuquerque alongside other land grants in the valley
(Pajarito, Alameda, Elena Gallegos, Ranchos de Alburquerque, Carnuel,
and the pueblos of Sandia and Isleta). The Atrisco land grant exempli-
fies various facets of a historical process including colonization, land

tenure, the settlers' social and economic activities, and legal adjudication following the Anglo American occupation of the Greater Southwest.

The evolutionary processes that defined Atrisco are evident in records of land transfers and other events occurring among heirs of settlers within the grant. Litigated disputes over ownership, sales, donations, and bequests of land culminated in the proclamation of Atrisco's status as a community land grant by the Court of Private Land Claims in 1894. By the mid-twentieth century, at least six thousand direct descendants of Don Fernando Durán y Chaves and other eighteenth-century progenitors claimed collective ownership to common lands along with their private properties within the Atrisco land grant. It is estimated that there are now more than thirty thousand descendants of the early settlers of Atrisco.

Oddly, scant literature exists to tell the Atrisco story in all its manifestations—whether as the Bosque Grande, Valle de Atrisco, Puesto de Atrisco, Atrisco Land Grant, or Town of Atrisco. To date, only two scholarly articles have been published about Atrisco, both in the *New Mexico Historical Review*: one by Richard Greenleaf, "Atrisco and Las Ciruelas" (1967), the other by *atrisqueño* land-grant heir Joseph V. Metzgar, "The Atrisco Land Grant, 1692–1977" (1977). Another (unpublished) study is a 1990 master's thesis by Eric Louis Palladini entitled "Don Fernando's Legacy: A Microhistory of Atrisco, New Mexico, 1692–1821" at Tulane University. In 1999, my own limited study in booklet form entitled *Don Fernando Durán y Chaves's Land and Legacy* was a precursor to the present volume, which attempts to give a fuller story of the Atrisco land grant and its significance to Albuquerque's rich past.

The current study is not intended to be a legal brief. Instead, it is a narrative about a people who learned to defend their heritage against all comers both inside and outside the land grant. It is a saga about intrepid pioneers and their land. Within that broad framework, their story is proof that, indeed, they lived on the land and owned it for more than three centuries. In the overarching canopy of time, stretching from the Spanish colonial epoch through Mexican sovereignty, over three hundred land grants existed in New Mexico. An impressive number of present-day Hispanic New Mexicans are descendants of land grant families and retain a special pride in their heritage.

The foundation for this study comes primarily from archival sources located in Spain, Mexico, and the United States. Much of the documentation is found in official records. For the colonial period, I relied on reports, correspondence, and land grant documents from the Archivo

General de Indias (AGI) in Sevilla, Spain; the Archivo General de la Nación (AGN) in Mexico City; the New Mexico State Records Center and Archives in Santa Fe; and other depositories. For nineteenth and twentieth century litigation, I consulted the Records of the Surveyor General and the files of the Court of Private Land Claims.[1] The latter cluster of sources contains transcriptions and translations of land grant records not only for Atrisco but also for dispositions of other land grants. For specific legal cases, I consulted the University of New Mexico Law Library.

A brief word is in order about diacritical marks, spelling, and Spanish paleography. The use of diacritical marks was not standardized during the Spanish colonial and early Mexican periods. In my text, accents comply with modern usage. In transcriptions of Spanish language texts, the original spellings are retained to reflect a faithful rendition of the words as they appear in the documents and also to convey a sense of the values of the periods under consideration. The Spanish place name of "Alburquerque," with the extra *r* in the second syllable, is the correct spelling and is used for the historic Spanish colonial and Mexican periods. The current spelling of "Albuquerque" emerged in error during the early Anglo American period and is used in chapters dealing with the post-1848 period and modern times.

Although the final responsibility for this volume rests on my shoulders, the present history of Atrisco could not have been accomplished without the assistance of a number of people and institutions. National Park Service staff at the Intermountain Spanish Colonial Research Center, located on the campus of the University of New Mexico, diligently assisted in editing portions of this work. Among them, Dr. Jerry Gurulé assisted me in surveying the collections at the New Mexico State Records Center and Archives in Santa Fe for materials related to Atrisco. Similarly, Dr. Bruce Erickson, former staff member, earned a debt of gratitude for his editorial assistance on this project. Edwina Abreu dutifully rose above the call of duty in editing an early version of this manuscript and, on her own time, prepared the appendix for this volume. Don Ramón Herrera, an important *atrisqueño* patriarch, kindly offered his ideas and shared a previously little-known document on *brincadores*, or claim jumpers, to fill a gap in the history of Atrisco. My longtime friend and colleague Dr. Félix D. Almaráz, Jr., professor of history at the University of Texas at San Antonio, is especially acknowledged for his incredible eye for detail in the editing of the penultimate copy of this volume. Matthew Bokovoy, acquisitions editor at the University of Oklahoma Press, deserves special mention for his editorial

and managerial skills in guiding the manuscript through all stages leading to its publication. Equally so, his colleague, Julie Shilling, Associate
Editor, pushed this volume forward to completion. Moreover, I wish
to acknowledge the staff at the New Mexico State Records Center and
Archives for their professionalism in assisting my research efforts. Staff
members at the Archivo General de la Nación (Mexico City) and the
Archivo General de Indias (Sevilla) were especially helpful in locating
documents related to Atrisco. Finally, I thank Peter Sánchez, Executive
Director of the Atrisco Heritage Foundation, for his generous support
in the production of the index for this publication.

JOSEPH P. SÁNCHEZ

ALBUQUERQUE, NEW MEXICO

Between Two Rivers

Introduction

> It is therefore ordered, adjudged and decreed by the court
> that the claim of the said plaintiff and petitioner to and
> for the said original and additional grants as aforesaid
> ... is hereby established and confirmed to said petitioner,
> The Town of Atrisco, in trust for the use and benefit of
> the inhabitants of said original and additional grants
> as their respective interests may appear, the said land
> so confirmed as aforesaid being in width from north to
> south, three leagues, more or less, for the entire length
> thereof from the Rio Grande to the said Rio Puerco
>
> CHIEF JUSTICE JOSEPH R. REED, 1894

Between Two Rivers is a history of the Atrisco land grant, which lies
west of Albuquerque between the Río Grande and the Río Puerco, as
it evolved from Spanish colonial times to 1968. That year, its owners transferred control of its assets to become Westland Development
Company. In 2006, Westland sold its Atrisco holdings to SunCal, a land
development company from California.

This history examines the creation of Atrisco as a frontier community
in the Spanish period (1692–1821) and Mexican period (1821–48) and
the persistence of its identity through the territorial period (1848–1912)
and statehood (1912–present). This study focuses on the continuities
and changes during the sovereignties of Spain, Mexico, and the United
States.

In 1692, Governor Diego de Vargas granted a large tract of land
known as Atrisco to Fernando Durán y Chaves in return for his help
with the reconquest of New Mexico after the 1680 Pueblo Revolt. Fourteen years later, in 1706, the Villa de San Felipe de Neri de Alburquerque
was founded. The founding of the Villa de Alburquerque has domi-
nated the history of the large valley that stretches from Isleta Pueblo in
the south to Sandia Pueblo in the north.

However, well before the arrival of Spanish settlers in the valley, pre-
historic pueblos existed there. The ruins of Piedras Marcadas in Albu-

3

querque's Río Grande Bosque are but one example of that fleeting past. The twenty thousand petroglyphs that Pueblo peoples carved into the basalt rock in the shadow of five extinct volcanoes to the west mark the spiritual boundaries of the ancient pueblos of the valley. By the mid-1600s, Spanish people had settled along the Río Grande in Alameda, Atrisco, and Pajarito. They, too, left symbolic petroglyphs on the basalt rock. The Atrisco settlements were below the southern portion of the bluff that today is visible from the intersection of Interstate 40 and the Río Grande.

Although Atrisco and Albuquerque are closely interrelated, Atrisco is undeniably older than Albuquerque. So are most places in Albuquerque's south valley—places that appeared along the Camino Real de Tierra Adentro, or Royal Road of the Interior, decades before the founding of the Villa de San Felipe de Neri de Alburquerque.

Shortly after the Villa de Alburquerque was founded, it subsumed Atrisco under the jurisdiction of its *ayuntamiento*, or municipal council. Both places were land grants, and their settlers intermingled for political, social, and commercial reasons as well as for defense. A network of settlements developed with other nearby land grants, and the Villa de Alburquerque soon became the hub for the general area.

Hispanics have continuously occupied Atrisco since 1692. That fact was its saving grace, because the Atrisco land grant that Governor Diego de Vargas conveyed to Fernando Durán y Chaves in 1692 evolved over time to resemble a community land grant. Nineteenth-century atrisqueños would argue in court that it had always been a community land grant, but they were unable or unwilling to produce the required documents. In the litigation of the 1890s, both the Atrisco and Río Puerco grants, jointly known today as the Atrisco land grant, were confirmed as one large community grant. Opposing lawyers argued that the original Atrisco grant given to Fernando Durán y Chaves in 1692 and the Río Puerco lands given to a group of atrisqueños in 1768 were nothing more than life estates conveyed to individuals, not community grants. The Río Puerco grant, however, contained special wording by Governor Pedro Fermín de Mendinueta:

> This grant of land . . . is made to the settlers of Atrisco . . . to their children and their heirs on the condition that they settle it with their livestock within the boundaries prescribed by Royal Law.[1]

Although the Río Puerco grant names specific atrisqueños as the grantees, it is evident from Mendinueta's words that he intended it to extend beyond the lifetime of the original settlers.

Governor Mendinueta also acknowledged that some atrisqueños had already attached lands from the Río Puerco to their holdings within the original Atrisco grant. He excluded their lands from the 1768 grant:

> I . . . do concede [said lands] in the name of his Majesty . . . to the settlers of the Puesto de Atrisco, with exception of those who already hold lands for ranches and pasturage of their herds, whom I exclude from this grant.[2]

One such owner of land between the *ceja* (brow or ridge) and the Río Puerco was Ana Sandoval de Manzanares, who had acquired her holdings there in 1716.[3] She and her family were among the original Spanish settlers of the Valle de Atrisco before fleeing the Pueblo Revolt of 1680. They had returned in 1692 to reclaim their lands in the valley. She is an example of how the ongoing process of bequests, sales, and other transfers caused the Río Puerco lands to become part of the larger Atrisco land grant.

Consequently, when the larger Atrisco land grant was adjudicated by the U.S. Court of Private Land Claims in 1894, the atrisqueños prevailed in their claim to both grants. They were able to show, through documented genealogical lines and historical land transfers, that they were descendants of the original settlers of the Atrisco and Río Puerco units. After all, their families had lived on both grants since 1692 and 1768, respectively. On September 4, 1894, the Court of Private Land Claims recognized the community grant characteristics of the "Atrisco Land Grant." The evolutionary historical process leading to that decision is narrated in this study.

That the original Atrisco land grant predates the founding of Albuquerque seems to have been buried in time and almost forgotten. Most Albuquerqueans know Atrisco only as the South Valley. To some, a long street called Atrisco that runs north-south through Albuquerque serves as the only reminder of that place name. Yet, any good map of Albuquerque still designates the Town of Atrisco as a historical entity.

Decades before Governor Diego de Vargas granted land to Fernando Durán y Chaves in 1692, Spanish settlers had already begun moving into the Valle de Atrisco. Legal descriptions of the time were based on physical attributes of the area. Juan de Perea, who lived on the bluff overlooking the Río Grande, was one of the early settlers in the area prior to the Pueblo Revolt of 1680. The original land grant from Vargas cited Perea's house as one of the northern corner markers. Thus, the "Barranca de Juan de Perea," on the bluff on Albuquerque's west side near where present Interstate 40 crosses the Río Grande, is noted in the land grant's legal description. Perhaps it is time to resurrect that name out of pride in the city's historical past.

Albuquerque's western horizon, known historically as La Ceja del Río Puerco, formed another boundary marker. The first land grant in 1692 ran west from the Río Grande to this ridge. The second land grant in 1768 ran further west from the ridge to the Río Puerco. The Atrisco lands were bounded on the south by other land grants such as Pajarito and Isleta, and on the north by Alburquerque, Ranchos de Alburquerque, Los Poblanos, and Alameda.

Roads constituted important elements of legal descriptions, particularly in Atrisco. The Camino Real de Tierra Adentro ran along present Isleta Boulevard on the west bank of the Río Grande. The road passed through Los Chávez, Pajarito, Armijo, and Atrisco, among other settlements; crossed the river near the present-day Central Avenue bridge; and continued toward Albuquerque's Old Town. In 2000, the U.S. Congress designated the Camino Real portion within the United States to be a National Historic Trail. The New Mexico portion of the Camino Real was blazed from Santa Bárbara (in present-day Chihuahua) by Juan de Oñate in 1598 and, after crossing the Río Grande at El Paso, ran to New Mexico's first capital at San Juan de los Caballeros. Santa Fe became the terminus of the Camino Real in 1609 when the capital of New Mexico was moved there. Atrisco, like hundreds of places between Mexico City and Santa Fe, is part of the litany of place names linked to form the Camino Real de Tierra Adentro.

After Spain was ousted in the independence movement ending in 1821, Atrisco existed quietly under Mexican sovereignty for the next twenty-seven years. Then, in 1848, as the United States absorbed New Mexico by war and treaty, Atrisco's ability to survive was again tested. Atrisco has tenaciously met all challenges to its title under the legal systems of three cultures: Spanish colonial, Mexican, and Anglo American.

The people of Atrisco, like other old New Mexico families, are of a hearty frontier stock. In the first 130 years of their history, they adapted to the challenges of settling and expanding their land grant. During this initial period, the people of Atrisco consolidated their interests in ranching, farming, and trade. They also endured the stress of a Spanish legal tradition of land tenure and protected their holdings against other settlers inside and outside of the land grant. In numerous ways, Atrisco contributed to the complex Hispanic cultural life and history of New Mexico.

Among the legendary Hispanos with roots in Atrisco were José

María Chaves and his brother, Julián Chaves, from Abiquiu. Their father, Francisco Antonio Chaves, was born in Atrisco. José María and Julián were direct descendants of Fernando Durán y Chaves. José María (1801–1902) built and lived in, until his death at more than a hundred years old, a house in Abiquiu known today as the Georgia O'Keeffe House. He served in the New Mexico militia under Spain and Mexico, and later under the United States during the territorial period. His brother, Julián, is remembered in the name Chavez Ravine, an area of Los Angeles that became the site of the old Dodger Stadium.

Both men participated in historical events in New Mexico and California. In the Rebellion of 1837, the brothers sided with Governor Albino Pérez in a lost cause. After the death of Governor Pérez, they and other supporters fled over the Old Spanish Trail from New Mexico to California. There the two brothers became involved in the California rebellion against Mexican authority, were captured in a gun battle, and were later released. Julián remained in California, dabbled in politics, and became a well-known landowner. During the 1840s, Brigadier General José María Chaves was instrumental in the pacification of southern Colorado against Utes, Comanches, and Apaches, which resulted in the settlement of the San Luis Valley by New Mexicans.[4] In his later years, José María, known as "El General," served in the New Mexico territorial legislature and as a probate judge in Rio Arriba County.[5] Atrisco abounds with such tales about individuals who participated in the history of the land grant.

After independence from Spain in 1821, residents of Atrisco, like those in other Hispanic areas in the Greater Southwest, adjusted to Mexican nationhood. Although much is known about broad historical trends during the period, how those trends worked at a local level in the Greater Southwest has been little studied for communities such as Atrisco. The Mexican period served as a transition for the next cycle of change, annexation as a U.S. territory in 1848. Hispanics in the Greater Southwest faced new problems as they adapted to a new government with cultural values based on English traditions and practices. Those changes culminated in the present contemporary society after New Mexico gained statehood in 1912.

Conditioned by their lengthy colonial experience, the people of Atrisco and other New Mexicans—men, women, and children alike—emerged as resilient, pragmatic, and largely self-directed frontier people. They contended with the arid topography, resisted warring tribes, struggled against certain avaricious newcomers from the United States, and adjusted their allegiance to two new sovereigns—first Mexico and then the United States—within a span of twenty-seven years (1821–1848).

Historically farmers and ranchers, Hispanic settlers cultivated wheat, corn, chili, potatoes, squash, grapes, and a variety of fruit trees—apple, peach, apricot, and cherry. They often dried foods to preserve them. In 1812, Pedro Baptista Pino bragged that "in New Mexico all the same crops are harvested that one finds in Spain, and they are much better quality than those grown in the rest of New Spain. In no other country of America (so travelers say) will you find wine with the taste and strength of ours."[6] New Mexicans gathered *piñón* nuts from the foothills and salt from saline deposits.

They excavated and maintained *acequias*, or irrigation ditches, that extended for miles from nearby streams. This ingenious method of diverting water to regulate and sustain basic natural resources helped assure the occupation and maintenance of their settlements. Acequias such as those found within Atrisco's historical perimeter defined a distinct place, forming community boundaries and entailing a rustic local technology to maintain them. Acequias also defined the social hierarchy required to maintain and regulate their use. Indeed, the acequia system created a requisite lifeline to sustain land tenure firmly for future generations. Other land-use practices similarly manifested deep roots in Spanish legal traditions.

Aside from farming, settlers raised herds of sheep, goats, cattle, horses, oxen, and mules in accordance with the Spanish Laws of the Indies and regulations established by the Mesta, an association of livestock owners that monitored transhumance, branding, pasturage, water easements, and breeding contracts.[7] Although the Mesta did not exist as a formal guild in New Mexico, its legal influence nonetheless constrained branding and herding there and throughout the Spanish Empire.

New Mexicans also supplemented their diet by other means. Settlers fished along local rivers and hunted in the mountains, plains, and mesas for small and large game, including quail, rabbits, partridges, wild turkeys, elk, deer, bears, buffalo, and mountain goats. As traders, they ranged far from home to exchange produce, leather goods, and animals for whatever items the outlying tribes had to barter. New Mexicans later participated in the two-way trade with the United States along the Santa Fe–Chihuahua Trail.

Like other New Mexicans, atrisqueños traveled along the Camino Real de Tierra Adentro, a network of trails fifteen hundred miles long connecting Mexico City with Santa Fe. During the Spanish colonial period, they hired on as guards and guides along the entire length of the Camino Real, part of which ran through Atrisco. The Camino Real was at once a trade and migration route. Along it traveled a pageant of colonial society, including friars, settlers, soldiers, American Indians, traders, governors, and a myriad of others.

Relationships formed during peacetime trading allowed Hispanic frontier people and American Indian tribes a period of truce to rescue their kin who had been captured and enslaved by either side in raids or war. Sometimes, captives could be ransomed or traded at annual *rescates* (trade fairs) at Taos, Pecos, Galisteo, or Las Salinas. As a community of frontier folk, the inhabitants of Atrisco, like other New Mexicans, defended their homes against marauders or intruders—Spanish or Indian, and later, Anglo American.

At home, in their quiet moments, New Mexicans prayed fervently, attended church, and performed domestic chores. They made their own clothes; preserved food; played musical instruments; narrated *chistes* (jokes), *cuentos* (folktales), and *dichos* (popular sayings); and tended to the family. The settlers helped each other construct houses and corrals. They gathered at the church for baptisms, weddings, and processions. On sad occasions such as funerals, they comforted the bereaved at cemeteries located within the confines of the land grant. Although many had chapels or altars in their homes, atrisqueños generally attended mass at San Felipe de Neri in the Villa de Alburquerque.

In the latter part of the twentieth century, Atrisco found itself in the middle of another historical challenge: urban development. Today, development of Albuquerque's west side implies much more than the construction of houses and roads; it is about caring for our national patrimony as the city expands. The preservation of that patrimony, and its intrinsic value, is tied to open spaces on the west mesa. Vacant lands on the west side are rapidly shrinking. However, some of the cultural resources on Albuquerque's west side that reflect historic land use by Hispanics—particularly the people of Atrisco—who lived along the Río Grande are being saved. Adjoining the northern boundary of the town of Atrisco is Petroglyph National Monument. In commemoration of Atrisco's cultural legacy, the southern portion of the monument is referred to as the Atrisco Unit. A portion of the Atrisco Unit was once part of the Atrisco land grant. Therefore, a small part of the Atrisco land grant will be preserved in perpetuity. In partnership with the City of Albuquerque, Petroglyph National Monument preserves and protects important elements of our Hispanic and indigenous past, inclusive of its spiritual significance to the many tribes that have used the area for such purposes. It is, indeed, a sacred place.

By the mid-twentieth century, the lands that formed the present

Petroglyph National Monument and the Atrisco grant were threatened by an encroaching city that should be as mindful of its past as it is about its future. Albuquerque's identity symbolically comprises the Sandia-Manzano mountain ranges to the east, the Río Grande Valley and wooded *bosque* in the center, and the volcanic mesa to the west. Aside from Atrisco, at least fifteen historic land grants stretch between the mesa and the mountain. Among them are Angostura, Alameda, Albuquerque (Old Town), Algodones, Bernalillo, Carnuel, Los Duranes, Elena Gallegos, Las Huertas, Isleta Pueblo, Pajarito, Los Poblanos, Ranchos de Albuquerque, Sandia Pueblo, Santa Ana Pueblo, and a few others long forgotten. They share a common history with Atrisco. Perhaps atrisqueños and other land grant heirs in the vicinity who have been equally adept at preserving their heritage have one more mission: the preservation of the national patrimony that the west side of Albuquerque represents.

The land grant phenomenon provides *Nuevo Mexicanos*—the descendants of Spanish and Mexican settlers—with a continuing legacy and cultural identity. Notwithstanding pressures and temptations to acculturate and assimilate, extant land grant communities in New Mexico and the Greater Southwest were, and continue to be, well-defined historic societies. The cultural heritage of all land grant heirs has long been under siege. *Tierra y agua*—land and water—are part of the patrimony.

CHAPTER 1

The Valle de Atlixco, 1540–1681

> We marched to a river which we named Nuestra Señora,
> because we reached it on the eve before her feast in the
> month of September. . . . This Nuestra Señora river flows
> through a broad valley planted with fields of maize. There
> are some cottonwood groves.
>
> HERNANDO DE ALVARADO AND
> FRAY JUAN DE PADILLA, 1540

The Río Grande Valley that runs through the city of Albuquerque was once home to Tiwa Indians. In the late sixteenth century, early Spanish explorers knew it both as the Valle de Tiguex and the Valle de Puaray. It is not known who first applied the place name "Atrisco" or "Atlixco" to the valley. The name derives from the Nahuatl word *atlixco* (also spelled *atlixo*), literally meaning "surface of a body of water."[1] An older place by that name exists in the central valley of Mexico and came into historical view following the conquest of Tenochtitlán by Hernán Cortés in 1521. The town of Atlixco, which sent tribute to Cortés, is located approximately twenty miles north of Izúcar in the present state of Puebla.[2]

Gilberto Espinosa and Tibo Chavez speculate that the name appeared in New Mexico early in the seventeenth century. "Across the river [from present Albuquerque]," they write, "was a settlement known as Atlixco (later Atrisco). Atlixco, in the Nahua language, means 'near the waters.' Probably the vicinity was originally settled by the Mexican Indians who accompanied Oñate from the valley of Atlixco, in Mexico."[3] However, there is no record that Mexican Indians or anyone from Juan de Oñate's 1598 expedition to New Mexico settled the valley at that time, unless a few stayed behind with Pueblo peoples living in the valley. Nahua-speaking Mexican Indians had accompanied expeditions to New Mexico as translators, auxiliaries, camp tenders, and burden bearers in 1540, as well as the 1580s and early 1590s. Tlaxcalans who accompanied Oñate could have given the valley its name as they passed through. The place name may have appeared then in the spoken word, if not the written word. Certainly, after Santa Fe was established in 1609, Tlaxcalans settled there in the Barrio de Analco, another Nahua place name. At any rate, during the seventeenth century a segment of the Bosque Grande between Bernalillo and Isleta became known as the Valle de Atrisco.

In 1540, Captain Hernando de Alvarado, a member of the expedition led by Francisco Vázquez de Coronado, made the first European sighting of the valley. Standing on the edge of a mesa just north of the extinct volcanoes that overlook present-day Albuquerque, Alvarado and his men, accompanied by Franciscan friar Juan de Padilla, looked down on a large valley that stretched from north to south as far as the eye could see. Through it ran the Río Grande, "which we named Nuestra Señora, because we reached it on the eve before her feast day in the month of September."[4] Along the river valley was a large Pueblo Indian settlement known as Tiguex. Soon after Alvarado's sighting of the valley, Coronado's large expeditionary force joined them, camping on the north end of the valley, near present Bernalillo, in the winter of 1540–41. During that time, hostilities known as the Tiguex War broke out between the Spaniards and the Pueblo people of Moho, Arenal, and Alcanfor in the valley. The Spaniards conquered, but did not settle, the valley.

Forty years after Coronado's expedition, a second expedition (1581–82) of soldiers and missionaries passed through the valley, led by Francisco Sánchez Chamuscado. They followed the Río Grande north from Santa Bárbara, near Parral in present-day Chihuahua. Continuing their march, they visited pueblos along the way until they came to the southern end of the valley, where present-day Albuquerque is situated on both sides of the Río Grande. There the group rested before proceeding north along the river. Hernán Gallegos, a chronicler of the Sánchez Chamuscado expedition, wrote,

> We halted two days in order to inform ourselves of what there was farther inland, so that we might continue our journey. There we learned more of what was in the interior, and that it was thickly populated, news of which gave us much satisfaction. . . . The people [in the valley] sustain themselves on corn, beans, and calabashes. They make tortillas and corn flour gruel [atole], have buffalo meat and turkeys—they have large numbers of the latter. There is not an Indian who does not have a corral for his turkeys, each of which holds a flock of one hundred birds. The natives wear Campeche-type cotton blankets, for they have large cotton fields. They raise many small shaggy dogs—which, however, are not unlike those owned by the Spaniards—and build underground huts in which they keep these animals.[5]

All along the river valley, the Spaniards encountered people who spoke various languages but followed a similar way of life. The Spaniards discerned only subtle differences between the Piros of the southern Río Grande in New Mexico and the Tiwas in the Albuquerque area. Gallegos noticed that all of the pueblos grew corn, beans, calabashes, and cotton. The Indians also made corn tortillas and atole as well as pottery and blankets.⁶ The pueblos they described were generally two, three, and four stories high, and the distinctions the Spaniards made were based on size. "The further one goes into the interior," wrote Gallegos, "the larger are the pueblos and the houses, and the more numerous the people."⁷ The Sánchez Chamuscado expedition named the Valle de Puaray after a prominent Tiwa pueblo in the valley; the mountain became known as the Sierra de Puaray.

Sánchez Chamuscado and his soldiers left the Río Grande pueblos and returned to Santa Bárbara, leaving missionary priests to convert the people of Puaray. Shortly thereafter, Tiwa warriors from Puaray killed the missionaries. The hope that they were still alive prompted Spanish officials to order another expedition northward.

In 1582–83, an expedition from Santa Bárbara led by Antonio de Espejo entered New Mexico. By late February 1583, after three months of travel, Espejo and his men reached Puaray. They were impressed with the number of pueblos, which stretched from one end of the valley to the other. There they learned that the Tiwas had killed the missionaries. Puaray had been abandoned, wrote Diego Pérez de Luján, a chronicler of the expedition. "The inhabitants of all these settlements had fled to the sierra because all had taken part in killing the friars. Some Indians soon came to find out what we wanted to do and we sent them to bring the others in peace."⁸ Espejo and seven men went to the sierra to bring the people back. Some came down, and by means of signs they agreed to return to their pueblos because their families were suffering greatly from the cold weather. Still, many refused to return for fear of Spanish reprisal. The memory of the Coronado expedition's attack on Moho, Arenal, and Alcanfor four decades earlier was still fresh in the lore of the people of Puaray.

The Spaniards inspected many of the abandoned pueblos and provisioned themselves with corn, beans, green and sun-dried calabashes, and other vegetables as well as roosters and hens. They also took some pottery to use. Perhaps to draw the Spaniards away from Puaray, Indians from other pueblos came with gifts and offered information about faraway provinces.⁹ Like Sánchez Chamuscado, Espejo presented information that would later attract Spanish settlers to New Mexico. In 1598, Juan

Pérez de Oñate led a large caravan of Spanish settlers north from Santa Bárbara to New Mexico. They settled at the confluence of the Chama and Río Grande rivers near San Juan Pueblo, but the settlements eventually expanded south, first to Santa Fe, then to the Valle de Atrisco. After the founding of Santa Fe in 1609, Spanish settlements began to dot the New Mexican map from Taos Pueblo in the north to the incipient settlement later known as El Paso del Norte in the south.

Documentation regarding the earliest Spanish settlements in the Valle de Atrisco is at best vague and fragmentary. In 1659, for example, a reference was made to a short-lived cattle ranch called Pajarito on the southern end of the Valle de Atrisco near Isleta Pueblo. The origins of Pajarito are nebulous, but it seems to date to the early 1640s. According to testimony given in a case against Governor Bernardo López de Mendizábal, a certain Franciscan friar named Salazar had dispossessed Indians of farmland around Isleta Pueblo in 1643.[10] Subsequently, Isletans began farming near the mountains, but Apache raiders made it quite dangerous to do so, and some Isletans were killed while farming there. One Isletan protested the Spanish occupation by cultivating a piece of land not far from Isleta that was claimed by a mestizo named Ramírez. Soon thereafter, a Franciscan claimed the land on behalf of a woman friend with six or eight children and established a stock ranch there called Pajarito. The family, known as los Gracias, was probably related to Andrés de Gracia from the El Paso area.[11] The land was about a league north of Isleta and was used for raising crops and herding.[12] By the eighteenth century, the area bore the name Puesto de San Isidro de Pajarito.

In the 1660s, Spanish officials considered settling the Valley of Atrisco. After the unsuccessful pacification of Quivira, which he claimed to have undertaken on his expedition to the Great Plains in 1662, Governor Diego Dionisio de Peñalosa Briceño y Berdugo planned to settle the Valle de Atrisco with twelve families. He testified that he had "attempted to found a *villa* in the midst of the settled region, in a valley called Atrisco, this being the best site in all New Mexico. [He] drew up an order to this effect, and twelve or fifteen persons who offered to make the settlement signed it with him on Pedro Varela's farm."[13] Whether the order was carried out is not clear, but the act may have empowered certain frontiersmen, possibly the likes of Juan de Perea and Juan Domínguez de Mendoza, to proceed with establishing farmlands in the area.

Spanish colonials, including farmers and ranchers, had settled in Atrisco decades before the Pueblo Revolt of 1680. It is likely that the Durán y Chaves family and others owned estates in that part of the Río Abajo (the Río Grande between Cochiti Pueblo and Socorro) as early as the 1660s.

Just below Cochiti, several haciendas also had been established along the river between present Bernalillo and Belen in the mid-seventeenth century. Following the Pueblo Revolt, Fernando Durán y Chaves returned to inspect and reclaim ancestral lands from Bernalillo in the north to the southern terminus of Atrisco, north of Isleta Pueblo, between 1681 and 1703.[14]

Spanish colonial documents recount the cold wind and snow that swept the Río Grande Valley in late November 1680, when Governor Antonio de Otermín marched north from El Paso to the Río Abajo, near what is now Albuquerque, with 130 soldiers, 112 Indian allies, and several priests. Their mission was to survey the destruction of New Mexico resulting from the Pueblo Revolt of that year. Having lost Santa Fe, the provincial capital, to rebelling Pueblo Indians in August, Otermín and approximately 2,500 Spaniards had abandoned New Mexico and settled in two refugee camps at El Paso.[15] Now, three months later, Otermín led the first of many sorties in an attempt to reconquer New Mexico, a quest that took twelve years. Their path from El Paso led to Atrisco and beyond.

During this journey, Otermín ordered one of his captains, Juan Domínguez de Mendoza, to take sixty mounted men and a number of Indian allies and reconnoiter the land north of Alameda as far as Cochiti.[16] Departing from Isleta, Domínguez de Mendoza first paused to survey the damage done to his hacienda in the Valley of Atrisco. Braving chilling winds and snow, he reached the hacienda on December 13.[17] One member of Domínguez de Mendoza's party wrote that the day

> dawned with extreme cold and a fierce hailstorm with pounding winds that blew all night and all day. Nonetheless, we marched to the estancia of the Maestre de Campo Juan Dominges [sic], three leagues away, where we found six estancias of Spanish settlers in this district deserted and burned and the cultivated fields full of stubble from the cut corn which the apostate traitors had gathered availing themselves of the lands which the settlers had possessed before the uprising.[18]

Domínguez de Mendoza himself corroborates the evidence that his hacienda was in the Valley of Atrisco.[19] He and his men "marched that night to his own hacienda, which was in the jurisdiction that they call Atrisco, three leagues this side of the pueblo of Alameda."[20] Their stay was short, lasting only long enough for the men to warm themselves by the fire. The rest of the march took place in the Valley of Atrisco somewhere between Isleta and Alameda. Proceeding with "all vigilance and secrecy," Domínguez de Mendoza arrived at the pueblo of Alameda at dawn and found it deserted except for "a lone Indian who had hanged himself," perhaps in despair at being left behind, or perhaps hanged by his people because he may have threatened to betray them to the Spaniards.[21]

In the next few days, Domínguez de Mendoza led his men past Sandia and San Felipe, where destruction met their eyes at every turn. Curiously though, he could not but notice that in the deserted pueblo houses, the natives of Sandia and San Felipe had kept some of the liturgical accoutrements taken from the churches of their former Christian priests.

In mid-December, Domínguez de Mendoza and his men camped a short distance from the rebel stronghold at Cochiti Pueblo. There they attempted to speak with the rebellious factions composed of many warriors from different pueblos. Despite peaceful overtures on both sides, Domínguez de Mendoza noted the hostility of one warrior faction and decided to leave before he was attacked. On December 19, after eleven days of scouting the area as ordered by Otermín, Domínguez de Mendoza returned to make his report to his commander, who was now camped at Alameda. Otermín had seen and heard enough, and decided that it was best to return to El Paso before he could be attacked. The Spaniards had caught their first glimpse of the province in revolt.[22] Entering the large valley south of Alameda, the small army followed the Río Grande, thus passing through the Valley of Atrisco on their return to El Paso. They would be back.

CHAPTER 2

The Durán y Chaves Claim to Atrisco and Angostura, 1681–1706

It shall be the will of the King, our Master, that this kingdom shall be settled, the said Don Fernando de Chaves shall be one of the settlers, and if he does not do this then this grant shall be void since I make it with this qualification and condition jointly with all his children and he shall enjoy the privileges of conqueror and settler and in order that it may so appear in favor of the said Don Fernando de Chaves, I signed it with the Civil and Military Secretary.

DON DIEGO DE VARGAS

Although the Valle de Atrisco was sparsely settled in the seventeenth century, farmlands along the Río Grande between Angostura and the Valle de Atrisco were beginning to attract settlers. Among them was *sargento* Pedro Gómez Durán y Chaves I, who had arrived in New Mexico in 1598 with Juan de Oñate's expedition. He was a native of Llerena, Extremadura, Spain. Although he claimed to have been one of the founders of the Villa de Santa Fe in March 1609, he was at Acapulco in February of 1610, taxing the cargo of a ship fitted for a voyage to the Philippines.[1] Indeed, many New Mexican frontiersmen were frequently absent from New Mexico as they hired themselves out as military escorts for trade caravans along the Camino Real de Tierra Adentro that connected Mexico City and Santa Fe.

One of the first incidents in which Pedro Gómez Durán y Chaves is mentioned occurred in May 1613, when Governor Pedro de Peralta entrusted him, along with Captain Pedro Ruíz, Gaspar Pérez, and others, with the collection of tribute at Taos Pueblo. They were to collect the annual tribute of corn and blankets. Passing through Nambe Pueblo, north of Santa Fe, they were intercepted by Father Isidro Ordóñez, prelate of the Franciscan order, who demanded that they return to Santa Fe to hear mass for the feast of the Pentecost. When they arrived in Santa Fe, the governor ordered them back on the trail to collect the tribute. Governor Peralta and Father Ordóñez met in the plaza and publicly argued over the matter.[2] The incident ignited a fierce struggle between civil and church authorities in New Mexico that would last for the rest of the seventeenth century.

For his military service in the Jémez Campaign of 1623, Pedro Durán y Chaves was promoted to *sargento mayor*. By 1626, he was *maese de campo*, field marshal in the Province of New Mexico. His wife was Isabel Baca de Bohórquez, about age forty. Isabel owned an hacienda at Arroyo del Tunque near San Felipe Pueblo. She appears to have been his second wife, "since she was some twenty years younger."[3] The date of death for Pedro Gómez Durán y Chaves is unknown.

His oldest son, Fernando Durán y Chaves I, inherited his *encomienda*, the right to collect tribute from a group of people in a specific locale under Spanish rule. During the late 1630s, Fernando Durán y Chaves served as lieutenant governor of the Río Abajo jurisdiction. In 1638 he accompanied Governor Luis de Rosas (1637–41) on an expedition to the Apotlapihuas in Sonora. Rosas was later murdered by conspirators in Santa Fe.

Fernando Durán y Chaves lost his encomienda during a political falling-out with the new governor, Alonso Pacheco de Heredia (1642–44).[4] Durán y Chaves had supported the friars in a struggle against the deceased governor Rosas. When the friars turned against the new governor, Durán y Chaves continued to side with them. For that, he earned the enmity of Governor Pacheco, who accused him of sedition. Durán y Chaves lost his encomienda when he fled New Mexico to avoid persecution and possibly execution.[5]

Durán y Chaves waited for the chance to return to New Mexico. When Captain Don Fernando de Argüello Carvajal, the appointee for the office of governor and captain general of New Mexico, was arrested for offenses against the crown, Spanish officials immediately appointed Luis Guzmán to that position and ordered him to his new post in New Mexico.[6] Durán y Chaves seized the opportunity to serve as a member of his armed escort.

From time immemorial, it had been the custom for officials to nominate frontiersmen residing in Mexico City to serve as guards and scouts on caravans traveling along the four major *caminos reales* leading from Mexico City to Veracruz, Acapulco, Guatemala, and New Mexico. Preference was generally given to frontiersmen who lived, or had lived, along a given route. In 1646, five of the fourteen men selected to escort Governor Guzmán were identified as New Mexicans.

In October 1646, the fugitive Fernando Durán y Chaves and several other frontiersmen who happened to be in the colonial capital of Santa Fe responded to the call to serve on an *escolta* or escort on the caravan bound from Mexico City to New Mexico. He and thirteen others were selected by the newly appointed governor Guzmán and the Franciscan custodian fray Tomás Manso to guard them and the mission supply caravan on the arduous and dangerous Camino Real de Tierra Adentro—a distance of nearly fifteen hundred miles. Fernando Durán y Chaves, Agustín de Chaves, Francisco Hurtado, Nicolás de Alcantará, Lorenzo de Solís, Lucas de Cubía Pacheco, Francisco de Aragón, Pedro Bentura de Gracia, Pedro Francisco Domínguez, Andrés de Loaissa, and Manuel Suárez were selected and offered 300 pesos each.[7] They formed the escolta under the command of 36-year-old captain Francisco López Palomino from Santa Fe, who had volunteered to return with the caravan because his wife and children were in New Mexico.[8] He replaced Alcantará, who could not make the trip, as captain of the escolta. At the last minute, Pedro Montoya volunteered to go on the caravan, completing the number of men in the escolta, which had been left one man short by Alcantará's departure. Montoya was paid 230 pesos. Indeed, Durán y Chaves had found a way to return to New Mexico in good standing.

By 1646, Fernando Durán y Chaves had returned to New Mexico under the administration of Governor Luis de Guzmán. It appears that the governor granted him amnesty for his service on the escolta. Under Governor Guzmán, his luck appeared much improved. His good fortune probably saved his brother Pedro's life. Pedro Durán y Chaves II had been involved as a conspirator in Governor Rosas's death. In 1642, Pedro was one of four masked men who had accompanied the assassin Nicolás Ortiz to the Palace of the Governors to murder Rosas. For his complicity in the assassination, Governor Guzmán (probably influenced by Fernando) banished Pedro from New Mexico, thus sparing him harsher punishment. Pedro, however, later returned.

Pedro married Elena Domínguez de Mendoza, the daughter of Tomé Domínguez de Mendoza and niece of the same Juan Domínguez de Mendoza who owned land in Atrisco (see chapter 1). In 1663, Pedro ran afoul of Governor Peñalosa and was imprisoned in the Palace of the Governors. Pedro had become embroiled in an issue regarding cattle, and a warrant was issued for his arrest. He avoided arrest by claiming the right of sanctuary in the church at Santo Domingo. Undaunted, Governor Peñalosa, in violation of the right of sanctuary, removed Pedro from the church and incarcerated him with his brother Fernando and Fernando's son Cristóbal in the Palace of the Governors. All three survived the ordeal.

Aside from their military backgrounds, Fernando and Pedro were large landowners with holdings in the Sandia jurisdiction that extended from San Felipe Pueblo to the southern end of the Valle de Atrisco. Pedro Durán y Chaves's land was described as being in the Valle de Atrisco, "four leagues north of Isleta." In 1680, when the Pueblo Revolt forced New Mexicans out of the province, he fled with his family to El Paso. This time, old and ailing, he did not return. As a refugee in El Paso, he influenced most of his family to move further south into New Spain. Pedro's third son, Fernando II, however, returned to New Mexico in 1692 to reclaim his father's and uncle's lands in the Valle de Atrisco.[9] Fernando Durán y Chaves II is the founding father of the succeeding generations of the land grant of Atrisco.

New Mexico–born Fernando Durán y Chaves II was heir to Pedro's land holdings in the Valle de Atrisco and claimant to his uncle Fernando Durán y Chaves's land in the jurisdiction of Sandía. Having served as *alférez* (ensign) of the jurisdiction of Sandia since 1671, he fled the Pueblo Revolt in 1680 with his wife, Lucía Hurtado de Salas, and their children. Before that fateful year, he had lived in the Valle de Atrisco, and he was the only one of his brothers to return with Diego de Vargas in 1692 to reclaim the family estate.

Vargas named Captain Fernando Durán y Chaves as his alférez, the standard-bearer of the army, in 1692. When Vargas triumphantly entered Santa Fe on December 16, 1693, Fernando Durán y Chaves proudly bore the banner of Nuestra Señora de los Remedios.[10] Vargas proclaimed of the event:

> I, the said Governor and Captain-General, about the eleventh hour of said day, made my entry into this Villa of Santa Fe . . . with the squadron of the march and in company of the very illustrious Council of this the said Villa and Kingdom, its high sheriff and color-bearing alderman, the Captain Don Fernando Duran de Chaves, carrying the standard referred to in these acts, and under which land was conquered.[11]

Soon after Vargas's reconquest of New Mexico, Captain Fernando Durán y Chaves presented him with a petition requesting two grants of land. Intent on asserting his gubernatorial powers, Vargas pointed out that as this was a new conquest, no one could claim land based on prior ownership.[12] Therefore, Durán y Chaves's petition began anew his family claim to lands in the Valle de Atrisco. His request begins:

> Captain Don Fernando Duran y Chaves resident of these Provinces of New Mexico appears before Your Excellency asking that all the privileges allowed by law be given him and says:
> Whereas I am now in company with Your Excellency on this estate called

Mejia in the prosecution of this New Conquest, and I hold the preeminence of Conqueror and am a native citizen of these Provinces of New Mexico and have the intention of returning to settle in the same as resident and in view of my large family consisting of my wife and seven sons and three daughters I am under the necessity of asking that Your Excellency will in the name of His Majesty the King our Master make me a new grant of the tracts of agricultural and grazing lands for large and small stock.[13]

Durán y Chaves's first request was for a tract at San Antonio de Angostura between the Río Santa Ana and the Río Grande. He described the boundaries of Angostura as follows: "One is where I used to live which is called San Antonio de la Angostura. Its boundaries are from the mouth of the Río Santa Ana to the narrows of the Río Grande. It is understood that the area runs south from the mouth of the Río Santa Ana until it meets the Río Grande. The Río Grande borders it on the east. It is understood that the Old Río Santa Ana borders it on the west side. I owned the said land for many years without any opposition."[14]

The second tract he requested, Atrisco, lay between the pueblos of Sandia and Isleta. Durán y Chaves described Atrisco as agricultural land with an acequia madre. It began on a bluff where Juan de Perea, a settler who had returned with Vargas, lived, and extended south along the west side of the Río Grande to some corrals formerly owned by his deceased brother-in-law, *maese de campo* Juan Domínguez de Mendoza.[15] His request for the second tract reads:

> The other tract is also on the lower Río Grande which is commonly called Atrisco. It is also agricultural land with its mother ditch [acequia madre]. This one runs south from a bluff where the old house [is] which Juan de Perea lived in to the river as far as some corrals that were owned by Juan Dominguez, my brother-in-law. My father, don Pedro de Chávez, lived within this tract, as well as some tenants. The said tract is uncultivated and vacant. For that reason, I give notice of it with all its entrances and exits, pastures and watering places. In view of the fact that I have a large family as I have said, I declare that I will settle it when this Kingdom is quieted and pledges its obedience to the King.[16]

After reviewing Don Fernando's petition and seeing the land, Governor Vargas granted the two tracts of land in 1692 in recognition of the services given by Fernando Durán y Chaves during the reconquest of New Mexico. In legalistic style, Vargas writes:

> Act of Concession: In so far as provided by law, I now make the grant that the petitioner requests of the two tracts which he claims were his: that at Angostura and that at Atrisco which belonged to his father, Sergeant Major Pedro Duran y Chavez, and his brother-in-law Juan Dominguez

de Mendoza. I make the said grant in the name of His Majesty to the said Captain Don Fernando Duran y Chavez for having accompanied me, the Governor and Captain General in the conquest of this Kingdom.[17]

The agricultural lands were granted to Durán y Chaves with all their appurtenances as well as pastures, marshes, woods, and watering places. There was one important condition to the grant. Vargas specified that the land had to be settled and that "Don Fernando de Chavez shall be one of the settlers, and if he does not do this then this grant shall be void since I make it with this qualification and condition jointly with all his children and he shall enjoy the privileges of conqueror and settler."[18]

During Vargas's second entrada, Fernando Durán y Chaves brought his wife, Lucía Hurtado de Salas, whom he had married in 1675, and their ten children from their refugee settlement at Guadalupe del Paso.[19] Sometime in the early days of the reconquest, Durán y Chaves had leased farmland on the south side of the Villa de Santa Fe from Juan Lucero de Godoy, his brother-in-law. Later, when Governor Vargas permitted settlers to leave Santa Fe, Durán y Chaves moved his family to Bernalillo, in the Valle de Atrisco.[20] Upon his return to his old lands in Bernalillo, he was named *alcalde mayor*, chief magistrate, and he reestablished the family claim to the land.[21]

Durán y Chaves warned the governor of an impending rebellion. In 1696, when the pueblos in the area rebelled, Vargas instructed Durán y Chaves to bring his Bernalillo settlers to Santa Fe if their safety were imperiled. When it did happen, Vargas advised Durán y Chaves that

> he was not giving him orders to march to Cochití and the other rebellious pueblos because he had faith in the strength and loyalty of the contiguous villas of Santa Fé and Villanueva. He directed him to ascertain whether the inhabitants of Bernalillo were safe, to watch over them, and if they were not, they were to retire to Santa Fé, with the soldiers as escort, for which purpose he gave the necessary orders.[22]

Durán y Chaves considered the instructions, and citing the impossibility of moving the settlers to Santa Fe, he opted to move them instead to San Felipe, which then stood on a high mesa. As a result of the strong Spanish presence there, San Felipe Pueblo was unable to join in the rebellion.

Once pacification of the pueblos had taken place, the Spaniards faced another, more formidable enemy: the Apaches. For the next few years, Apaches incessantly raided settlements in the Valle de Atrisco. In March 1704, Durán y Chaves and his neighbors suffered a devastating blow at the hands of the Apaches, who drove off nearly all of their livestock. After the Spaniards sent Governor Vargas a petition for military assistance, the governor led an army south from Santa Fe. The campaign began on March 30, 1704, and took place in the Sandia Mountains, an Apache stronghold. Misfortune struck the Spanish army as Governor Vargas soon fell gravely ill. He was taken to Bernalillo on April 2, where he died a few days later, probably at Durán y Chaves's house.[23]

The Apache raids on Bernalillo continued. Durán y Chaves asked Acting Governor Juan Páez y Hurtado to establish a *puesto* (military post) at Atrisco under the charge of Bernardo, his eldest son. The Puesto de Atrisco was established, probably around 1704, but Bernardo was killed in an accident.[24]

Meanwhile, in 1701, Durán y Chaves presented a petition to the new governor, Pedro Rodríguez Cubero, in regard to his land grants at Angostura and Atrisco. The governor ordered Captain Diego de Montoya, alcalde mayor of the Puesto de Bernalillo, to ensure that an act of possession be held in accordance with custom, and to make certain that no other claim to the land existed.[25] Cubero's decree stated:

> And I order Captain Diego Montoya, alcalde mayor of Bernalillo, the jurisdiction in which these grants lie, in accordance with the grants made to said Don Fernando Duran de Chaves by General Don Diego de Vargas, my predecessor, and by me, said alcalde mayor, to give him real possession which he asks for in this petition and without prejudice to any other person who may obtain better title, thus I order and sign, Pedro Rodriguez Cubero.[26]

That done, Governor Cubero approved the grant. Two years later, on October 14, 1703, Montoya went to Durán y Chaves's hacienda to present him with a title of investiture for the Angostura grant. Although the certificate of investiture for Atrisco has been lost, it was probably issued around the same time.

Seventy-three years later, in 1776, oral tradition corroborated that a certificate of investiture for Atrisco was presented to Durán y Chaves. Juan Candelaria, who was eighty-four years old and a descendant of Francisco de la Candelaria (one of the witnesses who signed the Angostura certificate of investiture) attested that Atlixco was "founded in 1703, in the month of March."[27] Juan Candelaria was born in 1692 and lived first in the Valle de Atrisco and later in the Villa de Alburquerque. His grandparents, Blas de la Candelaria and Ana de Sandoval y Manzanares, had at least two sons, Francisco and Feliciano. The family had lived in the Valle de Atrisco before the Pueblo Revolt in 1680. Blas died prior to 1680, and his widow, Ana de Sandoval y Manzanares, escaped with the family to El Paso during the Pueblo Revolt. Francisco de la Candelaria was born in the Río Abajo, likely in the Valle de Atrisco, in 1668. He and his brother Feliciano returned to New Mexico from El Paso after the reconquest and were among the founders of Alburquerque in 1706. Juan Candelaria, who lived in Alburquerque, was the son of either Francisco or Feliciano.[28] He wrote a somewhat flawed history of the Villa de Alburquerque, skewed toward his family interests, in which he recalled the founding of Atrisco as it had survived in family lore.

Ana de Sandoval y Manzanares, widow of Blas de la Candelaria, was one of the first atrisqueños to expand her holdings west to the Río Puerco. In 1716 she petitioned Governor Félix Martínez for land bounded on the east by the Río Grande, on the west by the Río Puerco, on the south by the hacienda of Tomé Domínguez de Mendoza, and on the north by a ruin just beyond the pueblo of San Clemente. Doña Ana claimed she had inherited the land from her father, Mateo de Sandoval y Manzanares. She stated that Governor Diego de Vargas "brought us hither in the year ninety-two for its settlement. He had promised to give to each one of the native citizens of this province who might come to settle and pacify the same, the tracts of land and fields, and stockraising ranches that we abandoned in the year eighty on account of the powerful insurrection."[29] She received the grant and was given possession by Don Félix de la Candelaria. Over the long haul, other atrisqueños would expand their holdings westward to the Río Puerco.

CHAPTER 3

Atrisco and the Villa de Alburquerque, 1706–1712

I certify to the king, our lord, etc.: That I founded a villa
on the banks and in the valley of the Río del Norte. . . .
and named it the Villa of Alburquerque.

GOVERNOR FRANCISCO CUERVO Y VALDÉS, 1706

New Mexico in 1706 was a different place from what it had been throughout the seventeenth century. The death of Governor Diego de Vargas in November 1704 caused concern among New Mexican pioneers. Vargas was a strong personality who had held office for most of the twelve years he was in New Mexico—longer than any previous governor. The church-state strife that afflicted relationships between civil authorities, friars, and pueblos prior to the Pueblo Revolt had been minimized. The encomienda system in New Mexico had disappeared as a result of the rebellion. With the Pueblo Revolt behind them, the settlers in New Mexico witnessed two significant changes. In 1706, the Villa de San Felipe de Neri de Alburquerque was established, and the Camino Real de Tierra Adentro, which had run on the west bank of the Río Grande through Atrisco, now crossed the river to the newly founded Villa de Alburquerque.

Following the demise of Vargas, fifteen Santa Fe settlers requested permission to leave New Mexico in 1704. They complained of poor living conditions, illnesses, constant Indian threats, difficulty eking out an existence, and other personal reasons.[1] Given the debilitated military, they feared another uprising. Spanish officials denied their request because they feared encouraging an exodus of Santa Fe's small Spanish population of approximately three hundred people.

New Mexico's defenses remained inadequate as Plains Indian tribes stepped up their raids on the new settlements. Reoccupation of New Mexico was the priority for Spanish officials. The poor defense of New Mexico, however, continued to plague settlers, who demanded a military solution to Apache depredations against them. Lack of money and manpower hindered the defense of Spanish New Mexico.

Vargas's successor, appointed by the viceroy of Mexico, was Governor Francisco Cuervo y Valdés. He offered a smooth administrative transition when he took the reins from Acting Governor Juan Paez Hurtado in Santa Fe on March 10, 1705.[2] The tension in Santa Fe, nonetheless, remained. Aside from settler unrest, the first task of Cuervo y Valdés was to address the problem of frontier defense and the continued fear of another revolt such as those of 1680 and 1696. To that end, Cuervo y Valdés prohibited settlers from living among the pueblos.[3] The Spanish population had been clustered in three main areas: Santa Fe, Santa Cruz, and Bernalillo, with scattered farms in the Valle de Atrisco.

Captains Fernando Durán y Chaves, Diego Montoya, and Manuel Baca were in command of thirty-four men and the general defenses at Bernalillo. Their junior officers included two alféreces, Cristóbal Varela Jaramillo and Pedro López del Castillo, and one sergeant, Juan González Bas.[4]

These frontier leaders and their families were among the first settlers of the Valle de Atrisco, principally in the Bernalillo area, and some of them were the first settlers of the Villa de Alburquerque. Diego Montoya, for example, had arrived in Santa Fe with Diego de Vargas and had lived there for a short while in 1693. Fearing another rebellion, he and other settlers moved down to Bernalillo sometime before 1696.[5] Similarly, Manuel Baca, who had lost family in the Pueblo Revolt, returned to claim lands in Bernalillo owned by his father, Cristóbal. Among the first settlers, he was in his late forties at the time of the founding of the Villa de Alburquerque.[6] Alférez Cristóbal Varela Jaramillo, who had fled the Pueblo Revolt at age sixteen, returned with Vargas and settled at Algodones. He was a member of the Confraternity of La Conquistadora.[7] The other alférez, Pedro López del Castillo, and his sister Juana López del Castillo, who returned to New Mexico with their families during the reconquista, were among the first settlers of Alburquerque in 1706. The sergeant, Juan González Bas, returned with Vargas and shortly thereafter settled in Bernalillo. By 1710 he was a captain, and two years later he was appointed alcalde mayor of Alburquerque. He, too, was a member of the Confraternity of La Conquistadora. His name is inscribed at El Morro along with his contemporaries, Salvador Holguín and José Naranjo.[8] As settlers, they contributed to the defense of the area as well as to the economic development of the Valle de Atrisco.

After 1706, with the founding of Alburquerque, the consolidation of the Valle de Atrisco into a defensive population cluster was begun. With it began a definitive identity for the Puesto de Atrisco. To shore up the defenses of the area, Cuervo y Valdés similarly established a defensive post at nearby Galisteo. He resolved to set up focal points of defense throughout New Mexico, particularly in the Río Abajo. The founding of the Villa de Alburquerque was one of his lasting achievements.

On April 23, 1706, Governor Francisco Cuervo y Valdés sat in one of the dimly lit rooms of the *casas reales*, the palatial adobe residences in the Plaza de Santa Fe, and dictated an official certificate to his secretary about the founding of two new settlements in New Mexico. Addressing his king and the viceroy, Governor Cuervo y Valdés stated:

> I certify to the king, our lord, etc.: That I founded a villa on the banks and in the valley of the Río del Norte in a good place as regards land, water, pasture, and firewood, about twenty-two leagues from the Villa of Santa Fe. I gave it as patron titular saint the glorious apostle of the Indies, Señor Francisco Xavier, and called and named it the Villa of Alburquerque. It has a good site and location.... Thirty-five families have been settled, including two hundred and fifty-two persons, large and small. The church is done; it is very capacious and decent. Part of the minister's dwelling is also finished. The principal royal houses are begun, the other houses for the settlers are finished, with their corrals and irrigation ditches in place and water running. The fields are sown; everything is in good order and there has been no expense to the royal treasury.... Francisco Cuervo y Valdez. Signature of the secretary, Alonso Rael de Aguilar.[9]

In the same statement, Cuervo y Valdés said he had also established a settlement at Galisteo with one hundred fifty families of Puebloans of the Tanos tribe. Emphasizing the legal nature of the founding of Alburquerque, Governor Cuervo y Valdés alluded to having established a municipality in accordance with the Laws of the Indies. But it was ascertained that he had overstated his accomplishments.[10] For reasons of patronage, he had named the new villa after the viceroy, Francisco Fernández de la Cueva, Duque de Alburquerque. After all, the viceroy had recommended Cuervo y Valdés for the governorship of New Mexico.[11] It was the viceroy who ordered Cuervo y Valdés to change the name of the new settlement from "Villa de Alburquerque de San Francisco de Xavier" to "Villa de San Felipe de Neri de Alburquerque" in honor of the coronation of Felipe V.[12]

Situated on high ground above the east bank of the Río Grande, a site selected by Captain Juan de Ulibarrí, the Villa de San Felipe de Neri de Alburquerque along the Camino Real was placed strategically in the valley, which was the object of Apache depredations. Directly to the east, twelve miles or so away, the Cañón de Carnuel (Tijeras Canyon) gave access to raiders from the plains beyond the Sierra de Sandia. With the site selected, Cuervo y Valdés announced an invitation throughout the province for settlers to join in developing the new villa. Troops led by Captain Martín Hurtado, accompanied by their families, arrived to create an important military presence in the valley. At first, as few as ten soldiers were stationed in the villa. They were not, however, sufficient to deter Apaches from attacking settlements in the Valle de Atrisco. In time, the valley, also known in the early post-reconquista period as "el bosque grande de doña Luisa,"[13] would be referred to as the Valle de Alburquerque.

Between 1703 and 1706, before the establishment of the Villa de Alburquerque, Fernando Durán y Chaves and his family moved from Bernalillo to the Atrisco area. Some of his children had moved there earlier. The relocation of the Durán y Chaves family to the Atrisco settlement in 1706 in effect anticipated Cuervo y Valdés's plan to establish a villa in the Valle de Atrisco. As settlers had already been moving into the area, the governor saw an opportunity to develop a defense-minded population cluster in the Río Abajo. Fernando Durán y Chaves's son Pedro III was a member of the "twelve first families" who founded the Villa de Alburquerque.[14] Another son, Antonio, moved to Atrisco and married Magdalena Montaño. She died before 1718, for that year Antonio married Antonia Baca from Bernalillo. He was one of the last surviving sons of Fernando and was the "possessor" of his father's last will and testament.[15] Like other families in the area, the members of the Durán y Chaves clan are considered pioneers of the Atrisco-Alburquerque area.

Apaches continued their incessant attacks on the settlements in the Valle de Atrisco. Nonetheless, the settlers of the Alburquerque-Atrisco area remained on their lands. During this period Atrisco became known as "Atrisco de Alburquerque,"[16] although atrisqueños often referred to it as "Puesto de Atrisco," signifying its military character.

In 1708, captains Baltazar Romero and Fernando Durán y Chaves petitioned the cabildo, or town council, of Santa Fe for more soldiers to be stationed at the Villa de Alburquerque. They claimed that Governor Cuervo y Valdés had given them privileges to the land, but that the force to protect them against the "danger from the enemies which surround us on all sides" was inadequate.[17] Cuervo y Valdés had temporarily assigned a squadron of soldiers from Santa Fe to protect the settlers of the Villa de Alburquerque while they established themselves in the area.

Even worse, reported captains Romero and Durán y Chaves, the present governor, El Marqués de la Peñuela, had taken away "the escort, for which reason the enemy, seeing our weakness, have dared barbarously to commit various robberies, every day carrying off our stock, taking it from our corrals . . . and seeing that they are not punished, they may surprise us and destroy us and our wives and children."[18] So dire was the situation that they suggested that if the troops were not forthcoming, they would be forced to abandon the area and "go where we may deem best."[19] The cabildo members presented the petition to the governor, "who said that he would apply the best remedy" to the request made by Romero and Durán y Chaves.[20]

The situation for those who lived in the Villa de Alburquerque and its adjoining districts changed little after its establishment in 1706. In 1754, Fray José Manuel San Juan Nepomuceno y Trigo wrote, "I might say the site of the Villa de Alburquerque, for the settlers, who inhabit it on Sunday, do not live there. They must stay on their ranches to keep watch over their cornfields, which are planted at a very pretty place three leagues distant, called La Alameda. There are no Indians in the entire territory, but the settlers pay their parochial dues, from which the father barely has sufficient for his daily needs."[21] Similarly, atrisqueños paid their tithes to the church, planted their fields, and guarded their lands from marauders day and night.

The importance of the Villa de Alburquerque, however, was its pre-eminent position in the valley. Its strategic location on the Camino Real, its relationship to Tijeras Canyon, and its military importance conveyed prestige to the twelve founding families, whose political influence was increasing. One of its citizens, Juan Candelaria, writes:

> On the seventh day of February, in the year of Our Lord, 1706, this Villa de Alburquerque was incorporated under the name of San Francisco Xavier. Don Francisco Cuervo Valdez was the governor. Friar Juan Minguez was first minister of this Villa. He had come as a missionary. Twelve families and the soldiers from the garrison residing in the town of Bernalillo came to colonize it. The heads of the twelve families were: Cristóbal Jaramillo, Juan Barela, Francisco Candelaria, Feliciano Candelaria, Nicolas Lucero, Baltazar Romero, Joaquín Sedillo, Antonio Gutierrez, Cristóbal Barela, Pedro Lopez del Castillo, Doña Bernardina Salas y Trujillo, a widow, and Juana López del Castillo. The soldiers were: Captain don Martín Hurtado, who commanded, chief Alcalde of this place, his secretary, Juan de Piñeda, Francisco García, soldier, Pedro de Chaves y Durán, Andres Montoya, Sebastian de Canseco, Antonio de Silva, José de Salas, Tomas García, and Xavier de Benavides. The Duke of Alburquerque was the Viceroy at the time of its founding and it derived its name from him. Friar Juan de Tagle was the custodian and Friar Manuel Muñiz, his assistant. The custodian resided at San Ildefonso. Governor Cuervo's administration had run two years. Friar Juan Minguez resided in his palace.
>
> The reconquest of this kingdom took place in 1696. This villa was founded nine years after. It covers four leagues of ground North of this place and

twenty-two leagues distant lies the villa of Santa Fe. The soldiers that came to colonize built a Presidio because of so few houses located on the side of the church to the north. Until today, it is known as El Presidio.[22]

The founding of the Villa de Alburquerque had changed the political veneer of Atrisco. Yet it was Atrisco that gave Alburquerque its enduring qualities of venerability and antiquity.

The early history of the Villa de Alburquerque was not without political intrigue. Don Fernando Durán y Chaves and his clan were politically powerful and influential. In general, they determined who would share power with them. In 1712, for example, when Captain Juan González Bas, who had been a pioneer in the Río Abajo, was appointed alcalde mayor, chief magistrate of the jurisdiction of Bernalillo, Durán y Chaves was not pleased. González was a member of the Bernal-Griego clan, which had somehow feuded with the Durán y Chaves family.[23] González sent a letter to the settlers of the jurisdiction of Alburquerque announcing that he would take office on the following Sunday.[24]

It seems that a gift-giving ritual by the settlers in the jurisdiction preceded the assumption of office. When González arrived at the house of Fernando Durán y Chaves to receive a few sheep, and, as he thought was his right, to assume possession of the house, a ruckus occurred. It is not clear, but it appears that Don Fernando was not about to accept the fact that his son-in-law, who had served as alcalde mayor, was to be replaced by an enemy of the family. Don Fernando barred González from entering the house, exclaiming that the governor had appointed an Indian to the post and calling him "*indio perro griego*," "*perro mulato afrentado*," and other epithets. Escalating the affront, Don Fernando shouted insults about González's father and family. Don Fernando's sons-in-law, Matías de Miranda and Antonio de Ulibarrí, restrained him from assaulting González. The humiliated González responded that he was not an Indian but a Spanish hidalgo like any other son of Castile. Don Fernando's son Francisco raised his musket and told González to leave.[25]

González quickly left the confrontation, but while he was at the house of a friend, Tomás García, Don Fernando's sons Francisco and Antonio Durán y Chaves arrived. Both were armed, one with a knife and the other with a sword. They threatened González again, using more profanity. A crowd gathered in support of González and helped him take refuge in García's house. Don Fernando's sons made it clear that their house did not belong to the Villa de Alburquerque, nor did González have the right to be alcalde mayor.[26]

Following the altercation, González pressed charges against Don Fernando and his sons, asking the governor to arrest them and bring them to justice. Don Fernando was arrested and placed in the house of a relative, Captain Martín Hurtado, and the two sons were taken to the house of alférez Cristóbal Jaramillo.[27]

At the trial, despite a number of witnesses on his side, González dropped the charges against Durán y Chaves and his sons, hoping for better relations with them. Despite his shaky start and the political influence of the Durán y Chaves clan, González went on to have a long and apparently prosperous career as alcalde mayor of the jurisdiction of the Villa de Alburquerque. He still held that post as late as the 1730s. The root of the problem may have been that Durán y Chaves was worried about the growing population in the valley and his family's waning power.[28] Or it may have been that Durán y Chaves was used to having his way and that González's appointment was contrary to his wishes. Nonetheless, life in the Valle de Atrisco was rapidly changing as the Villa de Alburquerque became the economic and political center of the area.

The relationship between the Villa de Alburquerque and Atrisco was more than an economic and political one, it was also a religious one. When the bishop of Durango, Pedro Tamarón y Romeral, visited Alburquerque in 1760, he noted that the villa was composed of 270 families, or 1,814 people. He said that the parish priest for the Villa de Alburquerque, Fray Manuel Rojo, also served the settlements on the west side of the river. Regarding Atrisco, the Villa de Alburquerque, and the crossing of the Camino Real de Tierra Adentro over the Río Grande, Bishop Tamarón wrote:

> Because some of his parishioners are on the other side of the river, this parish priest of Alburquerque, called Fray Manuel Rojo, is obliged to cross it when summoned. This kept him under apprehension, and above all he emphasized to me that when the river froze, it was necessary to cross on the ice. He elaborated this point by saying that when the ice thundered, he thought he was on the way to the bottom because when one crosses it, it creaks as if it were about to break.[29]

The founding of the Villa de San Felipe de Neri de Alburquerque proved historically significant, for what began as a small defensive post in the eighteenth century emerged as a major trade center in the succeeding period. The economic development of the area eventually depended on the fortunes of Spanish Alburquerque. Meanwhile, residents of Atrisco refused to take a back seat to the new villa.

CHAPTER 4

Betwixt Private Ownership and Communal Rights, 1712–1769

> On the 25th day of the month of April 1732, before me
> Captain Juan González Bas, Alcalde de Mayor and War
> Captain of the town of San Phelipe de Alburquerque
> and its jurisdiction, acting as Judge Commissioner with
> two witnesses of my attendance, for the lack of a royal
> or public notary, for there are none in this kingdom,
> appeared Doña Ysabel Montoya.
>
> JUAN GONZÁLEZ BAS, ALCALDE MAYOR
> OF THE VILLA DE ALBURQUERQUE

The eighteenth-century historical record of Atrisco is fraught with suits, as atrisqueños challenged each other and their neighbors over land and other property. Some sales or transfers of land started out innocently but ended in adversarial relationships. Land disputes followed a pattern: Generally, the alcalde mayor acted as arbiter and judge. In a given dispute, the two opposing parties and their witnesses submitted written statements about how they came to own the land in question. Some cases were prolonged and required the governor of the province to make the final decision. The judicial procedures the atrisqueños followed were no different from those practiced by other New Mexican land grant owners. It was, nonetheless, the land that had brought them together in the first place.

Depending on one's point of view, Atrisco was referred to as a *puesto* (post), a *sitio* (place), a *plaza* (town square), an *aldea* (village), or *ranchos*. Each term had legal significance. But Atrisco was not easily defined, for private land was kept separate from community land. Pasturage, woodlands, and water rights presented other problems for the administration of the community of Atrisco. Atrisco's economy in the colonial period was based on crops such as wheat, corn, and other vegetables. Wool was also a major industry; large numbers of sheep were tended in the uplands away from the agricultural bottomlands.[1]

Yet Atrisco could be defined by the diverse ways in which the land tenure pattern and its uses evolved. If it were true, as opposing litigants in the late nineteenth century would later argue, that Atrisco was a private land grant at its inception, it took on the character of a community land grant during this period. Alternatively, it had always been a community land grant, as the descendants of Don Fernando would claim and the Court of Private Land Claims would concur on September 4, 1894.[2] Atrisco's historical evolution, nonetheless, was already under way when Fernando Durán y Chaves died sometime in the second decade of the 1700s.

The Atrisco land grant in the eighteenth century comprised a number of individual settlements, each with its own plaza. The 1802 census showed four principal plazas that had developed in the eighteenth century, some named after the dominant family in each vicinity: Nuestra Señora de Guadalupe de los Garcías, San Fernando de los Chaves, San José de los Sánchez, and San Andrés de los Ranchos de Atrisco.[3] In contrast to Santa Fe, with its pattern of adjoining houses, Atrisco's settlement pattern described houses close together but detached, with only a few structures sharing common walls. Settlements were typically concentrated along the bottomlands with access to a communal acequia madre or main irrigation ditch for farming. Sheep ranching and grazing lands were located on the *mesilla* above the river.

Although genealogical records identifying settlers of the various parts of Atrisco are incomplete, certain settlers can be identified for each part. For example, settlers at Ranchos de Atrisco included Josefa Durán y Chaves (born in 1708); Francisco Sánchez (ca. 1726–58), who had taken part in campaigns against raiding Apaches; Juan Cristóbal Sánchez (1728–98), who also resided in Tomé; and Juana Tomasa Durán y Chavez (born in 1737).[4]

Settlers diligently kept track of their frequent land transfers. Almost all transactions were between kin, whether by blood, marriage, or *compadrazgo* (compaternity in an extended family).[5] It seems that even before the first owners of large estates in the Atrisco land grant had died, the land had begun to be broken up into smaller parcels. Paternal grants of land to sons and daughters occurred within the first generation of ownership. The names of owners changed as widows inherited land and some remarried.

The early history of most land transactions at Atrisco is easily traced. It is nevertheless difficult to ascertain the size of each land holding because the documents rarely quantify the land under consideration. Property transactions after the death of Fernando Durán y Chaves became increasingly complex, particularly between 1729 and 1757, as they took on a history of their own and set the pattern for future proceedings.

The children of Don Fernando Durán y Chaves—Bernardo (the eldest son), Antonio, Isabel, Francisco, Luis, Nicolás, María, Catalina, Pedro III, and Clara—tried at first to keep all transactions in the family. Don Fernando's youngest son, Pedro, who signed his name Pedro Gomes Durán y Chaves, married Juana Montoya. Their children were Manuela, Mónica, Josefa, Efigenia, Francisco Xavier, Quitería, Juana, Diego Antonio, María Luisa, and Eusebio (oddly, one of Efigenia's brothers, Pablo Chaves, was not mentioned on this occasion). Soon after Don Fernando's death, his sons Pedro and Nicolás sold their land to Bernabé Baca, husband of one of their nieces. Pedro also sold a piece of land to Antonia Baca, his brother Antonio's widow. Meanwhile, Pedro moved north to a place in the Río Arriba, and Nicolás moved to a site south of Isleta Pueblo.[6] The children of Bernardo Durán y Chaves sold their inherited land to their cousin Efigenia Durán y Chaves and her husband Jacinto Sánchez.

The brisk pattern of selling, buying, and transferring property eventually led to wider ownership of land in Atrisco. By the 1730s, the Atrisco land grant manifested a complicated web of ownership. In 1729, for example, Leonor Montaño, widow of Luis de Chaves, and her daughter, María Antonia de Chaves from Santa Fe, inherited land in the sitio of Atrisco. They sold it to a relative, Antonio de Chaves from Atrisco, for 239 pesos.[7] Sometimes the land was donated, as in the conveyance of land in Albuquerque by Diego Padilla to Diego Borrego in 1734.[8]

Each transaction followed a legally prescribed pattern. All sales, resales, divisions, subdivisions, inheritances, and transfers of land were required to be notarized. In the absence of a notary, it was customary to have the highest-ranking authority in the jurisdiction, usually the chief magistrate or alcalde mayor, serve as notary with the obligatory witnesses. Buyer and seller presented themselves before the notary or alcalde mayor. In 1732, for example, Isabel Montoya certified that she had sold a lot within the Atrisco land grant to Josefa Baca. Given the barter economy of the period in New Mexico, payment was made in kind, and in Isabel Montoya's case, poverty was the motivating factor. The sale was administered by Juan González Bas, the alcalde mayor of the Villa de Alburquerque. The history of ownership detailed in the transaction demonstrates the many ways in which title to a piece of property could be conveyed.

At this Hacienda of Santo Tomas de Villa Nueva on the 25th day of the month of April 1732, before me Captain Juan González Bas, Alcalde de Mayor and War Captain of the town of San Phelipe de Alburquerque and its jurisdiction, acting as Judge Commissioner with two witnesses of my attendance, for the lack of a royal or public notary, for there are none in this kingdom, appeared Doña Ysabel Montoya, widow of the stan-

dard bearer Miguel de San Juan, and Doña Josefa Baca, widow of Juan
Antonio García, whom I certify I know, and the said Doña Ysabel Montoya stated, to wit: that she gave and did give by sale to the said Doña
Josefa Baca a suerte [lot] of land that she has, which she obtained, which
her husband Miguel de San Juan had obtained as a gift [mejoría] from
his mother Doña Juana Baca, and her brother Antonio de Luna, for the
three of them had bought the same from Captain Juan Fernandes for the
sum of four hundred dollars [pesos] in silver and gold in order to be able
to make use of the sale. Partition has been made between the parties,
there accruing to each one of them their portion of 2,025 varas each, and
the said Ysabel sells her portion which said varas are measured out and
marked with monuments to the satisfaction of the parties and the said
party sells for the sum of 300 dollars [pesos] which she acknowledges
to have received to her satisfaction and contentment, upon which she
renounces her own right, house and residence, renouncing the laws that
may be in her favor in the general laws. . . . Whereupon neither the aforesaid party nor her heirs shall bring suit or claim against her, and should
it be brought up that they be not heard in court or out of it. Upon which
the said party . . . declares that because she is poor and without anything
to support her children and that she conveys and transfers as has been
stated, to wit: That those 300 dollars [pesos] she received in goods of the
country according to their market value, that is to say, the cows at twenty
dollars [pesos], the oxen at twenty-five dollars [pesos] each, the sheep at
two dollars [pesos], a pattern of serge with trimmings for thirty dollars
[pesos], a lock for six dollars [pesos], all to her satisfaction, whereupon
she binds her person and property now and in the future and she gives
it free from encumbrances, mortgage, without removing anything from
it, and there was present her son-in-law Juan de Chaves and she has the
consent of her heirs to sell, and the said lands are measured and re-mea-
sured for the first and second time, and that it may so appear I signed
with two attending witnesses and the grantor did not sign it because she
did not know how; at her request her son-in-law Juan de Chaves signed
it on the said day, month, and year as above. At the request of Doña
Ysabel Montoya: Juan de Chaves (rubric); Attending Witnesses: Joseph
de Quintana (rubric), Geronimo Jaramillo (rubric). Before me as Judge
Commissioner, Juan González (rubric).[9]

The archives from 1732 reveal a second transaction, this time between
Pedro Gomes de Chaves and Bernabé Baca, both citizens of the Puesto de
Atrisco (as mentioned above). Pedro Gomes de Chaves said that he had
sold to Bernabé Baca some agricultural land *(tierra de labor)* originally
granted to his father, Captain Don Fernando Durán y Chaves. The size
of the land was such that it could yield "about half a fanega of corn . . .
and it is bounded by the acequia madre on the north, on the south with

the boundary of his brother Antonio de Chaves, on the west with a small acequia that comes out of the acequia madre that waters the land of said Don Antonio de Chaves, on the east is a cottonwood which is near the acequia madre."[10] The land was sold for a hundred pesos.

In 1735, Francisco Xavier de Miranda of the Puesto de Atrisco sold a piece of land in Atrisco to Francisco Antonio Gonzales for 110 pesos. Miranda had a document stating he had purchased it from Juan Montaño. It was bounded "on the east, by an arroyo which was formerly an arm of the Río del Norte, and borders with lands of the said Juan Montaño, on the north by the lands of Phelipe Gallegos, on the west by the Río del Norte, and on the south by the lands of Joseph Montaño."[11] Montaño renounced, according to law, any future claim to the lands. In this case, the sale was administered by Captain Gerónimo Jaramillo, *teniente de alcalde mayor* of the jurisdiction of the Villa de Alburquerque.

Atrisqueños vigilantly kept track of each transaction in the sale or transfer of adjoining land to Atrisco. In 1734, Joaquín Sedillo acquired land contiguous with Atrisco near Isleta Pueblo. The transaction was notarized by Juan González Bas, the alcalde mayor of the Villa de Alburquerque. In 1768, Joaquín's son, Antonio Sedillo of Alburquerque, considered selling the land. Its boundaries were described as commencing "below the pueblo of Isleta. Boundaries, north, the league of the pueblo of Isleta; south, a twin alamo called 'Alamo de Culebra'; east, the Río Grande; west, the Puerco ridge. In the conveyance it is set forth that this tract was granted to the father of the grantor by the crown."[12]

In 1769, when Antonio Sedillo sold a tract from his inheritance to Diego Borrego, the atrisqueños looked on with great interest, for they turned out to witness the marking off of the boundary later that year. In the grant, given to Antonio Sedillo in 1769, the eastern boundary was described as a hill called "Cerro Colorado, which is the boundary of those of Atrisco ... The grant was made ... in the presence of Captain Baltazar Baca and Manuel Torres, and the settlers of Atrisco and the Rio Puerco, including Manuel Vaca, José Chaves, and Lieutenant Juan Bautista Montaño, and some 'Navajo Apaches.'"[13] The list of atrisqueños as witnesses indicates that they jealously guarded their boundaries whenever they were aware of a given transaction.

Another example of a land transfer took place in 1764, when Quitería Durán y Chaves, granddaughter of Don Fernando, wife of Bernardo Padilla, and mother of Pedro Durán y Chaves IV, divided her estate among her children as "Don Fernando Durán y Chaves had wished."[14] Pedro had asked his mother, who lived in the Villa de Albuquerque, to divide her lands in the Puesto de Atrisco into five equal parts (each 52 varas wide by 169 varas long) for himself and his brothers.[15] Pedro and his brothers were not the legitimate sons of Bernardo Padilla; thus he may have wished to protect his and his brothers' interests to the land and avoid a long legal battle in the future.

The evolutionary processes that defined Atrisco are evident in the variety of land transfers that occurred among the heirs of Don Fernando and other eighteenth-century settlers within the grant. Sales, donations, and bequests of land—in addition to litigated disputes over land and other property—were recorded forms of transfers that defined the historical evolution of Atrisco's community land grant status as proclaimed by the Court of Private Land Claims in 1894 (see chapter 12). By the middle of the twentieth century, at least six thousand direct descendants of Don Fernando and other eighteenth-century progenitors collectively claimed ownership to the common lands along with their individual ownership of properties within the Atrisco land grant.

CHAPTER 5

The Baffling Case of the Missing Sheep

The Partido System in Atrisco in the Late 1760s

> Well, sire, if such a thing as telling the truth hides the way
> things are, how much more could it hide that which can
> prejudice the attainment of justice?
>
> DOÑA EFIGENIA DE CHAVES, 1769

Apart from land transactions at Atrisco, other legal matters occupied the magistrates. In 1768 an economic problem erupted into a series of bitter legal battles that further defined and divided the community at Atrisco. Sheep raising was a major industry in Atrisco. The *partido* system, a pastoral institution dating from biblical times, had been transferred to New Mexico with the group who accompanied Juan de Oñate in 1598. Under the partido system, owners of large flocks usually turned over a certain number of ewes to a *partidario*, an individual who was contracted to care for them for a period of three to five years. The partidario was to make annual payments of lambs, rams, and wool to the lender at a rate of between 20 and 25 percent of the initial head count. At the end of the contract period, the partidario returned the original number of ewes to the owner and any outstanding debt associated with undelivered livestock or products. The partido system was an important element of New Mexico's economy, including that of Atrisco, where sheep raising was a major industry well into the twentieth century.[1]

The 1768 case of Atrisco demonstrates how the partido system worked and how the legal process functioned in Spanish colonial New Mexico. The final arbiter in a given case was always the governor of the province. The suit brought by María Ignacia Lucero de Godoy of Santa Fe against Efigenia Durán y Chaves of Atrisco clearly demonstrates the governor's role in the matter. It took several attempts by Spanish officials to untangle the confusion caused by the partidarios, or contracted sheepherders, who played a numbers game on their clients. Even the owners of the herds had a difficult time tracking the actual numbers of sheep they were owed. The case also offers a fascinating account of the role of women in New Mexico as seen through the cultural window of Atrisco.

About 1763, María Ignacia Lucero de Godoy, widow of Manuel Sanz Garbizu, continued the contract her deceased husband had made with Lorenzo Santillanes as partidario. Lorenzo was thirty-three and from the Villa de Alburquerque. Manuel Sanz Garbizu gave Lorenzo 700 head of sheep and 5 rams from their ranch at San Antonio for a five-year period. Lorenzo would mix them with his own sheep in order to increase the size of their flocks through breeding. In return, Lorenzo promised to pay Don Manuel (later his widow, Doña María) 200 sheep and 150 fleeces a year. Sometime in 1768 when Doña María proceeded to account for her husband's property, she discovered a shortage in their sheep flocks at Atrisco, as well as the absence of 150 fleeces a year.

Doña María observed that Lorenzo had kept his bargain until 1767, when he was unable to pay for two years. During the years of the agreement with her husband, Lorenzo had also contracted with his sister-in-law, Efigenia Durán y Chaves. As it turned out, Lorenzo had fallen on bad times and paid his sister-in-law first, with no sheep left to pay Doña María. In 1768, Lorenzo was able to pay Doña María 170 sheep, but he still owed 30 rams (*carneros*). In 1767, Lorenzo lost the entire herd in payment to Doña Efigenia. At that time he paid Doña Efigenia with 500 head of sheep.

Realizing what had happened, Doña María petitioned Governor Pedro Fermín de Mendinueta to investigate the matter and order Doña Efigenia Durán y Chaves to pay her the 150 head of sheep and the correct amount of fleece she was owed, along with the yearly increase and corresponding fleece. Saying that Lorenzo had no right to pay Doña Efigenia with her ewes (*ovejas*), she asked that payment be made by August, the month it was due according to the five-year contract with Lorenzo.[2] Doña Efigenia diverted the issue by raising the question of which partido Lorenzo should have paid first. In the end, the real issue revolved around Lorenzo's decision to pay Doña Efigenia with Doña María's sheep.

Summoned before Governor Mendinueta in May 1768, Lorenzo Santillanes stated under oath that he had, indeed, received 700 ewes and 5 rams from Doña María, and a contract in which he promised to pay 200 head of sheep and 150 fleeces a year.[3] He also said that he no longer had the 700 sheep, but he had paid the partido until 1767. In 1768, he admitted that he owed Doña María 50 rams. But the problem began in October 1767 when his contract with Doña Efigenia came due. At that time he simply did not have 500 sheep, so he took them from Doña María's flock. When asked by Doña María for her payment of 200 sheep, he told her that they had been lost. Asked to pay the debt, Lorenzo replied that he did not have any means to repay her.[4]

Having reviewed the testimony, Governor Mendinueta ordered Francisco Trébol Navarro, alcalde mayor *and capitán de guerra* (war captain) of the jurisdiction of the Villa de Alburquerque, to

> compel and obligate [E]figenia Chaves to show without delay, the 500 head of sheep, which the mentioned Santillanes has declared having given her and which belong to the said widow Doña María Ignacia, and give them to the said widow, or to whomever [the latter] may designate.[5]

Trébol Navarro went to Doña Efigenia's house and presented the governor's order. Doña Efigenia responded that she would immediately obey the order and pay the 500 head of sheep to Doña María.[6] Feeling that he had done his duty, Trébol Navarro reported back to the governor that the issue had been resolved. Just when the matter seemed settled, a few days later, Trébol Navarro received a brief from Joseph Hurtado de Mendoza, son-in-law of Doña Efigenia. Trébol Navarro must have shaken his head in disbelief. Was Doña Efigenia refusing to obey Governor Mendinueta's order?

Joseph Hurtado de Mendoza, from Andalucía in Spain, arrived in the Alburquerque-Atrisco area in the mid-1760s. In 1766 he married Feliciana Sánchez, daughter of Efigenia Chaves and Jacinto Sánchez.[7] The opportunistic Hurtado de Mendoza had some legal training and soon began to represent his mother-in-law's real estate interests. His credibility, depending on one's point of view, had been enhanced during 1767–68, when he was called upon to journey to Ciudad Chihuahua to investigate a rape case. However, he was severely criticized by the clergy there for overstepping his bounds.[8] Nonetheless, Efigenia had entrusted him to attend to all of her affairs.

Hurtado de Mendoza's brief, written in behalf of his mother-in-law, stated that she was in conformity with her rights. As ordered by the governor and in obedience with the mandate, Doña Efigenia said she would immediately show the 500 ewes as required, but they were the ones with which Lorenzo had paid her. Feeling that the governor had acted in haste, Doña Efigenia pointed out that some important facts had been overlooked. In her impetuousness to recover her losses, Doña María's complaint had "obscured the truth."[9] Neither Doña María nor Lorenzo had mentioned Doña Efigenia's flock, which he still had in his possession.

Explaining how Lorenzo had come into possession of her sheep, Doña Efigenia said that her late husband, Don Jacinto Sánchez from Atrisco, had contracted Joseph Jaramillo, now deceased, to care for his 400 ewes for a period of five years. The conditions were that at the end of the period he must pay 800 ewes. No rams or fleece was included in the deal. The debt came due on January 31, 1763, as indicated on the promissory note (*vale*). At that time, Jaramillo formally transferred the 800 ewes to Lorenzo, a transaction presided over by Don Balthazar Griego, *teniente mayor* (vice-mayor) of the Villa of Alburquerque. With that, Lorenzo had taken over the obligation to pay Doña Efigenia 800 ewes at the end of 1767.[10] Lorenzo made his arrangement with Doña Efigenia a few days before his arrangement with Doña María. Doña Efigenia made the point that, given the chronology, her agreement predated Doña María's.[11] Therefore, it seemed Lorenzo had paid the correct partido first. The real question remained unanswered: did Lorenzo have the right to pay Doña Efigenia with Doña María's sheep?

Doña Efigenia declared that Lorenzo had only paid her 600 ewes of the original 800 he owed her: "that's all he had in his corral." Thus, he still owed her 200 ewes. She noticed that before he counted out her 600 sheep, Lorenzo had separated out 40 or 50 head of sheep for himself. Not having the rest he owed, he paid Doña Efigenia the remainder of the debt with a piece of land, and she gave him a signed statement that the debt had been satisfied. Therefore, given the circumstances, explained Doña Efigenia, it appeared that Doña María's statement was not a true representation of what had occurred. In Doña Efigenia's view, Doña María should have acknowledged that "Lorenzo had my sheep, and that my contract predated hers."[12] Accusing Doña María of malice aforethought, she added, "I do not owe her anything."

Furthermore, according to Doña Efigenia's statement, Lorenzo did not turn the flock over to her, but to her brother Diego Antonio Chaves. As soon as she received the order from the governor to pay Doña María, she had gone to Don Diego Antonio's corral and begun counting the sheep that bore her mark. When she had counted up to 300 sheep, Don Diego Antonio stopped her, as he felt that the counting was agitating the sheep and causing them harm. In any case, Doña Efigenia said, Lorenzo had paid her with her own sheep, not with those of a different mark or brand. By mentioning the marks, Doña Efigenia had further confused the issue. So much time had passed in the mixing of the flocks that it would be next to impossible to separate out which mark belonged to whom. At first the governor thought that if Trébol Navarro could identify the marks, he could separate the flock belonging to Doña María.

Referring to Doña María's complaint, Doña Efigenia remarked with irony, in her statement to the governor, "Well, sire, if such a thing as telling the truth hides the way things are, how much more could it hide that which can prejudice the attainment of justice?" She asked that Doña María be prevented from bothering her further (*no me moleste, ni inquiete*).[13] As Doña Efigenia intimated that she had already given Doña María's son Manuel 500 ewes, she ended by petitioning the governor: "I ask and plead that you order the return of my 500 ewes, which I justly deserve, without delay."[14]

In response to the foregoing, Governor Mendinueta sided with Doña María, who argued that she had not received any sheep from Doña Efigenia. The governor said it was not Lorenzo's right to pay with someone else's sheep. On June 14, 1768, he ordered Trébol Navarro to check all the brands on the sheep in question and separate Doña María's from the rest of the flock. He instructed him to tell Doña Efigenia that if she wished to make any complaints, she could voice them to the alcalde mayor.[15] It appeared the case had been resolved. On July 20, 1768, a notification of the decision was sent to all parties, in which it was acknowledged that Doña María's son Manuel demanded that Doña Efigenia obey the governor's order.[16]

That same day, Lorenzo was asked to identify Doña Efigenia's mark or brand.[17] Lorenzo declared that all 400 head of sheep that Jaramillo had originally received from Efigenia's husband had one ear cut squarely at the top and the other split in the back.[18] After four years, the new marks on the 600 sheep included five marks: one with both ears split, another with both ears with their tops cut off, another with *ramal* and the other with *sesgo*, that is, cut at an angle. He also said that 103 of the rest had one ear cut and the other split. As proof of ownership, the 500 sheep belonging to Doña María had only four marks.[19] That could be proven with testimony by Juan Tafoya and Bernardo Mirabal, who witnessed Lorenzo giving his brother-in-law, Antonio Alberto Aragón, 250 head of sheep to breed. When he needed to pay Doña Efigenia, Aragón gave him 350 head of sheep that belonged to Doña María. The entire time, Lorenzo knew that the sheep belonged to Doña María.[20]

Antonio Alberto Aragón, thirty-seven years old, from the Villa de Alburquerque, was asked to verify Lorenzo's statement. On July 20, 1768, Alberto stood before Trébol Navarro and swore to tell the truth. Asked to identify the markings of the 400 sheep given by Doña Efigenia to Lorenzo, he responded that the ears had been marked accordingly: one had the top squarely cut off and the other ear was split. He verified the markings of the 400 sheep that Doña Efigenia's husband had given Jaramillo, who in turn had given them to Lorenzo, and said that 350 head of sheep of the 703 sheep returned to Doña Efigenia were so marked.[21]

The investigation dragged into 1769, when Bernardo Mirabal was called to testify. Mirabal recalled that when Lorenzo gave his brother-in-law Antonio Alberto Aragón part of the flock, he had noticed that they were the ones that Lorenzo managed for Doña Maria. As a mark, her sheep had both ears split. After Doña Efigenia asked for her payment, Lorenzo had asked Aragón to give back the sheep so that he could pay her the 703 head he owed.[22]

Finally, Trébol Navarro acknowledged frustration in the process of identifying Doña María's sheep, for it had taken nearly a year to do so. He explained to the governor that aside from trying to find witnesses and bringing them in to testify, he had met with difficulty in getting Doña Efigenia to cooperate in letting him inspect the flocks. Additionally, Trébol Navarro said that on May 23, 1769, he had received a statement that Don Juan Tafoya could not be present to testify in favor of Doña María. It seems Tafoya had suffered an accident and could not make the trip because of his advanced age and the long distance from his house to that of Trébol Navarro at Pajarito. Instead, Trébol Navarro summoned Ignacio Jaramillo to testify. That day, Jaramillo stated that he did not know the number of sheep Lorenzo had given Aragón, nor did he know the number he paid Doña Efigenia; he did, however, know that a portion of the flock belonged to Doña María.[23]

By June 3, 1769, Trébol Navarro had heard enough. He transmitted the testimony to Governor Mendinueta. Explaining the delay in carrying out the governor's orders, after a year of testimony, he said that since October 1768, he had made repeated requests to see the sheep and had been unable to do so for lack of cooperation by Doña Efigenia.[24] He had given up trying to identify the sheep, as the whole affair was "fruitless." He stated that he had tried both verbally and in writing to see the flocks but had been unsuccessful. He realized that Doña María had suffered economic losses, but at this point, he had gone as far as he could. Besides, added Trébol Navarro, in New Mexico, the practice was that a person could take sheep marked similarly to one's own.[25] He asked the governor to determine what he thought just, in this case.

Unimpressed by Trébol Navarro's effort, Governor Mendinueta asked him to send a copy of the file to Doña María so she could prepare a response. The governor let Trébol Navarro know that he had not changed his mind on the true ownership of the flock and commented that an order had already been served to Doña Efigenia to return the sheep.[26] Four days later, Trébol Navarro sent Doña María the file and asked her son to prepare a response within six days.[27]

Bernardo Sanz Garbizu wrote the response in behalf of his mother, Doña María. He minced no words in saying that Doña Efigenia's responses "gravely offend my mother." He called Doña Efigenia's actions malicious and unfounded, for the sheep unquestionably belonged to his mother. He reiterated that she had no right to his mother's sheep, as four witnesses had already proven the true ownership of the flock. He asked for the return of the flock in addition to the wool and accretions to the flock for the years 1768 and 1769. He declared her to be "in rebellion" against the governor's orders in refusing the inspection of the flock. In an emotional conclusion, he demanded the return of the flock and its products.[28] Acting as intermediary, Trébol Navarro transmitted the response to Joseph Hurtado de Mendoza, Doña Efigenia's son-in-law and representative.[29]

Hurtado de Mendoza responded with characteristic calm and in measured words. Lorenzo Santillanes's testimony was false in regard to the marks on the sheep, he said. Of the 703 sheep, Lorenzo had stated that 500 had four different marks and that 103 carried the mark of Doña María. He could prove the contrary. Up to that time, the marks on the flock had not been modified. At no time had Lorenzo given Hurtado de Mendoza's mother-in-law more than 600 head of sheep. After counting them, fewer than 13 remained in Lorenzo's possession—not 40 or 50 as Efigenia had stated earlier. Therefore, Hurtado de Mendoza contended, Lorenzo's testimony should be nullified, as should that of Antonio Alberto Aragón. Aragón had stated that 350 of the 700 sheep were marked with Doña María's mark: both ears split. It was known, argued Hurtado de Mendoza, that Lorenzo did not receive Doña María's flock until many days after he had received that of Doña Efigenia. He accused Doña María of deceit, calumny, and maliciousness in presenting her irritating allegations which were in themselves "offensive" to Doña Efigenia.[30]

Now, continued Hurtado de Mendoza, Doña Efigenia had promptly complied with the governor's orders. She now asked Doña María to return her 500 head of sheep. But Doña María's sheep were still in Atrisco more than three weeks later. Afterward, the sheep given to Doña Efigenia's brother, Diego Antonio Chaves, were taken to his ranch at Navajo on the Río Puerco. Three days later, when the sheep were already en route to Navajo, Doña María's son, Manuel Bernardo Sanz Garbizu, showed up at Atrisco to inspect the flock. Hurtado de Mendoza explained to him that he could just as easily inspect them at Navajo, but Manuel complained that it was too far. Therefore, stated Hurtado de Mendoza, there was never an intentional refusal to let Manuel inspect the flock; he had his chance, and the sheep had to be moved.

Doña Efigenia explained that it would be difficult to order the return of the sheep from Navajo to Atrisco because her authority did not extend outside of her immediate household. However, after the feast day of San Juan, the flocks would all be brought together for shearing. Doña Efigenia, through the power of attorney given her son-in-law, Hurtado de Mendoza, reiterated her undivided obedience to the governor's orders. She agreed that a year had dragged by, but that it was to Doña María's advantage—so that she could have time "to destroy the truth."[31] She pledged to cooperate fully and obey the governor's mandates. Hurtado de Mendoza added a statement that the practice in this kingdom regarding payment of livestock was to pay the first in line "even though the stock may have many marks on it from previous owners" and a statement signed by other Chaves family members reinforcing the sentiment.[32]

Trébol Navarro submitted all final arguments to the governor in July 1769.[33] In less than a week, he had his response from Santa Fe. Governor Mendinueta issued the *sentencia definitiva* spelling out his decision.[34] He recognized that Jacinto Sánchez, husband of Doña Efigenia, had lent 400 ewes to Joseph Jaramillo under the partido system. The contract between them ran the usual five years, after which Jaramillo would have paid Sánchez 800 ewes. The governor understood that the 800 ewes were passed on to Lorenzo Santillanes with the same obligation. Meanwhile, Doña María Ignacia Lucero de Godoy gave Lorenzo 700 ewes and 5 rams with the obligation that every year for five years he would pay her 200 rams and 150 fleeces.

Having completed his obligation for Doña Efigenia, Lorenzo paid her 600 ewes and a piece of land to make up for the 800 total he owed her. Lorenzo knew that by doing that, he would not have a single ewe to pay Doña María. She sued for the return of her flock, on the grounds that Lorenzo had no right to pay Doña Efigenia with her flock. Meanwhile, Doña Efigenia was satisfied that she had been paid, because her contract preceded Doña María's.[35]

The governor concluded that Lorenzo had corroborated that the flock he had used for payment belonged to Doña María. Aragón's testimony agreed with Lorenzo's that 350 head of sheep had been mixed in the flock, the greater number of which belonged to Doña María. More of her sheep had been mixed with those under care by Bernardo Mirabal and Ignacio Jaramillo.[36] Having established that payment had indeed been made with Doña María's flock, the governor proceeded with his explanation of his decision.

Doña Efigenia had attempted to discount Lorenzo's testimony by saying that more than 300 ewes had her mark and that Doña María had acted maliciously in her lawsuit. The governor stated that the issue, therefore, was not the right of first priority, but that Doña Efigenia had no right to be paid with someone else's flock.

Regarding malicious intent, the governor concluded that if anyone had acted maliciously, it was Doña Efigenia, who had self-righteously insisted that she had justly been paid.[37] He felt that her testimony demonstrated bad faith. Knowing the flock belonged to Doña María, she had proceeded to collect her payment. Moreover, continued the governor, she repeatedly refused to permit the inspection of the flock as had been requested in his order of June 14, 1769. The governor found fault with Doña Efigenia's math in the exchanges of flocks that supposedly took place. The governor, using information not in the files before him, reasoned that

> neither is she favored in the falsification ascribed to Lorenzo if the same words of her last response qualify for the truth. She says that Lorenzo swore falsely by declaring that he had given her 703 head of sheep . . . after counting them, there were 603 that were paid. Lorenzo's error in miscounting thirteen head of sheep was not enough to have falsified all the rest of his testimony. All of which demonstrates that he did so without malice aforethought.[38]

In his view, moreover, Doña María did not act maliciously in reporting the wrongful use of her flock, for she had legal grounds to question the use of her sheep as payment to Doña Efigenia.[39]

The governor ordered Doña Efigenia to deliver, without delay, 500 ewes along with the rams and fleeces due for 1768 and 1769 to Doña María and her son Manuel. He also gave Doña Efigenia the right to sue and collect payment from Lorenzo Santillanes.[40] The case was closed, or so it appeared.

Three days later, in faraway Puesto de San Isidro de Pajarito, Trébol Navarro summoned Doña Efigenia and Doña María's son Manuel to read them the governor's decision.[41] Having served them notice, Trébol Navarro issued the authorization for Manuel to collect the debt of 500 sheep, along with 156 rams for 1768 and 57 lambs for 1769, plus 200 head as payment for the corresponding years owed with 300 fleeces for both years.[42] That same day, a second notification of authorization was given Manuel because Doña Efigenia refused to return the flock. Trébol Navarro summoned her again and read her the governor's *sentencia definitiva*, and still she protested.[43]

Six days later, Trébol Navarro, after receiving notice that Doña Efigenia had not yet obeyed the order, went to the house of her brother, Diego Antonio Chaves, and summoned her. He reported to the governor that he found her "more and more rebellious."[44] Trébol Navarro returned to Diego Antonio's house, took the flock, numbering 500 sheep, and gave it to Manuel. But before the flock could be driven out, Diego Antonio told Manuel that the sheep were old and asked him whether he wanted them anyway. Manuel said no, he should be paid with the current flock.[45]

Hurtado de Mendoza, Efigenia's legal representative, wrote one last response in her defense. He said that she had merely raised a point of order that she believed to be correct. It would be a hardship for her to pay Doña María everything owed her in one year because it would wipe out her assets. Besides, she pleaded, as a widow, she had minor children to rear, and she would be left poor and helpless.[46]

On July 28, 1769, Trébol Navarro received a notice from Juan Domingo Sánchez, a son of Efigenia Chaves who had settled in the Río Puerco and was also a partidario. He said he had 400 head of sheep belonging to his mother. Now, as ordered, he was sending 400 head with 100 yearlings to give to Manuel, Doña María's son.[47] The gesture of payment seemed admirable, but the debt to Doña María was still outstanding. Lorenzo still owed 200 head of sheep and 300 fleeces.

On August 3, Trébol Navarro wrote that Doña Efigenia still owed 156 rams from the debt of 1768. Nor had Lorenzo paid off the 200 head from the 700 head of sheep that he was still obligated to pay Doña María from the year before, nor had 57 lambs and sheep been paid. The 300 fleeces owed for the past two years were also outstanding. Trébol Navarro went to Doña Efigenia's house and seized eighteen cows and one calf valued at 421 *pesos corrientes de la tierra*. They were equal in value to 156 rams at two pesos each and 57 lambs at about one peso each. Additionally, 50 pesos in fleeces were taken as part of the payment. In all, they totaled close to the 421 pesos owed.[48] Trébol Navarro ordered Doña Efigenia's brother, Diego Antonio, to give Manuel 100 ewes regardless of age. He also confiscated cattle from Doña Efigenia's corral valued at 45 pesos to pay legal costs.

Only after taking these harsh measures did Trébol Navarro feel satisfied that he had done his duty and accomplished the governor's dictum. Doña María was satisfied that the debt had been paid, though she had lost most of her flock that she could have bred for years to come. Finally, on September 4, 1769, Trébol Navarro, probably with a sigh of relief, submitted the final statement to Governor Pedro Fermín de Mendinueta along with the entire file of testimony, transmittals, orders, and reports of the final outcome.[49]

As this complicated court battle shows, partidarios helped each other to meet their quotas by mixing herds. It seems they believed that in the long run the numbers would come out even. In the case of Lorenzo, time ran out, and he was caught in the act of manipulating the number of sheep he held to pay off the debt. It fell on Efigenia and María to litigate the issue in order to untangle what they were owed. In the end, despite all the confusion created by the litigants and their witnesses regarding what was owed to Doña María, the numbers came down to 500 sheep, 156 rams for 1768, and 57 lambs for 1769, along with 200 head as payment for the corresponding years owed with 300 fleeces for both years.

The process by which the partido system worked is readily seen in the 1768–69 case at Atrisco. More important, it shows the system of justice at work: the procedure of taking testimony, the role of the magistrate, and the decision-making process involving the governor as arbiter. Each party was given an opportunity to see what had been entered into the record before it was submitted to the governor for final decision. Each side was given a voice in the matter and time to respond. When the case was finally resolved, it demonstrated that the Spanish colonial system of litigation had worked.

CHAPTER 6

Anatomy of a Scam

The Case of Las Ciruelas and Arbolito del Manzano, 1769

We dug the acequia through the middle of the lands of my brother Bernardo de Chaves and this is the truth, the same as if sworn, and I am ready to declare the same in front of the law.

NICOLÁS DURÁN Y CHAVES, 1769

The acequia ran on the east side, gave a half turn, and a little beyond there, stopped at a small plain with a rise that bordered it, and which Don Nicolás had told [me] formed a water tank. . . . That acequia, from the said ciruelas where it ran from to the place it reached his lands, was the boundary of the two lands it divided.

DECLARATION OF JOSÉ CHAVES, 1769

Although he had not said so in writing, the patriarch Don Fernando Durán y Chaves must have expected that the land from his original 1692 grant would remain intact in family hands. His 1707 will bequeathed his estate to his nine surviving children and the heirs of his deceased son, Bernardo. For over thirty years after his death, the family transacted land deals among its own members with few problems. But in 1757 a sale of a piece of land in Atrisco would test the strength of the Durán y Chaves family.

Problems began innocently when José Durán y Chaves from El Paso del Norte appeared in 1757 before the alcalde mayor of the Villa de Alburquerque and stated that he had sold land inherited from his father, Bernardo Durán y Chaves, son of Fernando Durán y Chaves. The buyer was Jacinto Sánchez, husband of Efigenia Durán y Chaves. As there were no claims against the property, alcalde mayor Antonio Baca verified and certified the sale at a price of 550 pesos. For nearly twelve years, the land underwent a series of divisions and transactions as it had previously—all within the family.

In 1769, after the death of Jacinto Sánchez, Joseph Hurtado de Mendoza, son-in-law of Doña Efigenia Durán y Chaves, read through Fernando Durán y Chaves's last will and testament and began to explore its advantages for his mother-in-law and her heir, Feliciana Sánchez, his wife. A piece of land in Atrisco was unaccounted for, and he pondered the possibility that it might adjoin those of his mother-in-law. He seems to have arranged for Nicolás Durán y Chaves, a son of Don Fernando Durán y Chaves, to make a statement regarding this property, known as Las Ciruelas.[1]

Nicolás Durán y Chaves claimed in his statement that Las Ciruelas, a tract bordered by lands of the Durán y Chaves family, belonged to the heirs of his brother Bernardo, who had died in 1705. Insisting that the acequia running through Atrisco at that time was not the original irrigation ditch used as the boundary of Bernardo's lands, Nicolás, who had lived in Atrisco for decades,[2] submitted that the wrong ditch had been used to survey the boundary. He suggested that the present owners of Las Ciruelas, the Romero family, illegally possessed the land. Nicolás said that he and his brother Pedro III had dug an acequia dividing the land after they had inherited it from their father, and that the original acequia had been covered from disuse.[3] In his statement, Nicolás affirmed:

> I, Nicolás Durán y Chaves, resident of the Puesto of Nuestra Señora de Guadalupe, declare that . . . as a person knowledgeable of the division of the lands in the place of Atrisco and having regarded the contradictions I have heard and so that my conscience is clear, I state that the boundaries that run down and border those of Pedro de Chaves; and to the other part that border with the lands of my sister Isabel and mine which are toward the south. . . . that the acequia which is between said lands was dug by me and my brother Pedro de Chaves after the distribution of the above lands. We dug the acequia through the middle of the lands of my brother Bernardo de Chaves and this is the truth, the same as if sworn . . . . Nicolás de Chaves.[4]

Nicolás's statement was enough to challenge the Romero claim to Las Ciruelas. Doubtless, Hurtado de Mendoza lost little time in explaining the significance of the statement to his mother-in-law, Doña Efigenia.

With Nicolás's statement in hand, Efigenia Durán y Chaves presented her petition to Francisco Trébol Navarro, the alcalde mayor of the Villa de Alburquerque. Legal proceedings over ownership of Las Ciruelas and its adjacent properties had begun.[5] In her own statement to Trébol Navarro, she described how the boundaries had been determined when her

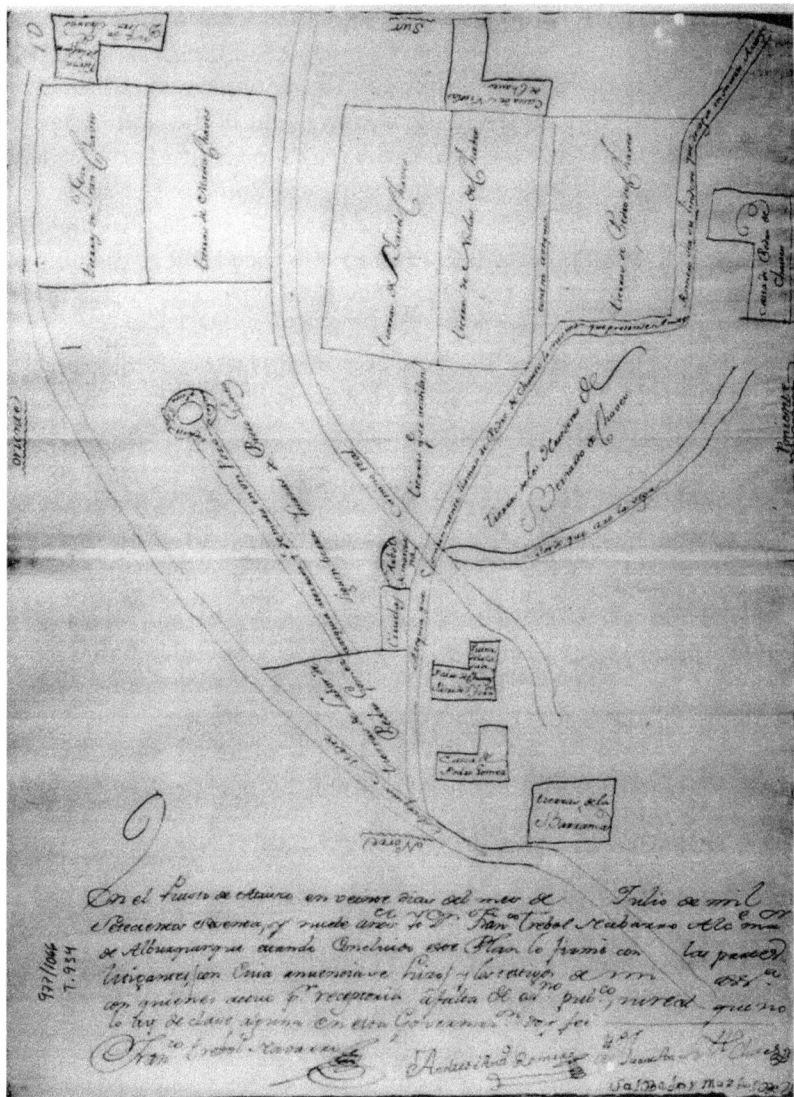

Map 2. Map of Atrisco drawn on July 20, 1769, showing the disputed lands at Las Ciruelas and Arbol de Manzano.

ARCHIVO GENERAL DE LA NACIÓN, MEXICO CITY

late husband, Jacinto Sánchez, had acquired the land from José Durán y Chaves in 1757. She noted that her husband had been sick in bed on the day the property was surveyed, and that her brother, Diego Antonio Durán y Chaves, had witnessed the measurement of the land.[6] Efigenia stated, furthermore, that the land divided by the acequia had therefore been illegally sold by Felipe Romero to Ignacio Romero. Her statement was that "in error, they showed him the [wrong] boundaries; a quarter of the land was what they sold."[7] Efigenia also stated that at the time of her statement, "Doña Luisa Durán y Chaves was now deceased, but at the time [of the sale] was absent from the said kingdom. She had given power of attorney to Juan Chaves, her brother, as well as to her sons, nephews, and heirs, and in the name of all, thus represented, the sale was made [to Efigenia's husband Jacinto Sanchez]."[8]

Doña Efigenia submitted as corroborating testimony the paper signed by Nicolás Chaves, who was deceased at the time of the hearing. The problem, she said, arose when Felipe Romero sold part of the disputed land to Ignacio Romero while her husband still owned it. She stated:

> And the said site being owned by my said husband [Jacinto Sanchez], Felipe Romero, also a resident of Atrisco, sold a piece of land which is divided by the acequia to Ignacio Romero, who not ignorant that the land was not his (rather, it was included in the whole purchase of said place), imposed a defense against nullification, upon which Don Felipe Romero offered that in case the lands were taken away by my said husband, the buyer, the referenced true owner of the land, he would replace it with an equal piece from his own lands.[9]

Doña Efigenia decried the continuous trespass across her lands as well as continued development and farming on it by the Romeros, and she urged the alcalde to establish the ownership of Las Ciruelas before it became impossible to prove her right to the land.

> Thus he has caused me much strife, as it seems, and considerable harm in his actions by rudely ruining my cornfields by opening foot and horse paths to get to the said piece of land.[10]

Alcalde mayor Trébol Navarro began the investigation into the ownership of Las Ciruelas in April 1769 by summoning the interested parties to testify. He reviewed a competing claim to the land by Lucía Ana Durán y Chaves (known as Doña Ana), widow of Felipe Romero. She was the daughter of Antonio Durán y Chaves and heir to his lands in Atrisco. Beyond her hereditary interests in Las Ciruelas and other lands in Atrisco, the desire to determine their ownership was magnified because her son, Andrés Antonio Romero, was living and farming in Las Ciruelas. On his shoulders would fall the burden of defending his mother's claim to the land against the interloper, Joseph Hurtado de Mendoza, and his eager mother-in-law, Efigenia Durán y Chaves.

Doña Efigenia, encouraged by Hurtado de Mendoza, countered by arguing that Doña Ana and her son were living on lands that had once belonged to the children of Bernardo Durán y Chaves. Those lands, she emphasized, had been sold in 1757 by José Durán y Chaves, son of Don Bernardo, to her husband, Jacinto Sánchez.[11] Doña Efigenia reiterated her demands: "With the expressed paper of Nicolás Chaves, you would be well served to go to the stated site and in the company of those referenced examine said land and its section and its boundaries and if said piece of land which Ignacio Romero purchased is mine and is included in the body of said site which my husband purchased, give me possession of it as it is part of the inheritance of my minor children. I ask you and plead."[12] Doña Efigenia further explained that once she received the land, Ignacio Romero would then be free to make a claim against Felipe Romero.

As requested by Doña Efigenia, Trébol Navarro went out to the site and walked the land in question accompanied by key witnesses and interested parties to the suit. Among them were José Durán y Chaves, the original 1757 seller of the land in question, who had come up from El Paso del Norte; Ignacio Romero; and Lucía Ana Durán y Chaves. All stood around Trébol Navarro in the ruins of a house once owned by Pedro Durán y Chaves II and responded to the alcalde mayor's questions.

Making a reconnaissance of the land, Trébol Navarro asked José Durán y Chaves to describe the lands he had sold to Jacinto Sánchez. According to Don José's response, the boundaries ran

> From the said ruins of the house where we were standing to Las Ciruelas, which is from east to west, and from the small road which runs from Las Ciruelas, which divides the lands belonging to Doña Antonia Baca, and on the north side from the said old house of the said Pedro de Chaves, and on the south with the lands of Don Nicolás and Don Pedro de Chaves, the elder. That the acequia which runs to the end of the said lands is the same which irrigates the lands of Don Diego Antonio Durán y Chaves and that these same lands are the ones that Don José Chaves states are the ones he sold, which with the rest comprise an integral whole with the lands around it owned by three heirs who are José Chaves, Juan Chaves, and Lucía Chaves and their heirs.[13]

Trébol Navarro was then set to make a decision. As he announced that the land belonged to Doña Efigenia, Doña Ana contended that there was one piece of evidence that had not been considered. It would prove that Pedro

Durán y Chaves III, Don Fernando's youngest son, had perjured himself in regard to the boundaries and sale of the land. It was a paper signed in 1722 by Pedro Durán y Chaves and executed by Alfonso Rael de Aguilar, lieutenant general of New Mexico.[14]

The document revealed that Rael de Aguilar had presided over a deal in which Pedro and Nicolás Durán y Chaves agreed to give their brother Antonio title to the land not mentioned in Don Fernando Durán y Chaves's will. Rael de Aguilar testified that everyone present comprehended the transfer of land to Don Antonio. "To that effect, among other ceremonies prescribed by law, I took him [Don Antonio] by the hand and walked him over the said lands and as a sign of possession he threw rocks and pulled up weeds."[15] The evidence was damaging to Hurtado de Mendoza's case. Trébol Navarro read:

> In the Villa of San Felipe de Neri de Alburquerque on the 27th of April, 1722, I, sargento mayor Don Alfonso Rael de Aguilar, Lieutenant General of this Kingdom of New Mexico, state that having appeared before me Don Antonio Durán y Chaves, settler of this said Villa and declaring that Captain Don Fernando Durán y Chaves, deceased, by means of his will which he made and stipulated before Captain Martín Hurtado, alcalde mayor and captain of war of this said Villa and jurisdiction, on February 11 of the past year of 172[1?] had, below, stated his final wish and disposition before his death. Because in one of the clauses [Don Fernando] states that as his legitimate son he demonstrates by means of his inheritance, that in accordance with the rest of his sons and Doña Lucía Hurtado his wife, and mother of said Don Antonio de Chaves, that from his landed hacienda in Atrisco which is mentioned in the will, he consigns to him one separate plot of land with structures which are within said lands that run down from the bluffs near the house of Juan de Perea to the three cottonwood trees on the acequia that border the lands of Luis de Chaves, his deceased brother. Although he had stated in said will that there is no other piece of land which he has and possesses; said father having left it out and having forgotten about it, not expressing it, [he states that] it is clear to Doña Lucía Hurtado and my brother that I am the legitimate owner and that it pleases me that the aforementioned appear before me and concur that the referred to piece of land is that which borders that of Nicolas Chaves and belongs to the heirs of Bernardo de Chaves. Thus, I asked that Doña Lucía Hurtado, Don Pedro, Don Francisco, Don Nicolas de Chaves, appear before me and concur and say that the referred to lands were and pertain belonged to said Antonio de Chaves who received them from said Captain Don Fernando de Chaves many years prior. [I, Alfonso Rael de Aguilar] agreed to what I had been informed in reference to the foregoing and that in this testament his said father granted possession to the said Don Antonio de

Chaves. To that effect, among other ceremonies prescribed by law, I took him by the hand and walked him over the said lands and as a sign of possession he threw rocks and pulled up weeds. And as a sign, he quietly and peacefully took possession which I gave in the name of his majesty without any contradictions. So that it be evident, I signed it along with the witnesses at my side as the Royal Magistrate. Alfonso de Rael Aguilar, Isidro Sánchez, Juan Rael de Aguilar, Pedro Gómes Durán y Chaves for Nicolás de Chaves.[16]

The document was authentic, for one of the signers, Isidro Sánchez, a military aide to Rael de Aguilar, was still alive and would later testify to its authenticity.

Don Pedro angrily alleged that the paper was false and that no one could prove the witness signature was his. The paper was important because it confirmed that Fernando Durán y Chaves had given his son Antonio Durán y Chaves, the father of Lucía Ana Durán y Chaves and grandfather of Andrés Romero, a plot of land adjoining that owned by Nicolás Durán y Chaves.[17]

Having considered the facts, Trébol Navarro dispossessed Doña Ana of Las Ciruelas and, by dint of that decision, dispossessed Ignacio Romero of his land as well (Ignacio had purchased a piece of land in the disputed area from Felipe Romero). Trébol Navarro forwarded his decision, with accompanying documents, to Governor Pedro Fermín de Mendinueta for approval.

Meanwhile, the clever Joseph Hurtado de Mendoza petitioned Governor Mendinueta to approve, as soon as possible, Trébol Navarro's decision granting the land to Doña Efigenia. Hurtado de Mendoza explained the salient elements demonstrating the hereditary rights of his mother-in-law, Doña Efigenia, and his wife, Feliciana Sánchez. Hurtado de Mendoza denied that Pedro Durán y Chaves had signed the paper executed by Alfonso Rael de Aguilar and claimed that Pedro's signature was forged. He even suggested that Felipe Romero was the author of the document (*Romero fue el amanuenze*).[18]

Ready to approve Trébol Navarro's decision, Governor Mendinueta remarked that new questions had been raised in this case and that he would like to see the referenced paper containing Pedro Durán y Chaves's supposed signature.[19] A week later, Mendinueta put a hold on the process, requesting more information on the case. He asked Trébol Navarro to advise Hurtado Mendoza about his right to respond.[20] Meanwhile, Andrés Antonio Romero appeared before the governor in behalf of his mother, Doña Ana, and stated that she was indeed one of the heirs to the land passed down by Don Bernardo Durán y Chaves. He stated that his grandfather, Antonio Durán y Chaves, had been in possession of those lands since 1722.[21] In clear language, he said that his great-grandfather, Don Fernando Durán y Chaves, had put in his will the following: "To the children of my son Bernardo, I leave the house that belonged to my father with its field at Las Ciruelas and one apple tree. I leave them, furthermore, one lot of land which runs from Las Ciruelas to where an irrigation ditch forms its boundary."[22]

Andrés Antonio Romero explained that the referenced piece of land that the other heirs were attempting to take from his mother was on the other bank of the irrigation ditch. If so, then it should be clear that the other bank of the irrigation ditch formed a distinct boundary for the land on that side of it. And that land, he explained, was vacant and not mentioned in Don Fernando's will.[23] Andrés submitted, therefore, that Pedro and Nicolás Chaves, brothers of Antonio Durán y Chaves, his grandfather, as interested parties and settlers in the Valle de Atrisco, had signed the paper in 1722 because they recognized that the land in question belonged to Don Antonio.[24]

As described in the document of 1722, the contested land in Atrisco comprised a lot with structures "within said lands that run down from the bluffs near the house of Juan de Perea to the three cottonwood trees on the acequia that border the lands of Luis de Chaves," and at the time that Don Fernando wrote his will, he believed that there was no other piece of land. But Don Fernando had "forgotten" that there was indeed another piece of land, and so he corrected his mistake by granting it to his son, Antonio Durán y Chaves, in front of witnesses. That piece of forgotten land was the land in question.

Andrés Antonio Romero made his plea: "I ask, in the name of my mother, that justice may be served, as do the [other] heirs seek, by using the boundaries left by my deceased grandfather and which my father used in the sale of the land in question to Ignacio Romero."[25]

In his statement, Andrés acknowledged that the transfer was made with the condition that Felipe Romero would give Ignacio Romero another piece of land in the event of a cloud on the title to the land. He said that the confusion rested on the "verbal allegations [agreements] made between my father [Felipe Romero] and Jacinto Sánchez. And, furthermore, although [Andrés and his mother] had, nonetheless, seen Don Fernando's will, they had never read it with a studied eye."[26] Until Hurtado Mendoza had pointed it out, it had not occurred to them that the land in question lay outside the terms of the will.

The paper allegedly signed by Pedro Durán y Chaves in 1722 took on new significance, for it was the only statement that recognized that the land lay outside of the terms of Don Fernando's will. Aided by her very able son, Andrés Antonio Romero, Doña Ana mounted a vigorous offensive—she had already told Pedro Durán y Chaves that "his signature was on the testament, that is, the paper that Don Alfonso Rael de Aguilar had drawn up."[27] Although Don Pedro vigorously denied it, the tide began to shift in favor of Doña Lucía Ana Durán y Chaves.

Attempting to recover his advantage, Hurtado de Mendoza drew up an interrogatory, which was accepted by Trébol Navarro, listing nine questions that he hoped would draw attention to the issue of the acequia.[28] These questions were to be asked of all witnesses.

1. If it is known to you that from Las Ciruelas downward are the lands of the children of Don Bernardo Chaves, that border those of Don Nicolás and Don Pedro Chaves.

2. If it is known to you whether the acequia cited in the clause of [Don Fernando's] last will and testament as the one that borders said lands, is the one that in the past ran from the Arbolito de Manzano, which was contiguous to Las Ciruelas and cut Las Ciruelas in half. And that from there the acequia ended in a water tank on the east side, continued on the east side, and came down toward the south in a straight line until it reached the lands of said Don Nicolás Chaves, ultimately reaching the ones bordered by said lands of the expressed children of Don Bernardo.

3. If it is known to you whether the old acequia watered the orchards and fields of Don Fernando Chaves, testator.

4. If it is known to you that while Don Fernando lived, there was no other acequia through said land except the old one of El Arbolito, which closely followed the little old road to Rancho de la Pastoria.

5. If it is known to you, or you have heard, that the motive for not having another acequia during the time of Don Fernando other than the old one, was because toward the west there were no lands being worked, and therefore, all the fields were on the east side of the old acequia.

6. If it is known to you, or you have heard, that the acequia that is now in the middle of the lands of said children of Don Bernardo, which runs north to south, was opened by Don Nicolás and Don Pedro Chaves long after the death of said Don Fernando, their father.

7. If it is known to you that this piece of land of Las Ciruelas is not designated nor does it belong by means of any title, to Don Antonio Chaves, father of said Doña Ana Chaves.

8. If you remember, know, or have heard tell, that at one time the witness, or his father, had signed a document of possession at the time that Don Alfonso Rael de Aguilar was lieutenant general.

9. If you know or have heard tell as common knowledge, at any time, either
   by said lieutenant general, or any other judge, that he had given
   possession of land in the Puesto de Atrisco to said Don Antonio
   Chaves.[29]

Hurtado de Mendoza called his first witness under the interrogatory, José Durán y Chaves, who presented himself before Trébol Navarro on May 9, 1769, at Puesto de San Isidro de Pajarito, south of Alburquerque. Don José, now sixty-four years old, swore to tell the truth before God, made the sign of the cross, and answered all the questions to the best of his knowledge.[30] He confirmed that although he had been gone from New Mexico since he was a young man, he remembered that his siblings Juan and Lucía Chaves had a piece of land that they had received from their father, Bernardo Durán y Chaves, and that after a long time he and they had finally agreed to sell the land in 1757.[31] That year, he traveled from El Paso del Norte to the Puesto de Atrisco to confer with his uncle Nicolás de Chaves, who had lived at Atrisco nearly all his life and knew the boundaries well. In regard to the first question of the interrogatory, Don José said the boundaries, according to Don Nicolás were as follows:

From the house which belonged to [my] great-grandfather, Don Pedro Durán y Chaves [II] which is now in ruins, he took me eastward, a little out of the way from said house where there was the huerta de ciruelas [plum tree grove] and the place where there was an arbolito de manzano [small apple tree] from which ran, very clearly, an acequia which, though many years had passed without it being used and which was overgrown and filled, could very distinctly be discerned. The acequia ran on the east side, gave a half turn, and a little beyond there, stopped at a small plain with a rise that bordered it, and which Don Nicolás had told [me] formed a water tank. From the tank, the acequia, with its same eastern side, ran straight to the south into a small hole, then upon exiting it, the said acequia, with its said east bank, ran straight south until it reached the lands of the said Don Nicolás. That acequia, from the said ciruelas where it ran from to the place it reached his lands, was the boundary of the two lands it divided.[32]

José Durán y Chaves went on to say that the acequia formed the boundary from Las Ciruelas to where it met with Don Nicolás's land. It was the boundary for the two pieces of land on either side. Northward, beyond the old house—Don Nicolás had told him—and west of there ran the lands that bordered with those of Don Pedro de Chaves. The lands described were those sold to Jacinto Sánchez.[33]

Regarding the second question, Don José said he had always believed that the boundary was the old acequia, as stated in Don Fernando's last will and testament. To the third question, he said that as he had not lived there since his boyhood, he could not remember whether Don Fernando irrigated his lands from the said acequia. He had no answer for the fourth question because he did not know anything, as he had left when he was young. Concerning the fifth question, he pointed out that Don Fernando's land lay east of the acequia, not west. To the sixth, he said that Don Nicolás and Don Pedro had constructed the new acequia because the water could not go up the steep grade of the old acequia. His answer to the seventh question was that Don Antonio Chaves did not merit the lands, because they were claimed by [José's] siblings and their heirs. Don Antonio's father [Don Fernando] had left him lands at La Barranca and, despite what he had been told, [Don Antonio] now wanted the lands in question. He had no knowledge regarding question eight. To the ninth question, however, he said that he remembered someone saying that even if Don Antonio claimed the lands in Atrisco, it must be known that they were not legally given him by a judge. As he had nothing else to add to his answers, the session ended and he signed his statement.[34]

Bernardo Chaves, son of Nicolás Durán y Chaves, was the second to testify and appeared at Puesto de San Isidro de Pajarito on May 13. His testimony supported that of Don José. He testified that Don Nicolás was born at Puesto de Atrisco and was knowledgeable about boundaries related to his own lands and those of José, Juan, and Lucía Chaves. He said that an acequia began at Las Ciruelas and ran from the acequia madre and behind the house that was now in ruins. The house, he said, belonged to his great-grandfather Pedro Durán y Chaves. The acequia ran from the corner on the east side of the house to the foot of a small apple tree near Las Ciruelas, where it gave a quick turn eastward and soon after turned south, following the old road which came out of Las Ciruelas to the former house of Don Fernando. The acequia then ran to the lands of Don Nicolás. The acequia served as the eastern boundary for the lands of Pedro Gomes, which were purchased by Doña Antonia Baca, and on the other side, toward the west, served as the boundary for José, Juan, and Lucía Chaves. He said that the lands of the aforesaid three persons began at the ruined house which was on a small elevation on the north side, and from the corner of the right hand which is west, he said, was a small, low-lying hill which had always been the entrance to Atrisco. Westward, beyond there, on the right, were the lands and house of Pedro de Chaves, whose lands were contiguous with those of Don Nicolás.[35] The rest of his answers to questions two through nine were similar to the responses given by Don José.

Although she did not testify, Antonia Baca, daughter of Pedro Durán y

Chaves, stated in a deposition that her father's signature on the document of 1722 had been forged. She also stated that she had heard that 1715 was the year that Don Fernando Durán y Chaves had died.[36]

On May 18, 1769, Pedro Durán y Chaves III appeared before Alcalde Mayor Trébol Navarro to give testimony. Don Pedro affirmed that the lands that came out of Las Ciruelas through that of the Arbolito de Manzano adjoined his and were the ones that his nephews José and Juan Chaves and niece Lucía Chaves had inherited from Don Fernando through their father, Bernardo. The lands were still identifiable because the house, now in ruins, belonged to his grandfather Pedro Durán y Chaves II, the first settler of Atrisco. Those lands, he said, reached as far as the entrance to Atrisco, which was on a small hill.[37]

He said that during Don Fernando's lifetime no other acequia existed except the acequia madre, which ran behind the house, and, after the *bordo de Arenal* (the embankment at Arenal), turned as far as the large field with trees which his father owned. There the acequia stopped. That was the acequia that ran behind his grandfather's house, which was now in ruins. Another acequia, the one that ran along some *arboles de ciruelas* (plum trees) were the lands that his father had left to his son Don Bernardo. That acequia terminated in a hole that formed a tank which was on the east side. Giving a half turn toward the east, it followed straight south toward the lands of Nicolás, his brother. The acequia watered the field of trees that his father had left him. Afterward, the acequia met with the old road that ran past the ruined house. His father, Don Fernando, had often told him that the acequia served as the eastern boundary of his lands and that the west side of it was the boundary to the land belonging to the children of his brother Bernardo.[38] He felt strongly that Felipe Romero did not in any way deserve the lands, "as much as he would like to say they are his."[39]

He reiterated that he had never placed his signature granting Don Antonio possession of the lands in question at Atrisco. He declared the paper false, for never in his life had he used the name Gomes, "because it was not his legitimate last name but one that is supposed." If his signature was forged, so was the paper granting Don Antonio possession of the land at Las Ciruelas.[40] Furthermore, he stated, at no time could he remember any judge ever granting possession of lands to his brother Antonio Chaves. He accused Felipe Romero of trickery by means of producing a false document that stated that everyone had agreed to give the parcel to Don Antonio because their father had forgotten to include it in his will. To Don Pedro, the proposition was based on a false premise.[41]

Hurtado de Mendoza called his final witness, Antonio Chaves II, another son of Don Nicolás. He tended to reaffirm all that the others had stated, and his answers added very little to the foregoing.[42]

Hurtado de Mendoza presented a summation of the testimony and documentation that had been produced to support his case in behalf of his mother-in-law, Doña Efigenia. He asked Doña Ana to produce the paper in which Rael de Aguilar had given Don Antonio possession of the land at Las Ciruelas so that it could be held up to scrutiny.[43] The inquiry being concluded, Trébol Navarro wrote Doña Ana de Chaves an order to turn over the paper within nine days.[44]

CHAPTER 7

Worn-out Statements

Las Ciruelas Restored

> With his worn-out statements, Don Pedro Gómez attempts to deny that which he gave before the competent judge when he was young and in his right mind, which his advanced age does not permit.
>
> ANDRÉS ANTONIO ROMERO, 1769

> This is the land that Don Alfonso Rael de Aguilar, with all the ceremonies empowered him, granted without controversy. The said heirs signed it, and I signed for Nicolás, and I remember that he was disappointed in me because I did not put "Don" with his name.
>
> ISIDRO SÁNCHEZ, 1769

Andrés Antonio Romero lost no time in renewing the legal battle to save his mother's claim to Las Ciruelas. At issue was who rightfully owned the land: the heirs of Don Antonio, as claimed by Doña Ana; or the heirs of Don Bernardo, as claimed by Doña Efigenia. The entire case hinged on the 1722 document authorized by Alfonso Rael de Aguilar that explained the location of the disputed lands.

Andrés appeared before alcalde mayor Francisco Trébol Navarro at Puesto de San Isidro de Pajarito and politely thanked him for having sent copies of the proceedings. The able Andrés had taken the time to study the documents, especially the interrogatories, and prepared a brief explaining that

> it is very clear that Don Antonio Durán y Chaves presented himself before the referenced lieutenant general petitioning that Doña Lucía Hurtado, legitimate mother of my referenced deceased grandfather Don Antonio Chaves and her other children . . . as required in the said possession. . . . that the piece of land belonged to my grandfather Don Antonio Durán y Chaves and with their statements the said lieutenant general proceeded to give him possession which was signed by the aforesaid, as

evidenced by their signatures. . . . With his worn-out statements, Don Pedro Gómez attempts to deny that which he gave before the competent judge when he was young and in his right mind, which his advanced age does not permit.[1]

With that opening statement, Andrés placed the entire episode in a new perspective.

Andrés minced no words in tearing his cousins' statements apart one by one. He brashly alleged that Don Pedro's testimony and Don Nicolas's written statement were made faulty by their advanced ages. Andrés questioned Don Nicolás's testimony, "if it is true that he gave it, for he was more advanced in age" than Don Pedro. As for the two sons of Don Nicolás who had testified, Andrés felt that Bernardo II was not in his right mind and had perjured himself, for on the first question, he had already answered falsely.[2] An astute student of the genealogy of Atrisco, Andrés pointed out that Bernardo had sworn that "he is the eldest son of Don Nicolás de Chaves, which is not so, because the eldest is Joseph Chaves, after whom was born Nicolás Chaves [II] . . . who died a few years later." Andrés said that "his testimony lacks truth . . . because he is such a limited individual that it is impossible that he is aware of what he has declared."[3] Employing the language of colonial times, he attempted to discredit the testimony of Don Nicolás's son Antonio Chaves II of Las Nutrias, because he was a "*genízaro*; his mother, a Jumana, was a servant to Don Pedro de Chaves. Therefore, he is incapable of understanding the gravity of his legal oath."[4] Andrés further declared that Antonio was not even the son of Don Nicolás, for his mother was unmarried.[5] Andrés submitted that Antonio's falsehoods were enough to dismiss his testimony.

Turning to testimony regarding the description of Las Ciruelas, Andrés declared that he placed no value on what Joseph Hurtado de Mendoza had submitted. He turned to Don Fernando's will and the document of 1722 giving Las Ciruelas to his son Don Antonio Durán y Chaves I. "Las Ciruelas is located on the east side" of Atrisco, he wrote. And the unattached land that Don Fernando left in his will "runs from Las Ciruelas to the west where the house belonging to Don Pedro Chaves stood. The clause in the will cites that the acequia is the boundary of the unattached lands running from north to south and borders the said lands on the east side. And the piece of land under examination is on the other side of the acequia that heads south."[6] That, he said, had already been proved and it did not belong to the heirs of Don Bernardo.

Andrés then played his trump card: he asked Trébol Navarro to permit him to submit "more proof, which is my right and that of my mother; I ask you, so that you may be better served, to summon Isidro Sánchez, settler of La Alameda." If anyone could clarify whether Antonio de Chaves was truly granted possession in 1722, it would be Isidro Sánchez, for he was there and had signed the document.

Andrés added that the lands Don José Chaves had sold to Jacinto Sánchez were not the ones in question. Regarding the sales contract made before Captain Antonio Baca, "I was the witness as demonstrated by my signature on the sales contract . . . that . . . permitted the past sale of the lands in question to be without contradiction." In other words, the lands Don José sold to Jacinto Sánchez were not the ones at Las Ciruelas and Arbolito de Manzano. His point was that the current acequia madre, not the ditch that was covered from disuse at Las Ciruelas, was the original boundary of the land in question.

Old and ailing, Isidro Sánchez could not make the trip from Santa Fe to the Villa de Alburquerque. He apologized that he was sickly and could not mount a horse to present himself before Trébol Navarro. His record was unblemished in the service to his king, for he had served as lieutenant of the pueblos of Jemez, Zia, and Santa Ana and the Puesto de San Francisco de Bernalillo, and he had helped the Franciscan friar Carlos Joseph Delgado establish relations with the Hopis that permitted the transfer of Natives to reestablish Sandia Pueblo in the late 1740s. He had also served as lieutenant at the presidio of San Felipe de Terrenate in Sonora.[7]

Sánchez wrote in a signed statement that in 1722, when he was stationed at the Real Presidio de la Villa de Santa Fe, he had accompanied Alfonso Rael de Aguilar and was a guest in the house of Don Antonio Durán y Chaves at the Puesto de Atrisco. Other heirs of Don Fernando Durán y Chaves were also at the house during that time, including Don Pedro, Don Nicolás, Pedro Gomes, and Doña Isabel Durán y Chaves, who had met for the purpose of executing the will left by the deceased Don Fernando. In the proceedings, the land in question came up and it was decided by everyone there to grant it to Antonio Durán y Chaves, which was done by Rael de Aguilar, as he had been empowered to do. To Sánchez's recollection, the land had little use. He described the boundaries with great precision:

> It borders on the west along the acequia which passes the house of Pedro de Chaves, on the south with the lands of Nicolas Chaves, on the east the Camino Real, and on the north with the vado or ford of the same acequia close to a small apple tree. This is the land that Don Alfonso Rael de Aguilar, with all the ceremonies empowered him, granted without out controversy. The said heirs signed it, and I signed for Nicolás, and I remember that he was disappointed in me because I did not put "Don" with his name; otherwise it was done quietly and calmly.[8]

Sánchez said that Rael de Aguilar had officiated over such proceedings many times, and as proof of this, anyone could check the archives in Santa Fe and see that Rael de Aguilar had been authorized to do so on various occasions.[9]

Nevertheless, Trébol Navarro informed Doña Ana Durán y Chaves that "at first view" he believed Isidro Sánchez's statement "was not sufficient proof" to support her case and that she ought to bring forth other witnesses.[10] Diego Antonio Durán y Chaves, forty-five-year-old brother of Doña Efigenia, stepped forward in Doña Ana's defense. He was asked if he knew

> that the piece of land of which Doña Ana Durán y Chaves has been dispossessed by Doña Efigenia Durán y Chaves at the Puesto de Atrisco, and which was currently owned by Ignacio Romero, is the same unattached land that was sold by the heirs of the deceased Don Bernardo de Chaves to Doña Efigenia Chaves. He answered that it was widely known, and he knew through hearsay, that the piece of land was vacant and that Felipe Romero, consort of Doña Ana Duran y Chaves, had spoken about the sale of a piece of land to Ignacio Romero.[11]

Regarding the most recent sale of the land to Jacinto Sánchez, Diego Antonio answered that the [covered-over] acequia was already there at the time of the sale. He said that Jacinto Sánchez, who was ill in bed, had asked him to go out with the buyers and the heirs of Don Bernardo because no one else knew enough about the boundaries of the land. Most of them had been raised outside of Atrisco. Furthermore, they only sold a piece of land that they had inherited from their father, a fact which agreed with that stated in Don Fernando's will.[12] As a witness to the sale of the land, Diego Antonio Durán y Chaves presented a clear and credible statement. Thus, he contradicted Doña Efigenia's claim. His testimony implied that the land in question belonged to Doña Ana Durán y Chaves.

Another witness, Ignacio Chaves, a settler of Atrisco, came forward to support Doña Ana's case. He said he knew the land in question well, and that Felipe Romero had sold a piece of land to Ignacio Romero by virtue of the instrument of possession that was made by Alfonso Rael de Aguilar in 1722. As long as he could remember, the acequia had always been there. Having sworn his statement, Ignacio Chaves declared that he was forty-three years old and had been raised at Atrisco.[13] Therefore, his testimony, too, had great credibility in the proceedings.

His case deteriorating, Joseph Hurtado de Mendoza made a desperate effort to salvage the legal position and interests of Doña Efigenia. In his written statement, he said that Don Diego Antonio Durán y Chaves and Ignacio Chaves had lied in their statements. Hurtado de Mendoza said that at the time of the sale, the lands were not vacant and that Don Diego

Antonio knew it because José and Nicolás Durán y Chaves, the sellers, were there and showed all interested parties the land in 1757 but testified to the contrary in 1769. Hurtado de Mendoza recalled that one afternoon, he and Don Diego Antonio had gone out to Las Ciruelas and followed the acequia to a hole that was covered up. They looked for the beginning point of the acequia, but it had been covered over by a cornfield in the immediate vicinity of Las Ciruelas.[14] His point begged the question: How could Don Diego Antonio be certain about the location of the acequia, if he could not even identify it on the ground?

Along a different line of reasoning, Hurtado de Mendoza said that soon after his marriage to Feliciana Sánchez, he was planting his field when Don Diego Antonio told him that the piece of land on the other side of the acequia that irrigated his cornfields was also his (Hurtado's, through his mother-in-law, Doña Efigenia). When the Chaveses were going to re-plow the fields, they had shown him the lands adjoining the old road and told him that although Felipe Romero had sold the piece of land, he had done so in bad faith. Hurtado de Mendoza continued:

> Therefore, I could easily claim it because it was mine. Similarly, summon if you please Ignacio Chaves, who under the same oath, says and declares that he is certain that the acequia is still visible, that it issues from Las Ciruelas, but it is covered up. Likewise, ask him if he is certain that when Felipe Romero went to sell the piece of land, that he wanted to buy it, but he did not because Tomás Chaves [Felipe Romero's brother-in-law] told him not to buy it because he would end up with nothing, for it did not belong to Felipe Romero.[15]

On June 12, 1767, Trébol Navarro, in an effort to clarify the charges leveled by Hurtado de Mendoza, summoned José Chaves, Diego Antonio Chaves, and Ignacio Chaves before him to clarify their answers.[16] Asked how much land was actually shown to Jacinto Sánchez and what its boundaries were, Don José answered that Nicolás de Chaves had shown him the land in question. Later, José revisited the land with his brother Juan and his brother-in-law Diego Antonio Chaves. They walked along the acequia until they came to the well at the end of it that had been covered with dirt. From there, they identified lands owned by Nicolás in relation to the old acequia.[17] The episode he described had done nothing more than reassure José that the land in question had been identified to his satisfaction.

Turning next to Don Diego Antonio Durán y Chaves, Trébol Navarro asked if it was true that he had made certain comments to Hurtado de Mendoza leading him to believe that the land at Las Ciruelas was his, and whether or not he had said that Felipe Romero had sold the land in bad faith. Don Diego Antonio responded that he "had not said anything like that, and if he did intimate anything like that, he did not remember it, nor does he have any recollection of such a thing."[18] When asked if one afternoon Hurtado de Mendoza had taken him out to the acequia at Las Ciruelas, which is filled and is still distinguishable, Don Diego Antonio responded that "it is certain that he entered the acequia at Las Ciruelas, where it originates, and, while in it, he followed it to the hole which he has declared before and that from there he turned around to Ciruelas by means of the same acequia," indicating that nothing else happened or was said.[19] The acequia he followed was short, covered over, and did not go anywhere; it merely terminated at the tank it formed. There was nothing special about it, especially as the lands around it were largely vacant. It hardly met the specifications of an acequia madre, much less one that would be used to define the boundaries of several heirs.

Ignacio Chaves testified for the second time but did not change his previous testimony. Asked to explain if he had decided against buying the land because Tomás Chaves warned him that Felipe Romero was selling it in bad faith, Ignacio clarified that the piece of land that Tomás Chaves had told him not to buy did not run from the old road, but from a new road that had recently been opened. Afterward, Ignacio became suspicious about whether that land was Felipe Romero's.[20]

Slowly, Trébol Navarro began to see how Hurtado de Mendoza had deftly twisted people's words at Atrisco. The testimony of Diego Antonio Durán y Chaves and Ignacio Chaves clearly showed an odd manipulation of facts by Hurtado de Mendoza.

Having lost some ground after the testimony of Diego Antonio Chaves and Ignacio Chaves, Hurtado de Mendoza called on Marcial Zamora and Juan Candelaria from the Villa de Alburquerque to testify in his behalf. They were unable to go to Pajarito because the Río Grande was running high and fast. Trébol Navarro delegated his commission to Francisco Perea, *teniente* of the Villa de Alburquerque, to carry out the inquiry.[21] They were subjected to an interrogatory of five questions related to their knowledge of the land at Las Ciruelas. Both verified that during Don Fernando's lifetime there was only one acequia of any consequence: the acequia madre.[22]

On June 14, 1769, Perea took the testimony of Marcial Zamora, who readily said he might not remember everything they wanted to know, but he did know that there was no other acequia at the time of Don Fernando besides the acequia madre. On the same day, Perea interviewed Juan Candelaria, who said virtually the same thing. The entire Valle de Atrisco had once belonged to Don Fernando, he said, and during Juan's lifetime there was only one acequia: the acequia madre. If there was another acequia, he did not know about it. Perhaps, he thought, they were referring to a small acequia that watered the lands of Pedro Gomes and ran only a short distance. Beyond that, he had little to say on the subject.[22]

Trébol Navarro was probably relieved to know that Hurtado de Mendoza did not have any more witnesses to present. Upon receiving the new testimony to review, Andrés Antonio Romero asked for six days to respond. Trébol Navarro granted the grace period.[23]

After reiterating his position, Andrés accused Hurtado de Mendoza of maliciously obscuring the facts and proving nothing. The new testimony showed that only the acequia madre existed at the time of Don Fernando. Therefore, the land in question could only be located in relation to it. Even some of the witnesses chosen by Hurtado de Mendoza had shown that. It followed from the testimony that Hurtado de Mendoza had misrepresented the facts. Everything that had happened to his mother, Doña Ana Durán y Chaves, in regard to her being dispossessed of her land—Andrés thought—could be traced to Hurtado de Mendoza. Andrés felt that Hurtado de Mendoza had stalled for time because he had plowed the land and was waiting to harvest it. He asked Trébol Hurtado to do the right thing and give the land back to his mother.[24]

Trébol Navarro now turned to making a recommendation to Governor Pedro de Mendinueta. On July 1, 1769, he transmitted the entire set of files to the governor for a decision. Governor Mendinueta responded four days later with a request that Trébol Navarro convene all the interested parties at the Puesto de Atrisco and draw a map of the land in question and its relationship to all other boundaries and acequias to the time of Don Fernando's will.[25] Trébol Navarro immediately complied (see map 2).[26]

Hurtado de Mendoza quickly shot off a protest cautioning that the map must be drawn with the utmost care, so as not to bias his case. He believed that those who drew the map were not knowledgeable about the land at the time of Don Fernando, and he would not endorse it. "How could I sign something I know nothing about, but only through hearsay?" He went so far as to suggest that the governor make his assessment in consultation with a lawyer before making a final judgment.[27] Obviously, the last comment would not sit well with the governor.

A few weeks later, Trébol Navarro called Hurtado de Mendoza and Doña Ana Durán y Chaves before him and read aloud the decision dated August 11, 1769. Governor Pedro Fermín de Mendinueta had determined that none of the heirs of Bernardo Durán y Chaves had shown the boundaries of the land in question to be theirs, nor had Hurtado de Mendoza.

Regarding the question of the acequia as a boundary during the time of Don Fernando, the governor wrote that Don Fernando, as the owner of the Valle de Atrisco, had left the land to the heirs of his son Don Bernardo. The only acequia that he could have used as a boundary would have been the acequia madre "which is the one that Andrés Romero says it is, not the one presented by Hurtado de Mendoza."[28] The first acequia, wrote the governor, runs southwest to the house of Pedro de Chaves, which was the one indicated by Don Fernando, but the second acequia in the small piece of land runs southeast, a very different direction from what Don Fernando had indicated. The acequia madre defined the lands of the heirs of Don Bernardo and Doña María Chaves as well as those of Isabel and Nicolás Chaves, and even those of Don Pedro de Chaves. Otherwise the whole thing appeared "absurd" (*es absurdo*).[29]

Regarding the contention by Hurtado de Mendoza that the paper of 1722 was false, the governor dismissed the notion. He said that a considerable analysis made of the signatures proved that the document was real. He had ordered them compared with signatures by Rael de Aguilar on other documents in the archives in Santa Fe and they were found to be authentic. The governor seemed somewhat concerned that Hurtado de Mendoza had signed every document regarding the claim made by Doña Efigenia Durán y Chaves and questioned his motives. Furthermore, he questioned Hurtado de Mendoza's impetuous planting of the land in question while there was still a legal cloud over it. It appeared to most observers that Hurtado de Mendoza was hoping to harvest the crop of corn and wheat in the fall and make whatever profit he could.

In his final decision, the governor stated: "Whereas this is my will in the definitive sentence, I declare and judge that the piece of land litigated in these proceedings is the same that was given to Don Antonio Durán y Chaves on April 26, 1722, and it belongs to his heirs and consequently to his daughter Lucía Ana Durán y Chaves, as the heir. Under the same supposition, it legitimizes the sale of land made by Felipe Romero, her husband." He ordered Doña Efigenia to return the lands at Las Ciruelas and Arbolito del Manzano to Doña Ana. Doña Efigenia was also ordered to pay all costs pertaining to the proceedings for having made a false claim.

Meanwhile, Las Ciruelas was now considered developed property, and Trébol Navarro, the consummate bureaucrat, sent two men out by order of the governor to evaluate the land and tax it. Hurtado de Mendoza paid the twenty-two pesos. Apparently, Hurtado de Mendoza and Doña Isabel reached an agreement concerning the fair distribution of the crops grown on the land between April and August 1769. Next, Trébol Navarro officially granted Doña Ana possession of Las Ciruelas and Arbolito del

Manzano. A copy of those proceedings was sent to the governor on September 4, 1769, to acknowledge compliance with the decision.[30] As part of the settlement, the governor ordered Hurtado de Mendoza to give his copy of Don Fernando's will to the Santa Fe archive in order to avoid a future controversy over those lands.[31]

The question of the acequia madre and the "acequita" of Las Ciruelas proved a deciding factor. The proof, for Andrés Antonio Romero, lay in three principal documents: one signed by Rael de Aguilar in 1722 granting his grandfather possession; another regarding Fernando's will stating that the only acequia used to designate the land to his heirs was the acequia madre; and the testimony signed by Isidro Sánchez, the only surviving witness of the 1722 signing. Once these documents were corroborated by testimony and an archival search to prove their validity, the governor could make a logical decision.

The astuteness of Governor Pedro Fermín de Mendinueta cannot be underestimated. He had quickly seen through Hurtado de Mendoza's scam of manipulating witnesses, documents, and the topography of the land in an attempt to get his way. The governor correctly reasoned that the land passed down to Don Fernando's heirs was based on the line established by the course of the acequia madre. That, he thought, defined Don Fernando's intent in the will. It stood to reason, then, that the land of Las Ciruelas was in the opposite direction of the course of the acequia madre. In the end, it did not matter that a second acequia had been cut at Las Ciruelas because those lands did not pertain to Don Fernando's will. Consequently, the heirs of Don Fernando in 1722 had acknowledged that those lands were separate and had accordingly agreed to give them to Don Antonio Durán y Chaves, the father of Ana Durán y Chaves.

The historical significance of the case is multifold. It reveals a process regulating land ownership that obtained in Spanish colonial New Mexico as well as other parts of the Spanish Empire. Legal procedure was diligently followed at every step, no matter how small. The record attests that even if the presiding official, in this case Francisco Trébol Navarro, did not agree with the plaintiffs, he nonetheless entertained seriously the question put before him. Although he had decided to dispossess Doña Ana Durán y Chaves, he dutifully recorded her arguments, which allowed the decision to be reversed.

Settlers in New Mexico during the colonial period evinced a high level of legal sophistication. They kept documents, were literate in terms of law and tradition, and kept watch over their property. Oral tradition was another source, for evidently witnesses knew the boundaries of their own land and those of their neighbors. Genealogical records were extremely important sources of information, and Andrés Antonio Romero made excellent use of his knowledge of the genealogy of the settlers of Atrisco. The documents written and signed by the litigants and some highly verbal witnesses also indicate that, contrary to popular twentieth-century belief, literacy was valued in colonial New Mexico. The case of Las Ciruelas and Arbolito del Manzano at Atrisco in 1769, along with other land grant issues throughout New Mexico during that period, reveals a number of extremely significant sources for the study of culture in New Mexico in the eighteenth century.

CHAPTER 8

Atrisco and the Río Puerco Grants, 1768–1772

Forced toward lands that have been vacant and unsettled since time immemorial, we take possession of them, settling them from the end of the Bosque Grande on the Río Puerco to the Cerro Colorado, where each one of us has made ranches and corrals.

JOSEPH HURTADO DE MENDOZA, 1768

This grant of land comprises the land within those boundaries shown and is made to the settlers of Atrisco with the exclusions stated above. It is made to their children and their heirs on the condition that they settle it with their livestock within the boundaries prescribed by Royal Law.

GOVERNOR PEDRO FERMÍN DE MENDINUETA, 1768

Dipping his quill into the dark ink, the talented but sometimes misguided Joseph Hurtado de Mendoza wrote the first words of a petition to Governor Pedro Fermín de Mendinueta in behalf of several settlers of Atrisco. "The settlers of the Puesto de Atrisco of this kingdom appear before the greatness of your lordship . . . and state that we are very oppressed, given the need for new lands to support our livestock."[1] The petition ushered in a new period (1768–72) for Atrisco. Land holdings would be consolidated and expanded toward the west beyond what is now Albuquerque proper. Even before the 1760s, atrisqueños had complained of the narrow boundaries of their grant, and for more than a decade, they had established ranches and grazed their livestock as far west as the Río Puerco. In 1768, they asked Governor Mendinueta for his assistance in that matter. The petition to the governor set the tempo and rhythm for these projects for the rest of the century.

The boundaries of Atrisco, wrote Joseph Hurtado de Mendoza, are adjoined

> on the north by the Río [Grande] del Norte and the Villa de Alburquerque; on the east the boundary runs very close along the said Río del Norte and Ranchos del Estero; and on the south are the lands of Captain Don Antonio Baca, which causes a bottleneck forcing us westward, not having anywhere else to go, not even to lands held in common. Forced toward lands that have been vacant and unsettled since time immemorial, we take possession of them, settling them from the end of the Bosque Grande on the Río Puerco to the Cerro Colorado, where each one of us has made ranches and corrals. [Those are the lands] we have been enjoying because of the pasturage for our livestock as well as the nearby firewood, there being no other place to provide for us all year long.[2]

Hurtado de Mendoza had succinctly explained a historical process: as the Valle de Atrisco became settled on the north and south, it constricted the atrisqueños inside the bounds of the original grant with no room to expand except westward. However, other competing settlements, such as one known as Nuestra Señora de la Luz de San Fernando y San Blas del Río Puerco, had been established in that area since 1753.[3] This large grant on the west bank of the Río Puerco, known as San Fernando, was settled by Bernabé Montaño and others. An earlier claim to land along the Río Puerco had been made by Ana de Sandoval y Manzanares, who received her grant from Governor Félix Martínez in 1716. It ran from the Río Grande to the Río Puerco and was bounded on the south by the hacienda of Tomé Domínguez Mendoza and on the north by a ruin just beyond the pueblo of San Clemente.[4] Given the friction between the atrisqueños and *sanfernandinos*, however, Hurtado de Mendoza and his associates needed to act quickly to claim the available land as far west as the Río Puerco.

The people of San Fernando had consistently accused atrisqueños of encroaching on their lands. Several infractions had occurred between 1759 and 1766 during the administrations of governors Francisco Antonio Marín del Valle and Tomás Vélez Cachupín. Each time, both sides raised the issue of boundaries. In 1768, Hurtado de Mendoza argued that the boundary question had to be settled in order for the atrisqueños legally to enjoy the benefits of their toil in the lands west of Atrisco.

The sanfernandinos pointed to the recent history of atrisqueño encroachment. In 1759 Agustín Gallegos, lieutenant of the settlement of San Fernando, succeeded in getting the ear of Governor Marín del Valle in a complaint about the problem.[5] The governor's response supported the sanfernandinos. The governor ordered that any grazing or watering of herds along the Río Puerco and adjacent lands must respect the rights of the settlers of San Fernando.[6] He ordered the alcalde mayor of the Villa de Alburquerque to announce his directive to citizens there so that it would be clear to everyone.[7] He strongly recommended that the settlers of San Fernando place landmarks of "stone and mortar" along their boundaries so there would be no mistake by any trespassers.

Still, longstanding questions abounded about the open lands south of San Fernando. In 1764, for example, Miguel Tenorio, a settler on lands along the Río Puerco, noted the existence of open land of little value that had no official owner. It was, however, being used by certain settlers of Atrisco as well as a man named Luis Jaramillo who had lands on the Río Puerco.[8]

The sanfernandinos, on their part, sought to reinforce the boundaries of their grant and any unclaimed land in the area. Their description of the boundaries appears to be inaccurate, especially in regard to the eastern and southern ends. In their petition to Governor Vélez Cachupín, for example, they said their boundaries ran from the stone ford of the Río Puerco on the north, to the Cerro Colorado on the west, to a *mesa prieta* (black mesa) on the east, and a *ceja* (ridge), the Ceja del Río Puerco, on the south. Actually, the ceja was southeast of San Fernando. The Ceja del Río Puerco could easily be seen from the Villa de Alburquerque: looking west, the atrisqueños could see that the ridge was a long horizon to the south of three extinct volcanoes. They stated that "at this time no one inhabits those lands." The *sanfernandinos* felt overcrowded in their present lands and somewhat threatened by the atrisqueños, who had not only grazed their livestock on the land south of San Fernando, but even established haciendas on it. They found they had no choice but to drive out the sheep and cattle herders from the nearby mountains as well as their haciendas.[9] As they had tolerated such trespasses since the days of Governor Marín del Valle, they asked that the boundaries be legally spelled out to better protect their claim.[10]

In his response in July 1766, Governor Vélez Cachupín flatly stated that trespassing was prohibited; like his predecessor, he forbade the atrisqueños to graze their herds on land belonging to the settlers of San Fernando.[11] He decreed that anyone trespassing on sanfernandino land would be fined thirty pesos to be paid with the equivalent head of sheep or cattle.[12] The money collected from the fines by the alcalde mayor of San Fernando would go toward the construction of a much-needed church at Nuestra Señora de la Luz de San Fernando y San Blas. The governor instructed Juan Cristóbal Sánchez of the Villa de Alburquerque to inform the settlers at Atrisco of the prohibition against trespassing.[13] Ignorance, he stressed, was no excuse. Thus the background was set for Joseph Hurtado de Mendoza's petition to Governor Mendinueta asking for recognition of the atrisqueño occupation and development of vacant lands along the Río Puerco.

Hurtado de Mendoza wrote that during the atrisqueños' expansion westward, they had always been careful not to encroach on lands along the Río Puerco claimed by the settlers of San Fernando. He explained that between the Bosque Grande and San Fernando lay an open space of at least a league and a half. No one had ever claimed or settled it, not even the sanfernandinos, who appeared not to need it because they had much more land in the other direction. Even though their population was four times greater than that of Atrisco, their land easily accommodated them.[14]

The settlers of San Fernando, on the other hand, viewed the expansion of the atrisqueños in their direction as a threat. Before the late 1740s, settlers along the Río Abajo—the lower segment of the Río Grande from Cochiti Pueblo south—had been migrating west. In addition to San Fernando, new migrants arrived and founded other towns along the Río Puerco. At the same time, other frontier folk were populating the area south along the Río Grande from Bernalillo to Isleta Pueblo. In 1760, the Río Abajo area near the Villa de Alburquerque had 270 families numbering 1,814 people, mostly of Spanish and "Europeanized mixtures." Atrisco had over 200 settlers. Land pressure caused the people of Atrisco to squabble over boundaries, genealogies, and land titles, or to seek new lands upon which to expand their already large herds of cattle and sheep as well as to gather firewood.[15]

Claiming encroachment, in the middle 1760s the sanfernandinos drove out the atrisqueños by force. Not to be denied, the powerful Durán y Chaves and Sánchez families joined forces and petitioned Governor Pedro Fermín de Mendinueta to grant them the vacant lands south of San Fernando.[16] Finding a spokesman in the articulate Hurtado de Mendoza, they explained their problems with the sanfernandinos, the unsettled land they claimed, and their service to the king as defenders of the frontier along the Río Abajo and the Río Puerco.

Although their relationship with the sanfernandinos had been troubled, the atrisqueños offered the governor a solution to the defense of the area. Hurtado de Mendoza argued that "the land we have been settling is on the usual path of the enemy Apache. We serve as a bastion for its defense."[17] Hurtado de Mendoza pointed out that not only had they suffered serious depreciation of their herds at the hands of Apache raiders, but the settlers of San Fernando, unaware of the protection the atrisqueños had given them, drove them off the land, causing even more losses to the herds. He stressed that the continuation of such experiences would lead to the ruination of many families from Atrisco. Such sacrifice, he suggested, should not go unrewarded, "especially in this kingdom; as willing subjects, we place ourselves at the great mercy of your lordship so that, like our true father, you will grant us the said land."[18] On April 28, 1768, the petition was presented to the governor. The atrisqueños realized that a new grant would solve their problems with the people of San Fernando.

Governor Mendinueta replied that he understood the reason for the atrisqueños' request for more land. He agreed that the limited amount of land along the Río Grande had forced them to seek new lands for pasturage needed to increase their herds. He also observed that the settlers of San Fernando del Río Puerco had rights to their lands. To the south was a strip of "no more than two leagues of land" that was available. The Cerro Colorado was the southern boundary cited by the sanfernandinos. Even though the atrisqueños did not have title to that strip, it was the same land where they had taken their herds to forage for many years.

Based on their prior and long-term usage of those vacant lands, the governor conceded them the strip of land between the Ceja del Río Puerco and the Río Puerco.

> I, Don Pedro Fermín de Mendinueta of the Order of Santiago, Colonel of the Royal Army, Governor and Captain General of this Kingdom of New Mexico, state: That I would and do concede in the name of his Majesty (may God preserve him) to the settlers of the Puesto de Atrisco, with exception of those who already hold lands for ranches and pasturage of their herds, whom I exclude from this grant, the lands which they apply for, with the understanding that for the settlers of San Fernando must be measured two leagues of five thousand varas castellanas from their settlement southward to the boundary. There, they will place a firm and durable landmark showing the boundary of the land owned by the settlers of San Fernando. Following the same direction southward, three leagues will be measured for the settlers of Atrisco, at the end of which they will similarly place a landmark on the north side showing the boundary of lands belonging to the settlers of San Fernando. Landmarks shall also be placed on the east side on top of the hill so named Ceja del Río Puerco, and on the west the Río Puerco itself. This grant of land comprises the land within those boundaries shown and is made to the settlers of Atrisco with the exclusions stated above. It is made to their children and their heirs on the condition that they settle it with their livestock within the boundaries prescribed by Royal Law. They may not sell it, nor alienate it under any title to any ecclesiastical person or without prejudice to a third party who may have a better right to it.[19]

The governor ordered alcalde mayor Francisco Trébol Navarro of the Villa de Alburquerque to proceed to the site and grant the atrisqueños posses-sion of the land described above.

On May 6, 1768, Trébol Navarro summoned the settlers of San Fer-nando to read them the governor's directive giving the land grant to the atrisqueños. Then he went out to the site and walked members from Atrisco and San Fernando through the measurement of the land and the placement of the "firm and durable" landmarks in the customary man-ner. Two days later, he went out to San Fernando and read the governor's grant to all the settlers so that there could be no misunderstanding of the proceedings.[20]

Hoping to overturn the governor's decision to grant the atrisqueños land along the Río Puerco, the settlers of San Fernando met with Trébol Navarro and a group of atrisqueños on May 9, 1768. Juan Bautista Mon-taño, lieutenant alcalde mayor and war captain of San Fernando, initiated the discussion by presenting an old document to Trébol Navarro show-ing that the sanfernandinos had a prior claim over the lands ceded to the atrisqueños, dating to the administration of Governor Tomás Vélez Cachupín in the 1750s.

Trébol Navarro studied the document and concluded that someone had tampered with it. Although it was a copy of an actual document signed by former governor Vélez Cachupín, Trébol Navarro's eyes were immediately drawn to the blotted-out words in the description of the boundaries claimed by the sanfernandinos. He said the words were "to-tally blotted out, not by scribal error, for when an error is made only a single line is drawn through it so that it is still legible. Then it is corrected at the end of the document, as is done in any tribunal or adjudication."[21] The alcalde mayor could not believe that it was caused by anything other than someone maliciously tampering with the document. He felt that he could only go by the testimony given by reliable witnesses concerning the boundaries, and nothing else.

Calling Juan Bautista Montaño before him, Trébol Navarro asked how the blots got on the document. Montaño, obviously thinking quickly, re-sponded before all present that "[the governor] Señor Don Tomás Vélez had blotted out the words."[22] Just then, one of the settlers, Antonio Can-delaria, spoke up. He said that even though he was a settler of the Villa de Alburquerque, he had served as lieutenant of the Puesto de San Fernando for a year and three months. During that time he had actually held the document in his hands and had noticed that the document did not have any blots on it "as it does now." Trébol Navarro then announced to all present that "these land grant documents have been maliciously blotted" and therefore were invalid.[23] He ordered the settlers of San Fernando to follow the mandates dictated by Governor Mendinueta in granting the vacant lands to the people of Atrisco.

Reviewing the boundaries, Trébol Navarro thought back to two large poplars on the western bank of the Río Puerco, where he had ordered a landmark placed. First, a long pole, about the height of a man, had been set into the ground. The landmark of stone and mortar was firmly placed as ordered. Trébol Navarro announced that the monument represented the boundary between the lands owned by the sanfernandinos and the atrisqueños. Only two leagues belonged to the settlers of San Fernando. No longer could they claim the land around Cerro Colorado in all directions as their own. They had forever lost the land south of it by dint of the governor's declaration that it was vacant and by his granting it to the atrisqueños. No one from San Fernando nor their heirs had any legal right to it. The atrisqueños' claim was based on their having occupied the land and thus having established an adverse claim.[24]

Trébol Navarro proclaimed his conclusion on the matter. Any claims by the sanfernandinos, he said, "are patently false and unfit to be presented before any tribunal. In my view, they can not and should not be heard as so ordered by royal law."[25] He reiterated that the pole with the landmark was where the measurement of three leagues granted to the people of Atrisco began. The measurement ran "straight south, to a poplar which is by itself on the bank of the said Río Puerco. I ordered the said settlers of Atrisco to use the poplar to mark their boundary. I pointed out that it is a firm and durable landmark. It has always been characteristically known as the *alamo gachado* or bent-over poplar.[26]

Joseph Hurtado de Mendoza was present throughout the entire proceeding and was clearly recognized as the legal representative of the settlers from Atrisco who had signed the petition for the grant. They were his mother-in-law, Doña Efigenia Durán y Chaves; José Sánchez and his brother Pedro Sánchez; Miguel Chaves; Manuel Baca and his brother José Chaves Baca; Ignacio Romero; Tomás García; José Chaves; Antonio Chaves Otero and his brother Santiago Chaves Otero; Felipe Jacobo Romero; and Andrés Romero.[27]

So that there would be no further question or appeal, Trébol Navarro took Hurtado de Mendoza by the hand,

> and in the name of the king, our Lord and in the name of the royal jurisdiction which I represent by virtue of the commission conferred on me by the governor of this kingdom, I gave him real and personal possession of the said site. I took him through the land, pulling up weeds, throwing dirt, and making other demonstrations as a sign of true possession, and figuratively, in behalf of the other grantees who were present. In

loud voices they declared "Long live the King!" "Long live our Lord!" "Viva!" Then they placed themselves under the advocacy of Saint Joseph, their patron, thus ending the proceedings. Together they pledged that no one of them should ever cause injury to any of the settlers of San Fernando.[28]

Afterward, Trébol Navarro assigned the lands to the atrisqueños. To Efigenia Durán y Chaves he gave land for a ranch for raising livestock. That land had formerly belonged to her brother, Diego Antonio Durán y Chaves. His new lands were some distance away, "more than one quarter league" from the boundary of San Fernando. Near the lands assigned to Diego Antonio, Trébol Navarro gave Hurtado de Mendoza a prime site for a ranch, apparently the northernmost lot. Trébol Navarro announced, "Having named and appropriated the ranch, and being that Don Joseph Hurtado de Mendoza now owned the first place, I ordered the rest of the settlers that they should follow suit in establishing their ranches to the south of his, so that they might avoid any injury to the settlers of the referred to San Fernando."[29] No one was assigned lands along the northern boundary in order to avoid any discord between the atrisqueños and the sanfernandinos.

Trébol Navarro read from a prepared statement. Admonishing both groups to live in peace, he explained that no settlers had the authority to cross their livestock into another's property under any circumstances. Any permission to cross into another's territory required the unanimous consent of the atrisqueños before Hurtado de Mendoza could give his approval. Such a requirement must be followed even if it involved a sibling, a parent, or a neighbor. He emphasized that this land was not inherited from a parent or relative, but specifically, a land grant for the benefit of a community of people. Anyone rebelling against this concept would answer to the governor by losing his land. No settler would be allowed "to sell or alienate his ranch through any entitlement, be it his relative, friend, or neighbor, as this land is conceded by his lordship, the governor, so that it would be productive and enjoyed for stock raising by the grantees. It was not intended for gain by sale."[30] Trébol Navarro signed the statement before the witnesses, Bernardino Chaves and Estevan Padilla, and submitted it to the governor as the last stage in the proceedings.

With the legal finalization of the grant, atrisqueño holdings now stretched from the Río Grande on the east to the Río Puerco on the west.[31] Hoping to begin a large-scale sheepherding industry, the atrisqueños began moving westward. Their efforts, however, came to a near halt for more than a generation when Navajo and Apache raiders stepped up their aggression and stymied the hopes of the Atrisco colonists.

As for the settlers of San Fernando, their troubles had only begun. If they had learned anything from the atrisqueños, it was that they could extend their northern boundary by carefully studying their own land grant and those of their neighbors to determine whether any vacant lands were nearby. Having lost the opportunity to expand south, they began to look north for land that would provide them with enough water for farming and ranching. A recent drought had caused them great hardship, and they sought relief from the governor.

As the founding settlers of the Río Puerco Valley, they had become accustomed to hardship. They petitioned Governor Mendinueta in 1767 to strengthen their defenses against Apache raids and to protect their rights to water and pasturelands.[32] They complained that the Apaches de Navajú on their far western boundary deprived them of access to water by cutting off the flow of the river to water their own crops. Similarly, the grants made to Juan de Tafoya and the pueblos of Jemez, Zia, and Santa Ana on their eastern boundary would also result in the diversion of water from the Río Puerco. They claimed that the flow of the river had lessened, especially in the springtime, because of increased agricultural use and a greater number of livestock being watered along the upper reaches of the river.[33]

They requested that no cultivation be permitted along the two tributaries to the river, the San Antonio and La Jara. To advertise their plight, they asked the governor to assemble all the settlers of the Río Puerco Valley and the pueblos of Jemez, Zia, and Santa Ana to assist them in this crisis. Otherwise, the settlement of San Fernando would eventually perish.

They had much to lose. Without water, they could not grow enough produce to feed their own livestock as well as those in their care under the partido system. They would have to trade their livestock for food, thereby reducing their herds. Their tithes to the church would be reduced, as the first fruits from their fields would be significantly decreased. They wanted assurances that their share of water would not be decreased.[34]

The governor read through their petition. His primary concern was to keep peace with both Navajo and Pueblo Indians. Governor Mendinueta refused their demand that the Navajos be removed, even if the tribe had not always resided in the area. He stressed that the Navajos were encouraged to settle and convert to Catholicism. Only fair and kind treatment would result in peace with them.[35] The people of San Fernando would be severely punished for any hostile act against the Navajos. As for the Pueblo Indians of Jemez, Zia, and Santa Ana, the governor similarly wrote that the alcalde mayor of the pueblos should work with the people of San Fernando, but only if it benefited the Indians. Their claim against the pueblos was dismissed when it was learned that the Pueblo Indians carefully worked throughout the year to preserve the weak flow of water.[36]

The sanfernandinos claimed that any water rights not held by Juan de Tafoya in his grant automatically belonged to them. Governor Mendinueta ordered the boundaries inspected and properly marked. While measuring the Tafoya–San Fernando boundary, he discovered that the Tafoya grant, then held by Salvador Jaramillo, properly owned its water rights. For their malicious charges against Jaramillo, the sanfernandinos were fined sixty pesos de la tierra (barter value of two pesos).[37] Undaunted, they continued to seek a remedy for their water problems.

In 1770, they again petitioned Governor Mendinueta. This time, they asked for permission to move to lands with enough water for their herds and, more importantly, for their families. Juan Bautista Montaño said they had constructed tanks to catch rainwater and had dug wells for drinking water but had been unsuccessful.[38] The recent drought had severely dried out the Río Puerco, and there appeared to be little hope of water throughout the year. They were in dire straits. So dry was the land that sand blowing incessantly through the area had covered their houses to the top of the walls as high as the roof beams.[39] They even consulted some boys known as *balisanes* who had a reputation for finding water, but they gave false hope, for all they did was "howl ignobly," and it cost double.[40]

Desperately, the settlers of San Fernando cast around for lands nearby that could solve their dilemma. In May 1770, Antonio Baca, a resident of the Puesto de San Isidro de Pajarito in the jurisdiction of San Agustín of Isleta, wrote the governor that it had recently come to his attention that the settlers of San Fernando had petitioned for his land "which the king, my lord, has given to me."[41]

Baca's lands bordered those of San Fernando along its north side, which ran from the ford on the Río Puerco, then along the road that connected the pueblo of Zia and the pueblo of La Laguna. He said that Don Bernardo de Miera y Pacheco, a settler of the pueblo of La Laguna who served as *juez comisionado*, or appointed judge, had given him possession of those lands. Baca merely asked that his boundaries be respected. He said he could call on other witnesses who would offer information and verify that the road he mentioned did run from the pueblo of Zia to La Laguna.[42]

Governor de Mendinueta reexamined the settlement patterns of the area in his review of the case. He recognized that the San Fernando boundary was contiguous with that of Antonio Baca.

> To the north, the road that goes from Zia to La Laguna and that shown by Don Antonio Baca southeast of the headland of Mesa Prieta which looks to the southeast where the Zia road crosses to La Laguna, but not

where the ford of stone that has been cited of the same road, but the ford in possession of the land given to Don Antonio Baca by Don Bernardo Miera y Pacheco makes it clear that the piece of land defended by Don Antonio Baca is his. If the settlers of Nuestra Señora de la Luz continue to insist on their northern boundary, this doubt is clarified with the judgment given by the legal assistant in the proceedings made by the said Baca with the concurrence of my predecessor Don Thomas Vélez Cachupín who all agreed that the land which formerly belonged to Joaquín Mestas be granted to Don Antonio Baca. And, I having seen the grant given to Joaquín Mestas by my predecessor Señor Don Francisco Antonio Marín del Valle, which is evident in his Libro de Govierno, in which it is clear that he gave a piece of land for cattle raising with the condition that it be fulfilled. Possession of the said grant was given him by Don Carlos Mirabal, then alcalde mayor of the Jurisdiction of Jemez, Zia, and Santa Ana. The boundaries as ordered are clearly stated: From the east it is bordered by the mesa which is called that of the Río Puerco; on the west with a small black hill which is by itself with a small pointed peak; on the north it reaches up to the boundary of Captain Joseph García; and on the south up to a point of a bald hill which is distinct from all the other hills and faces the Río Puerco, where a cross has been placed. It is clear from all that has been said that all that Don Antonio Baca possesses is the same that was possessed by Joaquín Mestas and no more. Even should one challenge the grant given to Don Antonio Baca and show an error in the boundary made by Don Bernardo de Miera y Pacheco on grounds that he did not have the right to exceed his commission; and it being impractical to show all the other boundary sides other than the principal ones. In this case, I am fully confident of the testimony presented by Don Carlos Mirabal and his witnesses Joaquín Mestas, Juan de Tafoya Altamirano, Bernardo Mirabal, Joseph García, Ignacio Jaramillo, and Antonio Gutiérrez, who were present in the proceedings of the possession of the lands given to Mestas.[43]

The governor repeated that the Mirabal commission had with great care and detail described the peak on the black hill on the west side, and the bald hill and the cross that was erected on the southern boundary. They were the landmarks that Antonio Baca should have known, especially since he had been alcalde mayor of the jurisdiction of Jemez, Zia, and Santa Ana when the original grant was made in 1753. As representative of Governor Tomás Vélez Cachupín, it was Baca who walked the settlers through their boundaries and gave them the right of possession.[44] Therefore, concluded the governor, the land south of the cross to the boundary of the settlement of Nuestra Señora de la Luz was surplus land. "In my name and that of his majesty, whom God preserves, I adjudicate that the said settlers renovate their landmarks so that they be fixed, except for the said lands which are included in the land grant to Luis Jaramillo."[45]

The cross was pivotal to proving where the vacant lands began. Curiously, the cross was no longer there. The settlers then sought witnesses who could verify that a cross had been erected on the site and tell where exactly it had been placed. Finally, they found a witness, Joaquín Mestas, and determined that Antonio Baca himself had removed the cross, probably to conceal the exact boundary and thereby obfuscate, for his advantage, where his line ran. When asked, Baca confessed that he had indeed removed the cross.[46] It seems the settlers hoped the governor would see that their need for land with water was more important than the right Jaramillo or Baca had to it, or for that matter anyone else's land that was not productive. But once the site of the cross was located, they could find the legal description of the vacant land.

On June 20, 1770, Carlos Mirabal, the juez comisionado, went out and gathered the interested parties before him and read the governor's decree. Before him stood Joaquín Mestas, Juan de Tafoya Altamirano, Captain Joseph García, Antonio Gutiérrez, Bernardo Mirabal, and Ignacio Jaramillo—all of the previous chief witnesses of the grant given to Joaquín Mestas. Collectively, they knew the boundaries and the location of the cross. Antonio Baca, the present owner of the grant, also attended. Among the witnesses were the settlers of Nuestra Señora de la Luz de San Fernando y San Blas del Río Puerco.[47]

Before all of the witnesses, Captain García and Antonio Gutiérrez swore to tell the truth regarding the boundaries of the grant originally given to Mestas. They described the land as starting at the stone ford, the point where the "camino real" from Zia to La Laguna crossed. Antonio Candelaria also testified that the stone ford pointing in a straight line from east to west indicated the boundary of the lands owned by Luis Jaramillo. Close by was a prominent rock near where the cross once marked the spot that designated where the open fields began.[48]

As was customary, Commissioner Mirabal led Juan Bautista Montaño by the hand over the boundaries, "pulling up grass and throwing rocks," signifying that he had given him physical possession of the land.[49] Antonio Baca then ceded any future claim to the land. It now legally belonged to the settlers of Nuestra Señora de la Luz de San Fernando y San Blas. Governor Pedro Fermín de Mendinueta approved the grant on July 1, 1770, after Don Bartolomé Fernández, alcalde mayor and war captain of the pueblos of Jemez, Zia, and Santa Ana, was notified of the grant, which used the Zia–La Laguna road as a boundary.[50]

In 1772, the poverty-stricken settlers of San Fernando petitioned the governor for additional land. This time, it was the sons of Juan Bautista Montaño—Antonio, José, Bernabé Manuel, and Juan Bautista—along with Ramón García Jurado, all residents of the Villa de Alburquerque, who complained about the lack of permanent water in the area of San Fernando, not to mention that they were overcrowded. The poverty there was so great that no matter how hard they worked, the produce was not enough to sustain them. In order to make ends meet, they were obliged to go out and work at the nearest Indian pueblos, sometimes weeding their fields, or taking them firewood from the mountains in exchange for a few ears of corn. The settlers of San Fernando requested additional lands with better pasturage for their herds. They reminded the governor that their "grandfathers and their fathers" had participated in expeditions and campaigns since the conquest and reconquest of New Mexico, as they too had done.[51] They then presented the original grant given their family by Governor Tomás Vélez Cachupín in 1753. The settlement had been placed under the jurisdiction of the alcalde mayor of Jemez, Zia, and Santa Ana. Owing to the constant Navajo and Apache raids, the grantees were temporarily forced to abandon the land. It was not until the late 1770s that the heirs of the original grantees returned to occupy the land.[52]

In March 1772, further division of the land around San Fernando occurred under the watchful eye of Governor Mendinueta. Having approved the petition to divide the lands, the governor authorized alcalde mayor Bernabel Manuel Montaño de Cuéllar to partition the lands among the settlers accordingly.[53] The distribution was made to the settlers so they could maintain their families.

Montaño wrote that the linear distribution of 300 varas of land was based on the measurement of "*varas regulares*," that is, approximately 32.5 inches per vara. Additionally, fixed landmarks were noted for each boundary. The settlers were given hereditary rights to the land, but they did not have the authority to sell the lands. The settlers who received the grant were Marcos Baca, Agustín Gallegos, Juan Bautista Montaño, Joseph de Jesús Montaño, Antonio Durán, Bernabé Montaño, Juan Candelaria, Mariano Gallegos (deceased), María Cuéllar (widow), and Gregorio Gutiérrez.

Also, two parcels of land, each measuring 120 linear varas, were given to Ignacio Jaramillo and Tomás Gurulé for the support of their families. Specifically, in Gurulé's case, he could only use his land for raising crops, particularly wheat, not sheep, cattle, or horses.[54] The proceedings were corrected, authorized, and approved by Governor Mendinueta and entered into his archive.[55]

It appeared that the boundaries of the settlements along the Río Puerco had been resolved. Yet, new problems would continue to arise as expansion took place. The land was harsh, and Apache and Navajo raiders compounded the precariousness of living in that desolate country. For at least a generation, the settlers of Atrisco and San Fernando were able to hold on. Were it not for the lack of water, the land grants appeared to be worth the risk. But eventually, the settlers would learn that the land could only support its natural carrying capacity. Despite the abundance of land in almost all directions, especially west of the Río Puerco, the land grant system limited expansion, for Indian pueblos and Hispanic settlers in the area jealously guarded their rights to grants of land given them by the king of Spain. The low water supply along the Río Puerco was a factor limiting the growth of settlements. To some extent, Hispanic expansion westward was curbed by rebellious tribes who, especially in times of stress, saw the large Spanish sheep and cattle herds as a solution to their dwindling food sources. In the end, it was the Spanish land grant that bound settlers to a given area. The settlers of Atrisco enjoyed their acquisition and expansion to the Río Puerco, despite the hardships they suffered.

Meanwhile, the efforts of the sanfernandinos were frustrated by decisions that went against them. Their petitions asking the governor to resolve their western boundary water rights with the Navajos and with Salvador Jaramillo of the Juan de Tafoya land grant; the dismissal of their claims against the intrusion of the pueblos of Jemez, Zia, and Santa Ana on their northern boundary; and their failed efforts to expel the atrisqueños on their southern boundary contributed to their frustration. The sanfernandinos and other settlers in the area continued to press their claim against the Navajos. The result was the devastating Navajo War of 1774–75.

In Atrisco, the actions of Joseph Hurtado de Mendoza had legally increased the ranchlands of those settlers named in the annexation of land extending to the Río Puerco. He had successfully proved that there were in fact vacant lands that were not included in the grant given to the settlers of San Fernando. As a result, Atrisco's new boundaries stretched from the Río Grande to the Río Puerco. It is clear that the Río Puerco lands were given to individuals. Like the lands in Atrisco that had been given to Don Fernando in 1692, the lands along the Río Puerco evolved through generations of land transfers to resemble a community grant. Within the historical context, the Río Puerco lands, moreover, were inextricably tied to the hereditary rights of those atrisqueños who held title to both lands.

CHAPTER 9

Atrisco in the Late Spanish Period, 1772–1821

At the spring our great-grandfather left us for the purpose of watering our stock . . . if . . . by chance any animal, because the farm of said gentleman is nearby, goes in and damages his planted ground, the fines he causes us to pay . . . are exorbitant, and which is done on a summary order, because the acting official is his son-in-law.

Francisco Antonio Chaves and
Bartolomé Montoya, 1786

While atrisqueños were developing their communal and private land-holdings between the Río Grande and the Río Puerco, other settlements in the province of New Mexico had likewise been expanding in all directions. By the 1720s, Abiquiu on the Río Chama had been established, albeit precariously. Abiquiu was the jumping-off point for a series of trading routes, later known as the Old Spanish Trail, to western Colorado, Utah, and eventually California. North of Santa Fe, Spanish plazas dotted the map as far as Taos. Spanish colonial settlements were strung along the Río Grande as far south as El Paso. As in the previous two centuries, Franciscan missionaries continued to evangelize among the Pueblo Indians and other tribes in the area. Meanwhile, military expeditions augmented by Pueblo Indian allies fought many battles with Apache, Navajo, Ute, and Comanche tribes. Traders, missionaries, soldiers, and other settlers passed by Atrisco on the Camino Real, stopping for food, water, and possibly lodging, on their way to the villas of Alburquerque and Santa Fe.

Like other colonials throughout the province, atrisqueños had participated in the expansion of Spanish interests in New Mexico, particularly along the Río Puerco. Thus, atrisqueños were part of a larger Hispanic settlement pattern in New Mexico, from scattered ranches near Taos Pueblo in the north to the town of El Paso in the south. Still, within the

86

pattern of expansion, atrisqueños continued to strengthen the evolutionary pattern of their communal traditions of land tenure at Atrisco by conveying lands within their domain.

Atrisco had been host to many notable Spanish colonial figures throughout its long history. Aside from the many Spanish governors, Franciscan missionaries, and church dignitaries who came up the Camino Real from Mexico City, military and ecclesiastical inspectors reported on Atrisco between 1725 and 1776. Francisco Álvarez Barreiro, a cartographer assigned to the expedition of Pedro de Rivera, had visited the Villa de Alburquerque in 1725 and made it a point to include Atrisco in his cartographic renditions of New Mexico. Likewise, in 1765, the Marqués de Rubí, leader of an expedition to inspect and survey the entire northern frontier of New Spain from Sonora to Texas, mentioned the Villa de Alburquerque in his report. His cartographer, Nicolás de Lafora, included Atrisco on his map. The leaders of the renowned Domínguez-Escalante expedition, Fray Atanasio Domínguez and Fray Silvestre Vélez de Escalante, rode by El Morro and Acoma on their return from their four-month expedition to Utah in 1776. Reaching the Río Grande near Isleta, they traveled north through the heavily populated strip of settlements between Isleta Pueblo and Alburquerque, which included Los Padillas, Pajarito, Armijo, and Atrisco.[1]

Still, life in Atrisco continued in its quiet and unpretentious fashion. In many ways, outsiders were politely treated but not invited to stay. Atrisqueños tended to mind their own business. Mostly farmers and ranchers, they were concerned with keeping their lands intact for their future heirs. By the time the Spanish period ended in 1821, atrisqueños were well versed in the legal language of land tenure. Not only did they maintain meticulous records of each transaction, they continued to keep tabs on transfers of land among their neighbors. Atrisqueños continued conveying their properties by selling, trading, donating, subdividing, and bequeathing them, as well as suing over boundaries to augment and protect their lands. By the late eighteenth century, the face of Atrisco no longer resembled the land grant from the days of Fernando Durán y Chaves. Many genealogical ties had been broken, as new settlers, some distantly related, others not related at all to the Durán y Chaves clan, had acquired interest to the land.

In 1790, the Viceroy Conde de Revillagigedo ordered a census of New Spain and its frontier areas.[2] As part of the Bourbon Reforms, which promised a more efficient government for Spain's overseas empire, the census would provide valuable information for taxation purposes.

Despite its weaknesses, the census of 1790 provided a profile of New Mexico in the late eighteenth century. It listed the occupations of male heads of households, names of wives, and ages and genders of immediate family members. Ethnic identity was also featured.

The total population of New Mexico in 1790 stood at 30,953, with major clusters at the Villa de Alburquerque (5,959), the Villa de Santa Cruz de la Cañada (8,895), the Villa de El Paso (5,244), and the Villa de Santa Fe (2,542). Given the remoteness of certain areas outside these population centers, it is likely that some people were not counted. Vagabonds, semi-sedentary tribes, sheepherders and their families in isolated places, and other such categories were not included in the census.[3] The census of 1790 was the only eighteenth-century census to list Atrisco and the Villa de Alburquerque separately.

Although the first census of the nineteenth century, compiled in 1804, appeared to be incomplete, it reflected a population of 224 settlers distributed among the four plazas of Atrisco: Nuestra Señora de Guadalupe de los Garcías had 51 inhabitants, San Fernando de los Chaves had 39 inhabitants, San José de los Sánchez had 52 inhabitants, and San Andrés de los Ranchos de Atrisco had 82 inhabitants.[4]

With their four plazas, the 224 atrisqueños formed a viable community. Of them, 117 (52 percent) were males and 107 (48 percent) were females in 1804. Among them were 109 children under fifteen years old and 57 young adults between the ages of fifteen and twenty-four years. Of the 224 inhabitants of Atrisco, 58 were over age twenty-four, indicating a high mortality rate between thirty and forty years of age.[5]

The 1790 census of Atrisco presents a picture of male occupations and ethnicity. Of the Spanish settlers, twelve were ranchers, seven were farmers, four were weavers, one was a shoemaker, and one was a musician. Of the mestizo (half-Indian and half-Spanish) settlers, the census notes one shoemaker, one carpenter, two carders, one day laborer, and one spinner. Two genízaros (generally defined as detribalized Indians) worked as shepherds. One *coyote* (a half-blood of Indian descent) worked as a carpenter, one was a carder, and two were day laborers. Only one Apache was living in Atrisco; he worked as a carder.[6]

Given the greater numbers of Spanish ranchers and farmers at Atrisco, atrisqueños encouraged marriages between persons of equal ethnic status in order to preserve family lines.[7] The pattern reflected a New Mexican society that remained ethnically stratified, like other areas of the Spanish Empire. Inheritance of land was commonly kept within the family or extended family.

In the late eighteenth century, New Mexicans seemed to be in continuous litigation over their lands. Spanish settlers in other parts of New Mexico, like the atrisqueños and sanfernandinos, attempted to increase their landholdings. During the period from 1772 to the end of the Spanish period in 1821, New Mexican frontiersmen and women pursued every opportunity to acquire land, grazing privileges, and water rights. Some were more successful than others.

In 1772, Juan Cristóbal Sánchez, alcalde mayor of the Villa de Alburquerque, tried to expand his right to graze his herds on a tract near Tomé owned by Nicolás Durán y Chaves.[8] In another case, expansion-minded settlers from the Villa de Alburquerque who petitioned for a settlement at Carnuel in March 1774 were denied (they would try again). On the other hand, Spanish settlers from the Pecos Valley successfully acquired a tract of land along the Pecos River at a place named San José del Vado del Río de Pecos in 1803.[9] In 1815, settlers successfully petitioned for lands known as Rancho de los Xemes near Vallecito. Later, upon review of the proceedings, they were denied because of errors in the documents they submitted.[10] There were other cases where redress of grievance was sought, as in 1815, when María Polonia Silva of La Ciénega, south of the Villa de Santa Fe, complained that her husband had sold land that belonged to her without her consent.[11] Of course, anything could happen to one's petition. An 1821 petition by Estevan Baca for lands on the Pecos River, for example, simply died for lack of action by Governor Facundo Melgares.[12]

Atrisco was no different from the rest of New Mexico during the period 1772–1821. The first generation after Don Fernando had kept a sharp and vigilant eye on its founding documentation. By the second generation, the sales, gifts, or donations of land had complicated the historical paperwork. By the third generation, some of the original documentation had been misplaced or destroyed, and careful notarization of new documents created a future basis for legal ownership of the land. This trend had been occurring in other parts of New Mexico as well as in other parts of the Spanish Empire.

The frequent conveyances of land at Atrisco created a maze of ownership. In February 1782, for example, atrisqueña Tomasa Tenorio, Salvador Jaramillo's widow, resident of the Villa de Alburquerque, and owner of a grant on the Río Puerco, presented a proposal to convey lands to her son. Her last will and testament expressed her intent to leave three wheat fields (*milpas de tierra labrada de pan llevar*) in Atrisco to her son, Miguel Jaramillo. Now, however, she wished to make a present of the lands to her son while she was still alive.[13]

The lands bordered those of Ignacio Chaves on the north, those of Diego Antonio Durán y Chaves on the south and west, and the Río Grande on the east. In anticipation of any litigation by heirs, Doña Tomasa promised to renounce any future claim she might have to the land. She also protected the transfer by validating that she was the sole owner of the land and that the title was clear.[14]

Still, there were other heirs who could file a claim. Through "a second marriage on the maternal side," the children of Doña Manuela Gregoria Armijo also had a claim to Doña Tomasa's land. To avoid problems with title, Doña Tomasa reached an accord with the interested heirs by "ceding and transferring all her interest of right and dominion" to Miguel.[15]

Given that other nearby lands in Atrisco might be involved, alcalde mayor Don Vicente Armijo stated that "none of the heirs shall ever bring suit against the said lands with their ditch [acequia] except Don Pablo Chaves, who is the proprietary owner of the lands with their ditch." Apparently the acequia formed the boundary with Pablo Chaves's neighboring lands. He therefore would have an interest in any changes to the acequia that would affect his lands. Regarding the lands of Doña Manuela Armijo, alcalde mayor Armijo stated that they "may be held hereafter by her children by her second marriage on the maternal side."[16] Thus certain lands in Atrisco changed ownership with the stroke of a pen. Doña Tomasa had avoided any legal problems for Miguel that would have resulted from a contested will.

An important legal action demonstrating the traditional relationships between landowners at Atrisco took place in 1786. The issue of commonage—that is, the right, inclusive of easements, to pasture animals on land owned by a town, village, or other community—is evidence of Atrisco's traditional communal character. Appealing their grievance to Governor Juan Bautista de Anza in the Villa de Santa Fe, Francisco Antonio Chaves and Bartolomé Montoya, both residents of the Sitio de Atrisco, represented themselves and several others in a suit against their distant cousin, Diego Antonio Chaves.[17] They complained that his actions to develop new farmland had blocked off entrances and exits to traditional watering places used by the settlers of Atrisco for their livestock. The suit by Francisco Antonio Chaves and Bartolomé Montoya charged that Diego Antonio Chaves had

> deprived us of the watering place, which we had free, at the spring our great-grandfather left us for the purpose of watering our stock, that, if for that purpose of giving them water we go to said spring and by chance any animal, because the farm of said gentleman is nearby, goes in and damages his planted ground, the fines he causes us to pay, and which we pay together with the amount of the damage, are exorbitant, and which is done on a summary order, because the acting official is his son-in-law,

and in as much as justice is of his house . . . we are forced to obey and keep silent, paying the damages and the fine, although we know what is imposed upon us is unjust, in that it results in our injury and causes serious damage to our rights and to those of others.[18]

They also complained that their livestock now had to cross a sandy stretch of land to get to water, which could cause injury to the animals. What they wanted was for Don Diego Antonio to make the exits and entrances to the spring accessible for their livestock.

Governor Juan Bautista de Anza at the Villa de Santa Fe reviewed the case. He noted that Francisco Antonio Chaves, Bartolomé Montoya, and Diego Antonio Chaves were descendants of Don Fernando Durán y Chaves. Don Fernando had stated in his will that all heirs would be provided free pastures and watering places without exception. Anza further cited his predecessor, Governor Pedro Fermín de Mendinueta, as ordering Don Diego Antonio Chaves in 1767 "not to prevent the entrances and exits of the town of Atrisco, specified in detail by the first founder or settler of said town which appear in his respective testamentary provision."[19] Anza directed Manuel de Arteaga, alcalde mayor of the jurisdiction of Alburquerque, to inform Don Diego Antonio.[20]

Alcalde mayor Arteaga convened all concerned parties at San Agustín de Isleta in April 1786 to hear Governor Anza's notification. Calling the meeting to order, Arteaga read the order of compliance to Don Diego Antonio in front of witnesses and the aggrieved parties. Arteaga made it clear to Don Diego Antonio that the others had the right to pass through the land using the proscribed easement. Don Diego Antonio, furthermore, was notified that they were not obligated to pay him any damages to crops in the path of the traditional right-of-way. That done, the matter was settled.[21] On April 17, 1786, Arteaga submitted a report of the proceedings to Governor Anza as required.

Sometimes title to land in Atrisco was lost or misplaced, and only with the approval of the proper authorities could land be sold. In 1798, for example, Domingo Chaves of the Villa de Alburquerque and Toribio Sedillo of Rancho de Atrisco presented a case before alcalde mayor Manuel de Arteaga.[22] Chaves explained that at one time he had given Manuel Baca, a settler of Rancho de Atrisco, now deceased, 700 head of sheep under a partido contract, but Chaves had lost the document. Baca paid Chaves with his right and his cultivated land in Rancho de Atrisco.[23] As the land was owned by Baca's wife, Feliciana Chaves, the law required her consent, which she gave.[24] The transaction was carried out before former alcalde mayor Francisco Trébol Navarro.

Domingo Chaves later gave the land to José Chaves, who sold it to

Salvador Jaramillo. Jaramillo misplaced the title to the land. He sold it to Toribio Sedillo for three hundred pesos with assurances that the land was his and the price was fair, and relinquishing any future claim to the land.[25] Sedillo was given full title by the alcalde mayor. In the absence of proof of ownership, the transaction was properly witnessed, and the alcalde mayor gave Sedillo possession of the land in the customary way.[26] Thus, new documentation was created that would serve in the place of the original title.

Another case in which no formal paper existed for the transfer of land occurred in May 1804, when Juan Chaves, a settler of San Andrés de Los Padillas, sold a piece of land and a house in Atrisco to Miguel Antonio Chaves. Juan had inherited the land from both his maternal and paternal sides.[27] Juan's siblings, Pedro, María Guadalupe, and Ventura, were the children of Diego Antonio Chaves. Juan shared rights to the land with his sister María Guadalupe (then deceased). Similarly, Juan owned only a half interest in the house and its appurtenances, to which he shared rights with his sister Ventura. In order for Juan to sell the property, he had to show sole ownership of both house and land.

Juan claimed he owned the entire tract of land, for prior to her death, María Guadalupe had sold Juan her share. Because the deal was accomplished in good faith, "both of them being satisfied," only a simple paper was signed before two witnesses, including their brother Pedro Chaves and Jacinto Rodríguez from La Joya de Sevilleta. Thus, when Juan Chaves sold his land to Miguel Antonio Chaves, Pedro appeared before alcalde mayor Arteaga to validate that María Guadalupe had sold her part to Juan.[28]

Regarding the house, Juan said he had bought the house and garden from his sister Ventura.[29] He said he had purchased both shares of the house and land belonging to his sisters for a total of four hundred pesos.[30] Once satisfied that they belonged solely to Juan, Miguel Antonio Chaves bought all rights to the land, garden, and house.

In the absence of formal paperwork demonstrating Juan to be the sole owner, the procedure required that witnesses to the deal present themselves and divulge all they knew about the transaction. This was done in front of the alcalde mayor of the Villa de Alburquerque, Don Manuel de Arteaga. With the new document, Juan Chaves relinquished all rights to the property with all of its improvements. Juan stated that if the property and house should be worth more than Miguel paid for it, he would make "him a present and donation," *inter vivos*. He promised to cede and transfer his own right to the lands to Miguel Antonio Chaves "in order that he may enjoy them for himself, his children, heirs, and successors, and that no suit or cause shall be brought by the said vendor nor his heir and that in case any should be brought that they be not heard in court or out of it as from the present time to that time he relinquishes all and any laws which may be in his favor."[31]

Alcalde mayor Manuel de Arteaga then presented the formal documents as an instrument that "might serve as a title and by it he may take possession of said lands, and may sell, exchange, or alienate them to the person or persons he may desire, and in order that it may be of record." It was signed by all parties.[32] The document was notarized by Marcos Lobato, justice of the peace, who affixed a seal to it before two witnesses.[33]

One of the last transactions at Atrisco during the Spanish colonial period took place in January 1815 before alcalde mayor José Mariano de la Peña of the Villa de Alburquerque. Francisco Antonio Chaves from Abiquiu had decided to sell some land in Ranchos de Atrisco. The purchasers were Salvador García, Antonio Sedillo, Toribio Sedillo, Julián Sedillo, Rosa Gutiérrez, Juan de la Cruz Castillo, Ignacio Gabaldón, Juan de Jesús García, Miguel Anaya, and Manuel Jaramillo, all settlers from Ranchos de Atrisco.[34] Francisco Antonio had inherited the land from his father, Tomás Francisco Durán y Chaves from Atrisco, who had acquired it from his brother José.[35]

The land adjoined that of Antonio Chaves on the north and that of Santiago Chaves on the south. On the east was the Río Grande, on the west the Ceja del Río Puerco.[36] The land measured 564 linear varas.[37] In the sale, Francisco Antonio Chaves gave up all rights and customs to entrances, exits, uses, and rights of passages through the land. He swore that the land was free from ground rent, mortgage, or any encumbrances, and should it be otherwise, he would return the amount paid for the land as well as any value accrued from any development from that date forward.[38] Don Francisco Antonio sold the land for 282 pesos, whereupon he renounced any future claim to it.[39]

Such conveyances demonstrated Atrisco's landholding patterns in evolution. Records of the continuous occupation of the land reveal the tradition and practice of private land ownership, while the conveyances also imply joint uses of the land, such as common lands, acequias, pasturage, and wooded areas, that point to a communal tradition. The Río Grande was more than the eastern boundary of the Atrisco land grant; its use, like that of all rivers in the Spanish Empire, emanated from the traditional concepts of sovereignty and privilege, as vested in the king of Spain.

Although much had happened at Atrisco during the Spanish period, one notable birth, among many, took place. On October 18, 1818, Julián Chaves and María Luz García bore a son whom they christened Manuel

Antonio Chaves.[40] As Chaves grew into manhood, his life took on heroic proportions. In 1862, during the Civil War, he commanded the New
Mexico Volunteers against Confederate forces led by Henry Hopkins Sibley at Apache Canyon. In a reckless attack, Chaves and his men routed
Sibley's rear guard. News of the attack caused panic among Confederate
forces, who were defeated by Union forces at Glorietta Pass. His biogra-
pher, Marc Simmons, summarizes the significance of Manuel Chaves as
follows:

> He was called El Leoncito, The Little Lion. . . . Manuel Antonio Chaves
> earned that name in more than a score of battles with hostile Navajo,
> Ute, and Apache. . . . Chaves' life straddled three periods of New Mexi-
> can history: He was born at the tag end of the Spanish colonial period,
> he grew to manhood in the rough and heady days of the Santa Fe trade
> during the quarter century of Mexican rule (1821–1846), and he spent
> his mature years under the territorial regime established by the United
> States. Through the working of fate, or by mere chance, his career was
> interwoven with practically every major historical event of the epoch
> in which he lived. Yet, because history is a capricious mistress, Manuel
> Chaves' name has been virtually forgotten.[41]

Chaves's life was one of hardship, for in 1827, when he was nine, his atrisqueño parents moved forty miles away from the overcrowded Río Grande Valley
to Cebolleta beyond the Río Puerco (near present Mount Taylor). In that
war-torn country, beset by attacks by Navajo and Apache warriors, young
Chaves grew to be a tough frontiersman.[42] His adventurous life took him far
afield to Missouri, New York, and Cuba. He died at San Mateo, New Mexico,
in 1889.

   Chaves was well known for his defiance of Archbishop Jean Baptiste
Lamy of Santa Fe. Lamy had threatened to excommunicate Chaves in
a fence and boundary dispute concerning Guadalupe Chapel in Santa
Fe. The church bordered Chaves's land. As the story went, Chaves and
his relatives showed up with their weapons at Sunday mass. Sitting in
the front pew, they awaited the archbishop's pronouncement of excom-
munication from the pulpit. Lamy wisely backed off. Chaves was im-
mortalized in Willa Cather's *Death Comes for the Archbishop*, published
in 1927. In her novel, Cather describes Manuel Chaves as

> the handsomest man of the company, very elegant in velvet and broad-
> cloth, with delicately cut, disdainful features,—one had only to see him
> cross the room, or to sit next him at dinner, to feel the electric quality
> of his cold reserve; the fierceness of some embitterment, the passion for
> danger. . . . He had estates in the Pecos and in the San Mateo mountains,
> and a house in Santa Fé . . . He loved the natural beauties of his country

with a passion, and he hated the Americans who were blind to them. He was jealous of [Kit] Carson's fame as an Indian-fighter, declaring that he had seen more Indian warfare before he was twenty than Carson would ever see. He was easily Carson's rival as a pistol shot. With bow and arrow he had no rival; he had never been beaten.[43]

Cather continues with more prose dripping with stereotypes concerning Manuel Chaves and his life. Still, Manuel Chaves may well be the only atrisqueño to be commemorated in American literature.

At the end of the Spanish period, nevertheless, while Manuel Chaves was still in his infancy, Atrisco and Alburquerque were busy pushing their claims beyond the Río Puerco to Cebolleta. On the cusp of a new era between the end of the Spanish period and the beginning of the Mexican period, the atrisqueños and sanfernandinos were very concerned about the defense of their Río Puerco holdings.

On October 21, 1821, they watched, with great anticipation, the results of a punitive campaign against the Navajos in the Cebolleta campaign led by Juan Armijo.[44] His expedition went as far northwest as the Chusca Mountains. Apparently, Navajos had raided the Alburquerque-Belen area, taking livestock and some "Christian" captives. Under Juan Armijo was a complement of militiamen from Alburquerque and Belen. These troops likely included atrisqueños led by Francisco Armijo of Alburquerque.

In his report of October 23, 1821, to Governor Facundo Melgares, Juan Armijo wrote that his troops had begun their march from the Puesto de Cebolleta on October 3. Marching in good order, they reached the Paraje de San Lucas, where they set up camp with sentinels guarding the herd of horses and their position. At that point, Francisco Armijo presented Juan Armijo with a paper announcing that a promised complement of men for his unit was incomplete, and raising his voice, Francisco declared that his unit would no longer continue on the campaign. The men from Belen and Alburquerque pulled out with Francisco Armijo.[45] Juan Armijo accused Francisco of insubordination, mutiny, and desertion.

Marching without that complement of militiamen, Juan Armijo continued the campaign with auxiliaries comprising units from Isleta, La Laguna, and Acoma pueblos. The expedition camped at Siete Ojos. Soon, Juan Armijo reported that Francisco Armijo and his men had rejoined the expedition. Francisco explained that they had reconsidered their duty to the expedition and that he had represented the earlier consensus of his men. They further explained that the military park with powder and cannon under Juan Rafael Ortiz should be brought. In agreement, and glad to get his men back, Juan Armijo added sixty men to Francisco's command as promised. Then he dispatched Francisco and his men to bring up the military park, which was expected to take a few days.[46]

By October 11, Juan Armijo could wait no longer and decided to backtrack in the direction of the military park, all the while wondering whether his men had deserted him again. Eventually, Francisco Pino, lieutenant of the urban militia of Belen, rode into camp and resigned his commission, saying he could no longer serve on the expedition. It was painfully clear that the mutiny continued. Juan Armijo wondered if he would ever meet up with Francisco Armijo and his command.[47]

Concerned about the desertion and mutiny, Juan Armijo held a council with the remaining men, who expressed their lack of concern with the disagreements among the troops but said they feared entering Navajo country with so few men and arms. Juan Armijo nevertheless continued his march to Cañada de la Rica, reaching it on October 12. There, his heart skipped a beat. Francisco Armijo and his men were waiting for him with the military park which Juan Ortiz had turned over to him at a place called Peña Blanca in a field owned by the Navajo Calletano. Francisco asked for and was granted six men so that he could bring back those who had deserted with Pino. Francisco caught up with Pino and was able to persuade most of the deserters to return to the expedition.[48]

By October 15, the expedition was back in order and had picked up new signs of the Navajos they had been tracking from Cebolleta. Juan Armijo, as commander, punished the deserters by having them march on foot with their weapons slung on their shoulders. They marched day and night until they reached the *cañones de la agua chiquita*, where they stopped to sleep. The next day at five o'clock in the morning they began their march until they stopped to make camp at the *cañon de la mesa quemada*. Juan Armijo reported that in all that time, they had not engaged the enemy.[49]

Still not having forgiven the deserters, Armijo said he continued to make them march on foot with their muskets on their shoulders on October 17, until they reached the *cañones del agua salada*, where they camped at one o'clock in the morning, nearly dead on their feet from lack of sleep. On October 18 they continued their march until reaching the *carrizo a orillas del Valle de Chusca*. From there, they marched toward the mesas of Ojo del Oso.[50] That same day, they marched late into the night, picking up recent signs of the Navajos.

On October 19, about eleven in the morning, they caught the Navajos off guard and attacked them, killing six. Armijo was surprised that in the volleys fired at the Navajos, none of the "Christians" were harmed. Similarly, none of the men in his command were wounded by enemy fire. Two more Navajos were killed trying to run off with five horses. By noon, Armijo, feeling he had met his objectives, turned the expedition around and headed back to Cebolleta. By October 22, the expedition had returned to the Plaza de los Ranchos, and the next day he reported that he had returned home to Alburquerque.[51]

If anything, the expedition demonstrated that hostilities were unabated between the settlers of the Alburquerque area who were defending their claim to the Río Puerco, and the Navajos who were defending their own claim. During the Mexican period, 1821–48, Hispano-Navajo relations would be little improved.

Over the long Spanish period, Atrisco had established its legal hold over the land between two rivers. The many land transactions established a pattern of ownership among the Durán y Chaves family and other powerful allies such as the Sánchez and Baca clans. Each transfer, donation, sale, or partition conveying land in Atrisco developed paper trails demonstrating the successor of each transaction. Heirs maintained the lists of owners and validated their claims based on wills and bills of sale. When settlers took possession of the land, they received a certificate of investiture showing that an official, usually the alcalde mayor, had personally walked the new owner over the boundaries in the presence of several witnesses. The governor, to whom all papers were remitted for final inspection, put his final signature on the matter.

Such documentation became critical to the ownership of land in the long term as sovereignty over the Americas changed. After 1810, a new order was at hand when Padre Miguel Hidalgo raised the standard of revolt against Spain. By 1821, the Spanish colonial period in Mexico and Latin America was over. New Mexico now belonged to the new nation-state, Mexico, which held sway over the area between 1821 and 1848. Atrisqueños, like most land grant owners throughout the defunct Spanish empire, would be challenged by new rulers to provide legal proof of ownership to their land. The incipient Mexican nation-state would begin land grant processes anew, for those who still had the energy to do so.

CHAPTER 10

Nuevo México Infeliz

New Mexico under the Mexican Eagle, 1821–1848

O year of eighteen hundred
and thirty-seven—be damned!
Miserable New Mexico
What has happened to us?

ANONYMOUS NINETEENTH-CENTURY
BALLAD ABOUT THE 1837 ASSASSINATION
OF GOVERNOR ALBINO PÉREZ

After leaving Albuquerque, we continued our march
through a succession of cultivated fields and pastures.

GEORGE W. KENDALL, 1844

Do not find it strange if there has been no manifestation
of joy and enthusiasm in seeing this city occupied by
your military forces. To us, the power of the Mexican
Republic is dead. No matter what her condition, she was
our mother. What child will not shed abundant tears at
the tomb of his parents?

ACTING GOVERNOR JUAN BAUTISTA VIGIL Y ALARID,
SEPTEMBER 18, 1846

The Mexican period (1821–48) in the Greater Southwest of the present
United States effectively began on September 27, 1821, when Agustín
Iturbide, mounted on a black horse, triumphantly marched his revo-
lutionary army into Mexico City and accepted its surrender from Juan
O'Donojú, the last royal representative. O'Donojú had signed the Treaty
of Córdoba on August 24, 1821, and Mexican independence from Spain

was attained. Iturbide then turned to establishing the Republic of Mexico. In that twenty-seven-year period, New Mexicans witnessed great historical changes as an emerging Mexican nation reorganized its political and economic institutions. Another source of change with great cultural ramifications was the United States, as trade and immigration from the east increased via the Santa Fe Trail. The short-lived period of Mexican rule served as a transition to eventual acquisition by the United States.

The changeover from Spanish practices to Mexican legislated policies began when Agustín Iturbide took Mexico City on September 27, 1821, and appointed a *junta provisional,* or provisional council, consisting of thirty-six members with Iturbide as president and commander-in-chief. Meanwhile, on February 13, 1822, Spain recognized Mexican independence. A week later, a recently elected National Congress assembled in Mexico City to write a constitution. After much debate, the Congress elected Iturbide as emperor in July 1822. By October 1822, Iturbide had dissolved the Congress and installed a *junta nacional,* or national council. Just as quickly as Iturbide appeared as emperor, he was overthrown by General Antonio López de Santa Anna, who created the Mexican Republic and restored the Congress.

Because Atrisco sat astride the old Camino Real de Tierra Adentro, its inhabitants had the opportunity to witness and often participate in events as they developed between 1821 and 1848. Merchants, missionaries, and couriers with news of change, as well as governors, soldiers, and other Mexican personnel, passed through on their way to and from Santa Fe. In 1837, atrisqueños participated in quelling a rebellion against Governor Albino Pérez, and in 1841, they gave food and water to poorly treated Texan prisoners of war who passed through their land on their way to Mexico City. They watched a unit of the Army of the West march south along the old Camino Real toward El Paso during the Mexican War. Throughout the period, fast-developing events emanating from far away determined New Mexico's fate.

As a distant outpost of Spain, New Mexico had been far removed from the center of power for centuries. That aspect changed little under Mexico. New Mexico, like other outlying provinces such as Alta and Baja California, Texas, and the extreme fringes of the northern Mexican states and the Yucatan Peninsula, would seemingly be treated as equals within the new legislation under Mexican rule. In reality, however, Mexican officials did not regard those areas as nationally significant.

When Spanish sovereignty ended in 1821, Atrisco had been in existence for at least 129 years. For the people living there, the actions of the Mexican government would not change the ownership of their land grant, or for that matter, any transfers of land within it requiring litigation. Philosophically, the Spanish legal tradition remained intact, at least momentarily. Bureaucratically, the administration of justice and government followed a new organization chart that would evolve over the next two decades. But for the most part, during the Mexican period, atrisqueños, like other New Mexicans, attended to their own business as they had during the Spanish colonial period.

In 1821, New Mexicans had scant understanding, and cared little, about the meaning of a republic. Once they received news that independence from Spain had been achieved in 1821, atrisqueños patiently watched the budding Mexican nation unfold. Spain's ouster took on a new perspective when, in October 1821, the nascent Mexican government sent a decree throughout the nation to celebrate "independence" immediately. Owing to the slow overland mail service along the dangerous and arduous Camino Real, official news of the celebration did not reach New Mexico until late December 1821. Although atrisqueños were aware of Mexico's struggle for independence from Spain, it was not until the end of 1821 that they realized the impact of the revolution. A mounted courier passed through Atrisco and the Villa de Alburquerque, as he had along other villages of the Río Abajo, on his way to Santa Fe. On December 26, 1821, at the Palace of the Governors, the courier dismounted and handed a mail pouch to Governor Facundo Melgares. It contained official correspondence demanding that New Mexico's governor and other officials take an oath of allegiance to the recently established Mexican government.[1] Five days later, New Mexicans celebrated the event despite the cold weather that blew in over the Sangre de Cristo Mountains.[2]

Two festivities, a week apart, marked the event in the Santa Fe plaza. The first was a gathering on December 31, 1821, to commemorate the significance of the revolutionary goals known as Las Tres Garantías (The Three Guarantees): Religion, Union, and Independence. The event, organized by Governor Melgares, was called a *loa*, a dramatic presentation with (in this case) three designated speakers praising the three guarantees. A stage was constructed in the plaza near the portal of the Palace of the Governors. Postmaster Juan Bautista Vigil y Alarid, working with various Santa Fe artisans, was chief planner for the construction of the stage and artwork. He left no detail unattended. Nailed high in the center of the plaza, a white flag with a tricolor heart could be seen by all.[3]

The stage was designed with attention to the symbolism that the presenters of the loa would highlight in their homage to the new sovereign. Adorned with the finest draperies of taffeta and a variety of exquisite cloth, the stage had a backdrop painted with three symbols: a lion and lamb embracing, signifying union; a tree of liberty watered by four streams fed by a cloud; and a likeness of Mexico's founding father, Agustín Iturbide, portrayed with a crown of laurels and the words "Religion," "Union," and "Independence." The flag of Mexico was raised high above the stage.[4]

Onstage, Santiago Abreu paid homage to the independence movement, Juan Tomás Terrazas performed a reading on religion, and the presidial chaplain, Fray Francisco de Hozio, proclaimed the significance of the Mexican Union. At the end of the presentations, the crowd acknowledged their appreciation of the actors.[5] Governor Melgares later reported that the celebration had been a quiet and somber affair.

The second event, nearly a week later on January 6, 1822, the feast day of Los Reyes (the Magi), was less orderly. Virtually in the dead of winter, New Mexicans braved freezing temperatures to celebrate into the wee hours. Some observers said the event lasted past four o'clock the next morning. The celebration included parades, orations, patriotic dramas, music, Catholic masses, ringing of church bells, firing of muskets, dancing of Pueblo Indians, and a ball in the governor's palace. Twenty years after the event, Thomas James, who had assisted in raising the Mexican flag in the Plaza de Santa Fe, dimly recalled that the all-night celebration appeared sordid and crude to him. He described the street celebration as "licentiousness of every description," with crowds of gamblers enjoying "unrestrained vice" at dice and faro tables. Gambling, though illegal, was described as "the national sport of Mexico."[6] The tradition of commemorating Mexican Independence (also known as Diez y Seis de Septiembre) in New Mexico had its origins in Santa Fe during the winter of 1821–22.

New Mexicans received other official notices concerning political reform throughout Mexico in the period 1821–48. The Department of New Mexico, with its capital at Santa Fe, was divided into two districts (*distritos*). Each district was divided into sub-districts (*partidos*). Each sub-district was further subdivided into blocks (*manzanas*) for the purpose of identifying voters and law enforcement needs. The partidos were administered by a local municipal council (*ayuntamiento*) whose presiding officer was the *alcalde constitucional* and who served as both mayor and magistrate judge.

The First District had two partidos, with capitals at Taos and San Ildefonso (not the Indian pueblos but Hispanic settlements near them with the same names). The Second District similarly had two partidos, with capitals at Albuquerque and Los Padillas. Albuquerque and Los Padillas each had an ayuntamiento and an alcalde consitucional who administered the respective partidos. Atrisco belonged to the second partido of the Second District and thus reported to the ayuntamiento of Los Padillas. At the southern end of New Mexico, El Paso served as capital of a partido administered from Ciudad Chihuahua. Las Cruces and surrounding towns in southern New Mexico were within El Paso's jurisdiction.

The main difference between the Mexican and Spanish periods in that regard was that the alcalde constitucional, unlike his predecessor, the alcalde mayor, was elected and made decisions in consort with the ayuntamiento. Under the old Spanish system, the alcaldes mayores were appointed and held judicial, executive, and legislative powers.[7] The alcaldes mayores of the Spanish period made decisions or recommendations on their own as judicial officers without benefit of a council. In New Mexico, alcaldes mayores, as appointees, were obligated to carry out orders from their governors without question. To that end, alcaldes mayores like Francisco Trébol Navarro of Albuquerque deferred to decisions made by the governor. More than once, Trébol Navarro was overruled by Governor Pedro Fermín de Mendinueta.

As a township within the partido of Los Padillas, Atrisco now held occasional elections for delegates to the ayuntamiento. In 1833, for example, one such election for president and secretary took place in accordance with the Law of July 12, 1830, Articles 19 and 20. Under this legislation, Atrisco was described as "La Plaza de los Ranchos de Atrisco de las manzanas números 35 y 36," indicating blocks 35 and 36. Toribio Sedillo won for president with fourteen votes cast in his favor. Four secretarial positions were also decided. The first secretary, José Baca, received twelve votes; the second secretary, Toribio Sedillo, received eleven votes; the third secretary, Matías Castillo, received nine votes; and the fourth secretary, Tránsito Román Sánchez, received the remaining votes.[8] The record does not clarify how Toribio Sedillo could serve as both president and second secretary.

As a Spanish period land grant, Atrisco's survival in the Mexican period would be tested. To that end, Atrisco depended largely on the political influence it exerted over the ayuntamiento of Los Padillas as well as that of Alburquerque. The regulatory provisions of Mexican law did not significantly affect the ability of atrisqueños to maintain or convey their lands in any manner they wished. Atrisqueños adjusted to the changing times. They watched the new order unfurl with new laws, largely regarding the reorganization of political and economic institutions. For the most part, the structure of the budding Mexican nation would have more of an effect on the political organization of settlements, like Atrisco, as participating units in national politics. Atrisqueños, like other land grant occupants, watched to see if any laws dealing with land tenure would have an effect on their future.

In effect, during the early Mexican period, definitions of land tenure used under Spain were retained under the new sovereign as duly defined by the Mexican Constitution of 1824. Under Spanish law and custom, for example, public lands known as *tierras realengas* (crown lands) or *tierras baldías* (vacant lands) had theoretically belonged to the monarch. Under Mexico, they belonged to the constitutionally defined government. In the preceding era, the king, as the ultimate source of law, had granted *tierras concejiles* or *propios* to towns or individuals, as he did to atrisqueño Joseph Hurtado de Mendoza and others in the Río Puerco area in 1768 (see chapter 8). Public lands were available as common lands with available water for grazing or for temporary planting by individuals, who could not claim them for their own. The Mexican government continued to grant land from available public lands to individuals or towns who applied for them.

Under Spain, for example, propios were properties owned by a community or municipality as private property. Propios could be rented out by town councils (*cabildos*) for revenues that were used for public works. The *Recopilación de leyes de los reynos de las Indias* provided for the regulation of propios. In the establishment of the Villa de Santa Fe, the instructions of 1609 to Governor Pedro de Peralta similarly provided mention of propios. Toward the end of the Spanish period, officials issued a condensed guide to land policy known as the Plan de Pitic, which took into account the significance of common lands, propios, acequias, pasturage, and other land uses as defined in the *Recopilación de leyes*. Under Mexican rule, the Plan de Pitic served as a precedent for the establishment of ejidos (common lands).[9]

The main changes in the litigation of land issues would occur with a new bureaucracy that would handle such issues. In the long run, atrisqueños realized that the Mexican government would largely leave existing grant owners to carry on their business as they had under Spain, but landowners would have to learn how the Mexican political system worked. Change was in the air; landowners learned a new political vocabulary that blew northward from Mexico City.

Spanish colonization laws pertaining to new settlements and land tenure also carried over into the Mexican period. Spanish policy, particularly in Texas, had allowed Anglo-Americans to enter and settle in Spanish territory provided that they converted to Catholicism and settled a prescribed number of families on the land. Additionally, the policy obligated them to show progress toward cultivating the land. Such policies continued into the Mexican period, as Anglo settlers crossed the Sabine River on their way to San Antonio. Mexico desired, as did Spain, to populate the wide open spaces along its northern frontier with settlers who they hoped would be loyal to Mexico.

In the Colonization Law of 1823, the Mexican Congress authorized the central government to enter into contracts with *empresarios* (entrepreneurs) who would introduce two hundred families into Mexican territories. In return for services rendered, an empresario would receive three haciendas and two farm fields (*labores*) for every two hundred families settled. The most an empresario could receive was nine haciendas and six labores. Settlers who declared themselves farmers would receive one *labor*, and stock raisers would receive at least a *sitio* (six square miles) of land. This law authorized any duly ordained ayuntamiento to grant land within its jurisdiction.[10]

This was followed by the Colonization Law of 1824, which provided for a stronger role by the states in the granting of land. That role was reinforced when, in 1828, the central government issued a new policy, consistent with the Colonization Law of 1824, authorizing governors to grant land within their jurisdictions to any Mexican citizen or foreigner who properly requested land for cultivation or settlement.[11] In 1835, the central government attempted to withdraw this authorization from its governors but found it difficult, as it had earlier relinquished this power to the states.[12]

The contradiction in Mexican land policy seemed to depend on who was in power. The Colonization Law of 1824, for example, applied when Mexico defined itself as a republic. When a dictatorship with a centralized government consolidated its power under Santa Anna in 1834, the authority of the states was curtailed. Therefore, under the centralist form, a valid grant could not be made locally. In an attempt to straighten out the confusion, the Mexican government in 1854 declared void all grants made in the periods October 3, 1835–August 4, 1846, and March 17, 1853–July 7, 1854.[13] However, as New Mexico would become part of the United States in 1848, the effect of this nullification on New Mexico land grants was moot.

The broad colonization legislation of the Mexican Congress had little effect on old Spanish land grants in New Mexico such as Atrisco. Understanding the new chain of command, however, was essential. Once a transfer of land was completed, for example, the contracting parties would now take the documentation to be validated by the alcalde constitucional; in the case of Atrisco, he was located in Alburquerque. At

Atrisco, foreigners did not figure into any of the land exchanges, which continued to be made among family members, close friends, and relatives in the extended clan.

One example of day-to-day business at Atrisco occurred in 1823 when the family of Miguel Jaramillo reviewed his last will and testament. Jaramillo named as executors Antonio Chaves, Bartolomé Chaves, and Rafael Sánchez, all residents of Atrisco.[14] Jaramillo noted in his will that he had been married four times. His first wife, Francisca Lucero, bore four children: José Miguel, Catarina, Manuel, and María de los Reyes. At the time of his death, all four were married. His second and third wives, María Manuela Trujillo and María Antonia Sánchez, bore him no children. His fourth wife, María Gertrudis Candelaria, bore six children: Juan Antonio, Miguel, Bárbara, María Guadalupe, Fernando, and María Antonia. Although his first three wives did not bring "any dower or fortune" into the marriage, María Gertrudis Candelaria brought in some personal property and a calf.[15]

Don Miguel left a house in Atrisco, which he described as his residence, to the children of his first marriage. He also owned a strip of land in "the meadow," which had been donated to him by his grandmother, Tomasa Tenorio, in 1782. He said it should go "to the children whom I had by my wife María Gertrudis Candelaria, one-half to them and one-half to my said wife since the land referred to as La Casa Vieja I hold by purchase made during the time of this last marriage about two hundred varas and of which property my said wife made a relinquishment in favor of my first children wherefore I have given her one-half of la vega [the meadow] to compensate for the said property."[16] Jaramillo also mentioned a share of a tract of land called El Torreón on the other side of the Río Grande, which, if proven his, appeared to go to Doña Gertrudis.

The rest of his property included two mules. The one called La Chiquita was ordered to be delivered to Doña Gertrudis "to replace the cow with her calf which she brought me." Jaramillo's shotgun, still in possession of his son Manuel, went to his son Juan Antonio. Jaramillo also listed one ax and one reed (part of a loom) for weaving blankets. He acknowledged a debt of one sheep to Francisco Xavier Chaves with the words "let it be paid."[17]

The will was validated on March 30, 1823, by Juan Armijo, the alcalde constitucional of the jurisdiction of Alburquerque. Jaramillo's burial costs were taken from the sale of the piece of land known as La Casa Vieja. Jaramillo said that La Casa Vieja contained

> a little more or less [than] four hundred varas and the same amount of uncultivated land which I acquired by inheritance from my parents, I

order that of the best of the said cultivated land these be taken one hundred varas to pay for my interment and . . . masses with the condition that they may be taken by any of the legatees who may be willing to pay for them, and all that remains in this place, it is my will that it shall go to my said children by my first marriage.[18]

According to the terms of his will, Miguel Jaramillo's land grant would continue intact for another generation. Such was the mundane nature of business at Atrisco during the Mexican period.

The political reorganization of Mexico would soon prove to be more relevant to the atrisqueños. Prior to modifying its colonization policies, the Mexican Congress passed the Constitutive Act, which provided for the election of representatives to Congress. It defined Mexican sovereignty as the "supreme power" formed by the legislative, executive, and judicial branches. The territories of Mexico would be directly subject to the supreme power. During that period, the Congress created large states, which included provinces within them. By dint of the Constitutive Act, on January 31, 1824, Congress created the internal states of the East, West, and North, the latter including the provinces of Chihuahua, Durango, and New Mexico.[19] Later, Mexico discarded the word "province" and substituted "territory." Thus the Decree of July 6, 1824, created the Mexican Territory of New Mexico.[20] New Mexico remained a territory under the Constitution of 1824 until December of 1836. The new constitution of 1836 provided that the Congress would create departments instead of states. Under the Decree of December 29, 1836, New Mexico became a department under the Republic of Mexico.

By the early 1840s, the departmental governments comprised governors, juntas, prefects, sub-prefects, common councils, alcaldes, and justices of the peace.[21] The governor's duties by now were fairly traditional. The role of the governor continued to be crucial to litigated issues faced by New Mexicans.

The last major reform of New Mexico's government under Mexico took place with the Decree of June 13, 1843, which would have an effect on departmental governments and tweak the responsibilities of governors. One new provision, for example, called for the reduction of the governor's term from eight years to five years. Departmental councils, like that of Santa Fe, also underwent reform. The decree created *asambleas*, or departmental assemblies, composed of eleven members with a minimum of seven allowed. The asambleas were charged with establishing taxes with congressional approval, regulating spending, and appointing necessary employees. In regard to property, the members of the asamblea regulated the acquisition, alienation, and exchange of property with legislation in accordance with colonization laws. Attending to the departmental infrastructure was a priority, and the asamblea provided for opening and maintaining roads. Among the many responsibilities of the asamblea were the promotion of public instruction, the recruitment and maintenance of the army, and the establishment of municipal corporations. Still, Congress retained the right to review and, if need be, annul legislation or actions by the asambleas.[22] Members were to be elected by the outgoing juntas so that their terms would be staggered. At first, some of the members would serve for two years, while the others served for four. To serve in the asamblea, members had to be a full twenty-five years of age.

The electoral process, from the partido to the national level of politics, had evolved quickly during the early republic. Caleb Cushing, U.S. envoy to China, passed through Mexico on his return trip from the Orient in 1844 and made some observations about Mexico's social and political conditions. Cushing's observations explain how the changes affected units, such as Atrisco, within a partido. Exactly how the process Cushing describes worked in New Mexico is difficult to ascertain. New Mexico, as a part of the Mexican body politic, nonetheless played a role in national and local elections.

Cushing's observations offer glimpses of the political ambience throughout the Mexican Republic in the 1840s. Cushing writes that popular elections were held throughout Mexico every two years in the months of August, September, and October. Throughout the Republic of Mexico, he wrote, the inhabitants of the partidos, which he also called "sections," voted for primary electors, who in turn chose members of the electoral college, who selected representatives for the National Congress and the departmental asambleas. Married males over eighteen could vote; unmarried males had to be twenty-one years old to vote. In the vote, the partidos, generally consisting of not fewer than five hundred people, chose only one primary elector each. The primary electors were designated, Cushing writes, "*de primer voto.*" After the election of the primary electors, they met and chose secondary electors ("*de segundo voto*") who collectively constituted the electoral college of each department. Particularly in the more heavily populated areas of Mexico, the primary electors "choose secondary electors, in the proportion of one secondary to every twenty of the primary electors."[23] The electoral college of each department elected deputies to the National Congress and chose the members of the asamblea for their respective departments. All representatives to the National Congress or the departmental asambleas had to be at least twenty-five years of age. Cushing reports that the departmental assemblies elected the president of the republic and two-thirds of the senators.[24] This explains the role of the partido in national politics as well as in local affairs.

Politics in the frontier areas did not always run smoothly. Rebellions took place throughout the 1830s in Yucatan, Sonora, California, Texas, and New Mexico. The last ten years of Mexican rule in such frontier areas proved troublesome to officials in Mexico City. Issues such as the appointment of outsiders to serve as governors, the territorial or departmental status accorded frontier areas instead of statehood, and the imposition of taxes hampered relations between these areas and the National Congress. In the frontier areas, politics were localized at the lowest level of government. Mexican officials hoped to remedy the situation by extending judiciary control to those local areas.

In the Spanish period, the alcalde mayor had reported directly to the governor. Under the Mexican Constitution of 1836, the administration of justice was further upgraded by the establishment of *prefecturias*, large districts administered by a prefect with judiciary control. Thus, between the office of the *jefe político* (formerly the governor), who administered the departamento, and the ayuntamiento, which monitored the affairs of the municipio, another layer of decision-making was added with the *prefectos*, who had political power over the districts called prefecturias— before a given case reached the governor.

The change in the bureaucratic administration of justice added a degree of procedural authority to the granting of land to Mexican citizens. Unlike the Spanish period, when only governors and higher officials such as the viceroy could grant lands, Mexican law provided that governors were "authorized, under the law . . . to grant the public lands of their respective territories to the contractors, families or private persons, Mexicans or foreigners, who may apply for them, for the purpose of cultivating them or living upon them."[25] The language of the regulations specifically stated that "every applicant for land, whether contractor, head of family or private person, shall apply to the Political Chief [jefe político or governor] of the respective Territory, with an application [in] which is given his name, country, profession, the number, religion and other circumstances of the families or persons whom he desires to colonize, and shall also mark as distinctly as possible and describe on a map the land he applies for."[26] Lesser officials could now make concessions of land, provided the governor approved them.

Local prefects, who were appointed to their coveted posts by the governor, controlled the assignation of common lands, among other duties. The Law of March 20, 1837 empowered them to "regulate administratively and in conformity with the laws, the distribution of common lands (*tierras comunes*) in the towns of the district, provided there is no litigation pending with regard to them, the right being reserved to the parties in interest to apply to the Governor, who without further appeal, shall decide what is most proper, with the concurrence of the departmental council (*junta*)."[27] Interested settlers, however, had to apply to the governor for land.[28] In any case, the transactions were, of course, subject to his approval. At the end of their proceedings, they made a certified copy validating their actions and usually obtained the approval of the governor.

Centralization of political power was the aim of Mexican authorities under Santa Anna. Quickly changing the form of government from a federal republic to a dictatorship, the National Congress in Mexico City early in 1835 abrogated the self-governing powers of the states. Each state or department, thereafter, was permitted a five-member council that reported directly to the Congress. In November 1835 a provisional departmental council met in New Mexico in accordance with Mexican directives. The convocation of a provisional council signaled New Mexico's preparation for departmental status. Seven months later, the first permanent council of New Mexico was recognized under the Constitution of 1836.[29]

The political atmosphere created by a vigorous Mexican authority proved stressful to New Mexicans. They were keenly aware that Texas and Yucatan had rebelled over issues related to their status. Frustrated and angry about changes that appeared abusive to them, New Mexicans openly rebelled against the centralist Mexican government. At the time, atrisqueños had no idea that they would participate in events surrounding the restoration of New Mexico in the wake of the rebellion against Governor Albino Pérez.

Albino Pérez was appointed to the military governorship of New Mexico by President Antonio López de Santa Anna in 1835. As a native of Veracruz and an outsider to Santa Fe politics, he was publicly opposed by New Mexicans. Arriving in New Mexico in April 1835, Pérez had high hopes of improving the situation that confronted him, but he succeeded only in encouraging the resentment harbored against him by those who considered him an outsider.[30] Pérez's unquestioned loyalty to the central government of dictator Santa Anna, his noble qualities, and his military experience made him a fine choice for the New Mexican mission.[31] Pérez's objective—to prepare the people of New Mexico for the change from an outlying provincial territory to a department or state—inspired opposition from New Mexican frontier people who interpreted the change to mean that they would surrender local power to a distant central government.[32] Consequently, an explosive political issue regarding home rule undermined his mission.

Soon after his arrival in Santa Fe, Albino Pérez began an inspection tour of northern New Mexico. He reported his findings to the people in the patriotic, romantic language then current:

> Compatriots: A series of extraordinary circumstances have come together to furnish me with the most pleasant references to speak to you for the first time. As of today it is thirty-four days that I have the honor to govern you, and already I can count thousands of examples of your gentleness, your love for order, your submission to justice and a true complement of many civic and moral virtues which God has joined here so as to illuminate His Omnipotence in this majestic retreat.[33]

Pérez spoke of the "patience of a truly paternalistic government, proud of its Mexican origin and . . . heroic . . . because it is supported by the unanimous vote of the Nation." The speech was published and circulated throughout New Mexico, but it was received with indifference.

Meanwhile, Governor Pérez went about the business of implementing the "departmental plan" of government, which resulted from the establishment of a strongly centralized government under Antonio López de Santa Anna, president-dictator of Mexico. By that time, New Mexico had been divided into several districts, each administered by a *prefecto* with judicial and political powers.[34] The prefectos reported to the jefe político (in this case Albino Pérez), who in turn was directly responsible to the National Congress. Subsequently, once the prefect system was established, the chain of governmental command linked local control with the central government.

Yet, controversy shrouded the department system in New Mexico, and Albino Pérez's leadership became the focal point of attention among New Mexicans. The causes of discontent resulted from legislative action Albino Pérez initiated, plus the consideration that he was not a native of the area he governed. Chief among the issues was that the Pérez administration imposed direct taxes on the inhabitants of New Mexico. Demands he made on the people for aid against marauding Indians were another area of complaint, for the people felt that the central government should provide military assistance. The upshot of such discontent was a lack of cooperation by New Mexican frontiersmen.

Don Albino's activities, no matter how practical, became increasingly unpopular. On October 16, 1835, for example, he announced legislation regulating trade with Indians. The October law threatened the lucrative illegal Indian trade, which the jefe político blamed for increased

Comanche, Apache, Ute, and Navajo attacks by well-supplied raiders. The law provided that:

1. Foreigners from the north be prohibited from trading in New Mexico with all classes of Indians
2. Both foreigners and citizens of New Mexico not be permitted to trade arms and ammunition to barbarian nations who surround the territory and raid into Chihuahua
3. Trade with Indians be permitted only with a license issued by the departmental government
4. No Mexican citizen, native or naturalized, be permitted to trap beaver without license from the departmental government
5. No citizen be permitted to use his license to trap beaver for any foreigner.[35]

Pérez also specified that monies be used to outfit troops for combat against raiders. But New Mexicans viewed the law as an example of Pérez's role as an agent of the centralist government bent on destroying home rule.

Pérez announced another regulatory law eight months later in June 1836. This time foreign merchants were the target. The law, weighted with details, provided that taxes would be levied on each wagon hauling foreign merchandise into Santa Fe, on each animal involved in freighting, and on each horse or mule brought into New Mexico for sale.[36] The June law also provided for taxes per head for driving herds of cattle or sheep through the streets of Santa Fe. Cutting timber required a license, and fees for attendance at theaters and dances were charged in accordance with the law. The June legislation, far-reaching in scope, made it mandatory for all foreigners as well as natives of New Mexico who resided outside of Santa Fe to report to the alcalde within three days after their arrival in that city, and that all persons state their business and occupation under penalty of fine. The prefects of the territory were instructed to keep a list of all inhabitants within their respective districts, listing their occupations. Unemployed individuals who could not prove that they subsisted by legal means were to be punished. Justices failing to comply with the requirements of the law were to be censured, fined, and removed from office. Notwithstanding the practicality of Pérez's actions, the earlier October law and the June enactments affected many facets of the New Mexican economy. Having little discretion over the matter, Albino Pérez signed the law into being.

Although the law placed the burden of taxes on foreign traders, they in turn passed the burden on to their New Mexican customers by raising prices. Josiah Gregg, an American trader in Santa Fe, noted the attitude of the people when he stated that, although it was "necessary for the support of the new organization to introduce a system of direct taxation . . . the people . . . would sooner have paid a *doblón* through a tariff than a *real* in this way."[37]

While his economic reforms were causing debate among foreigners and citizens, Governor Pérez turned his attention to other problem areas. Knowing of the up-and-down history of education in New Mexico, Pérez proposed a remedy. The jefe político did not have to look far for examples of illiteracy; the 1836 report of the ayuntamiento of Santa Fe showed that two of the seven deputies could not read or write.[38] Describing the state of education in the department as deplorable, Pérez said that children running in the streets, as well as youths who were given to "evil dispositions, abandoned to laziness, and practicing vices" ought to be in school. Moreover, he described the prevailing "thievery, immorality, desertion, and poverty as the most humiliating shame of the city."[39] In July 1836, Pérez proposed the establishment of two schools for primary instruction in Santa Fe. All children ages five to twelve were to attend school under penalty of fine. The fines ranged from one to five pesos, double for the second offense and triple for the third. Anyone who could not pay the fines was subject to arrest for a minimum of three days. The time of detention increased with each arrest.[40]

Failing to consider the already depressed attitude of the people, Pérez detailed how his compulsory education system would work. Several commissioners of public instruction stationed in every block of Santa Fe made lists of inhabitants and kept track of school-age children and their attendance in school. Aside from making monthly attendance reports, the commissioners selected students for academic or vocational programs.

If there existed any doubt concerning Pérez's authority to suggest or decree taxation provisions of laws, it soon disappeared with the Decree of April 17, 1837.[41] The decree from Mexico City spelled out the role of jefes políticos in directing their departments toward improved fiscal efficiency. Granting investigatory, advisory, and appointive powers to department governors, the decree allowed Albino Pérez to supervise officials of the Hacienda, or Treasury. As witness to the monthly and annual cash statements made by officers of the Treasury, Pérez could observe omissions and abuses. As a result of Pérez's accretion of authority, the undercurrent of opposition began to move swiftly, gathering the discontented and opportunistic elements of New Mexico's political society. The optimism portrayed in Pérez's inaugural speech began to disappear. Slowly, his political enemies revealed themselves.

In the backlands of northern New Mexico, trouble brewed for the Pérez faction. A seemingly obscure court case in out-of-the-way La Cañada de Santa Cruz began a chain of events that led to the political confrontation with the jefe político, Albino Pérez. Presiding over a trial involving relatives, Juan José Esquivel acquitted them. The case was reviewed by Ramón Abreu, a supporter of Pérez, who not only reversed the decision but had Esquivel arrested when he refused to comply with the reversal. Public sympathy soon rallied around Esquivel, who sat in jail serving out his term. Moving swiftly, a mob formed outside his cell, liberated him, and escaped to a mountain stronghold. Observing the situation, Josiah Gregg noted that it was "an occurrence that seemed as a watchword for a general insurrection."[42] At that moment, the escaped Esquivel became not only the protagonist in the struggle against the jefe político, but also the pretext for a rebellion.

On August 3, 1837, a revolutionary junta was formed consisting of twelve men who called their district the Cantón de La Cañada. They drew up their position statement, which mentioned nothing about the Esquivel incident:

> Long live God and the Nation and the faith of Jesus Christ. The principal points that we defend are as follows:
>
> 1. To be with God and the Nation and the faith of Jesus Christ
>
> 2. To defend our country to the last drop of blood in order to attain victory
>
> 3. Not to admit the Departmental Plan
>
> 4. Not to admit a single tax
>
> 5. Not to admit the bad order of those who are trying to effect it.
>
> God and the Nation. Santa Cruz de la Cañada.
August 3, 1837. Encampment.[43]

The term "encampment" suggested the existence of insurgent headquarters, a signal that the rebellion had begun. The Hispanic rebels gathered at the encampment with their Indian counterparts, "the principal warriors of all the northern pueblos."[44]

As word reached Pérez of impending trouble, he hastened to gather a militia but could muster only "a hundred and fifty men including the warriors of the pueblo of Santo Domingo."[45] With his small force, Pérez left the capital on August 7, 1837, to suppress the rebels. They spent the night at the Indian pueblo of Pojoaque, continued the march to Santa Cruz, and were attacked en route by the rebels, reported Francisco Sarracino, "in a disorderly manner . . . giving us a lively fire . . . Colonel Pérez approached the cannon and said to me these words, 'Friend Sarracino do not abandon the cannon.'"[46] Needless to say, the cannon was abandoned, the battle was lost, and most of Pérez's men were captured or defected to the rebels. Pérez was chased back to the outskirts of Santa Fe, where, on August 9, he was caught and brutally killed.

The rebel forces gathered strength. Two thousand strong, mostly Pueblo warriors, they marched on Santa Fe. The inhabitants fortified themselves in their homes, preparing for the worst. The rabble entered the city and elected a governor, José Gonzales, whom Gregg described as a "good honest hunter, but a very ignorant man."[47] Two days after their entry into Santa Fe, they left. With Gonzales and the rebels at large, New Mexico was in a state of rebellion.

News of the rebellion reached the Hispanic villages on the Río Abajo. Despite their dislike of the Pérez administration, the people of the Río Abajo, which formed the Second District of New Mexico (including Atrisco), could not or would not support the rebels. On September 8, 1837, members of the Second District held a meeting at Tomé, south of Albuquerque, and called for the suppression of the rebels, who by then had established themselves in Santa Fe. Sensing that the tide of sentiment for rebellion had ended, the Albuquerquean Manuel Armijo joined them in announcing his opposition to the uprising.[48] At the meeting in Tomé, Mariano Chaves announced, "I know of no one better qualified to lead our army than Manuel Armijo."[49] After nominating Armijo, he asked the assembly to declare Armijo leader of the army.

Armijo reported the situation to Mexico City and asked for reinforcements. By the end of the year, Mexican officials sent three hundred more men under a Colonel Justiniani, who commanded the Escuadrón de Veracruz and presidial troops from Chihuahua.[50]

As soon as he could muster a fighting army, drawn mostly from the Second District, Tomé, and Alburquerque, Manuel Armijo, self-appointed governor, attacked and routed the rebels just north of the Santa Cruz Valley. On January 27, 1838, at the Battle of La Cañada, Armijo captured and executed José Gonzales, thus crushing the revolt. He reported to the central government that the situation was under control and there was no need to send more troops northward. Armijo, already recognized as commander-in-chief, petitioned for the governorship and received it. Granted that concession, New Mexico was restored to its native sons.

After the untimely death of Albino Pérez in the rebellion of 1837, archrival Manuel Armijo thus became governor of the politically fragmented department of New Mexico until the American invasion of 1846. But the death of Albino Pérez seemed to haunt New Mexicans, for he was commemorated in the oral tradition and the historical records of New Mexico.

A ballad memorializing Pérez's tragic death appeared in northern New Mexico. It was a *décima glosada,* a poetic form in which each stanza has ten lines of eight syllables in a fixed rhyme pattern. In the décima "Año de mil ochocientos treinta y siete desgraciado," the balladeer portrays Albino Pérez as an innocent victim of circumstance who died as a result of "vengeance and hatred" on the part of the people he tried to govern. Angry yet wistful, the balladeer criticizes a generation for the misfortune wrought on New Mexico.

Año de mil ochocientos	Year of eighteen hundred
Treinta y siete	And thirty-seven—
desgraciado	be damned!
Nuevo México infeliz	Miserable New Mexico
¿Qué es lo que nos ha pasado?	What has happened to us?
Ya murió el juez de distrito	Our district judge is dead
Murió el prefeto y el jefe	So too our prefect and our chief
Y así, ninguno se queje	Let no man cry in grief
Cuando pague su delito	For the guilt upon his head
Estaba desvueladito	This innocent man was led
Cuando pagó el inocente	To doom, sleepless and exhausted,
Y que padezca la gente	Now let the storm be inflicted
Este crecido tormento	On the people, let them dread;
Siempre te tendré presente	You will always be remembered,
Año de mil ochocientos.	O year of eighteen hundred.
Junta de departamento	Departmental council convoked
Constituida por la fuerza	Convened by force;
¿Quién ha de tener a bien	Who can, as a matter of course,
La inicua desobediencia?	Accept such a wicked revolt?
¿Quién será aquel que no tema	Who will now not fear to speak
Hablar por su territorio	For his land, having seen
Viendo la venganza, el odio	The vengeance and hatred
De lo que nos ha pasado?	Which upon us they did wreak?
No quisiera haberte visto,	I wish I had never seen you
Treinta y siete desgraciado.	Eighteen hundred thirty-seven,
	be damned.

Desgraciado territorio	Miserable territory
¿Qué hicistes con la paciencia	What became of your patience
Con la cuerdura, obediencia,	Your good judgment, the obedience
Que era tu único tesoro?	That was your only treasure?
Es lo que más siento y lloro:	That which I lament and mourn
Verte hoy desacreditado	Your reputation soiled,
De la fuerza cautivado	By violence despoiled,
Sin defensa ni salida;	Defenseless and forlorn;
Llora, llora tu desdicha,	Cry, cry for your misfortune,
Territorio desgraciado.	Miserable territory.
Conquistadora feliz,	Contented Conquistadora
Tú has de traer el consuelo	You must bring your consolation
Y que no permita el cielo	That heaven not permit
La discordia entre nosotros;	Discord among us
Madre mía, nuestro amparo,	Mother mine, our true salvation,
Siembra tú la paz y unión	You sow your peace and
Entre nos, tus moradores	unity among us,
De este reino conquistado,	Your dwellers in this conquered land
Yo estoy confuso y no sé	I am confused and don't know
Qué es lo que nos ha pasado.	What has happened to us.[51]

The tragic event received renewed attention in the twentieth century when, on a June afternoon in 1901, a group of New Mexicans met in Santa Fe to dedicate a monument to the memory of Albino Pérez.[52] According to a newspaper of the time, the First Cavalry and the New Mexico National Guard Band led a parade from the plaza to a point along Agua Fria Street and stopped near the spot where Governor Pérez had fallen sixty-four years before. The Daughters of the American Revolution and members of the Rough Riders, followed by the National Guard, firemen, and a contingent of interested citizens, reached the place of dedication. As they gathered around, gusts of wind and dust swirled around the spectators, while overhead, clouds began to darken the late-afternoon sky. One of the participants unveiled a marble boulder polished on one side, with the inscription:

On this spot, Governor Albino Pérez . . . was assassinated
August 9, 1837[53]

The paraders listened to speakers while wind and dust disturbed them and the rain clouds became ever more menacing. After a round of introductory remarks, Demetrio Pérez, son of Albino Pérez, expressed his appreciation for the honor extended to the memory of his father. As he ended his speech, a driving hailstorm scattered the crowd and cut short the ceremony.[54]

With Pérez dead in 1837, New Mexicans could ignore directives from

the central government in Mexico City. Earlier, the government of president-dictator Antonio López de Santa Anna had suffered political and
military defeats in the Texas and California revolts of 1836. Instability
in Mexico allowed New Mexico to revert to its customary pattern of
isolation. But, for the next decade, New Mexicans fared poorly under
subsequent Mexican administrations, and sentiment for annexation to
the United States as an alternative to Mexican rule began to grow. When
Stephen Watts Kearny and his Army of the West marched into Santa
Fe during the War of 1846, members of the New Mexico upper class
welcomed them. A new, troublous era had begun for the Hispanos of
New Mexico.

For the next few years after the death of Albino Pérez, Governor Manuel Armijo entrenched himself as sole ruler of New Mexico. With the
one-man rule imposed on New Mexico came stability, but the trade-off
was that Mexico City had little involvement in New Mexico throughout the 1840s. New Mexico went through a laissez-faire period during
which Mexican officials kept their distance as long as Manuel Armijo
controlled affairs in his jurisdiction.

In the wake of rebellion, a strange event took place that would solid-
ify Armijo's powers with the central government in Mexico City. Tend-
ing their sheep and farms, atrisqueños were touched by an event that
historians would later call "the Texas invasion of New Mexico." A group
of adventurers had decided to invade New Mexico and make it part of
Texas. They claimed that the Río Grande was the boundary, and that
the entire east bank from the San Luis Valley to the the Gulf of Mexico
belonged to the Lone Star Republic. The Texans theorized that New
Mexicans were just waiting for an opportunity to declare independence
from Mexico. If true, it would be their duty to release New Mexicans
from Mexican tyranny, especially those living on the east bank of the
Río Grande. The Texans also theorized that if the invasion were successful, trade along the Santa Fe–Chihuahua Trail could be diverted
through Texas channels.[55]

In spring 1841, Mirabeau Buonaparte Lamar, president of the Republic of Texas, without the support of the Texas Congress, approved an
expedition of about three hundred men. The expedition advanced toward New Mexico under Colonel Hugh McLeod, accompanied by three
commissioners who made proclamations explaining the advantages of
freedom from Mexico.[56] Traders, adventurers, and some travelers who
did not understand the purpose of the expedition also went along. One
author writes of the ill-fated 1841 expedition, "This 'wild goose chase'
was sponsored by President Lamar for the express purpose of territorial

expansion, of acquiring control of New Mexico—by peaceful means if possible; by military force if necessary. The expedition was assembled within the shadow of the Texas capital and with the advice and aid of the Texas President himself."[57]

In the guise of traders along the Santa Fe–Chihuahua Trail, Colonel McLeod led his men across the arid lands of west Texas.[58] On the morning of June 19, 1841, they left Brushy Creek, fifteen miles north of Austin, bound for New Mexico. Poorly supplied and equipped, they planned to live off the land. After a week, the expedition was in unfamiliar land. They reached the vicinity of present-day Amarillo by the first week in September. The men were discontented and fatigued from the march through a treeless plain and wanted to abandon the expedition. One committed suicide, a few others suffered from fever, and some were killed by Indians. By the time the expedition reached New Mexico, the survivors were near starvation, dehydrated, ragged, and dirty.

On September 17, the arrival of New Mexicans with messages electrified the camp. Peter Gallagher, a member of the ill-fated expedition, wrote in his journal: "About 8 o'clock, one of the Mexicans . . . together with three others from New Mexico, arrived in camp bringing letters informing us that all was right and that we should destroy all that we could not bring and take those Mexicans for guides to the settlements."[59] The next day, seven wagons and all unnecessary baggage were burned. They followed the guides through the waterless Llano Estacado for nearly two weeks when, on October 4, a fully armed Mexican escort commanded by Colonel Damasio Salazar met them at Laguna Colorado. Lieutenant Colonel Juan Andrés Archuleta presented them with terms of surrender: first, that they lay down their arms; second, that their life, liberty, and personal property would be protected; and third, that they would be escorted to San Miguel el Vado, several days away. Believing that their arms would be returned to them, the Texans capitulated.

On October 6, they camped at a point on Pajarito Creek. There the officers were separated from the men and all were taken to San Miguel. Two days later, after marching sixty miles, they arrived at Anton Chico, where they were fed and incarcerated in an old house. The next day they marched twenty miles to San Miguel el Vado, where they were again kept under guard. Women came to sell them food, which, lacking money, they traded for with the buttons off their shirts.[60] Meanwhile, Captain William P. Lewis, acting as translator, betrayed the Texans in order to save himself from imprisonment and possibly a firing squad.

In Santa Fe, meanwhile, Governor Armijo appointed prefect Antonio

Sandoval as acting governor while he personally attended to the invasion.[61] Armijo had already informed New Mexicans that the Texans intended to "burn, slay, and destroy" on their march through the department.[62] At first, Captain Lewis told Armijo that they were merchants
from the United States. Having dealt with merchants on the Santa Fe–
Chihuahua Trail, Armijo pointed to the star and the word "Texas" on
Lewis's uniform. Turning to the Texans, he said, "You cannot deceive
me; United States merchants do not wear Texas uniforms."[63] Armijo's
ire was evident, his patience thin.

Armijo dealt with the Texas invasion of New Mexico for what it was.
Some members of the expedition were executed. The majority were sent
to Mexico City for trial and imprisonment. Among them was José An-
tonio Navarro, who had supported the Texas Rebellion of 1836 against
Mexico. He was regarded as a traitor by Mexican president Antonio
López de Santa Anna and imprisoned for nearly four years.

Damasio Salazar was the officer in charge of the prisoners. He marched
them south from Santa Fe along the old Camino Real to Alburquerque,
then through Atrisco, Pajarito, and Los Padillas, past Isleta to Socorro.
Most of the Hispanos pitied them, gave them food, and wished them
well, making the sign of the cross and praying for them. *"Pobrecitos"*—
"poor things"—rang in the Texans' ears as they headed south.

George W. Kendall, one of the prisoners and also a Louisiana newspaper reporter, recalled that on October 22 they entered Alburquerque,
"famed for the beauty of its women, besides being the largest place in
the province of New Mexico, and the residence of Armijo a part of the
year."[64] The people turned out to see the *"estrangeros."* Kendall wrote,
"As we were marched directly through the principal streets the inhabitants were gathered on either side to gaze at the estrangeros, as we
were called. The women, with all kindness of heart, gave our men corn,
pumpkins, bread, and everything they could spare from their scanty
store as we passed."[65] Kendall wrote that after they departed from Albuquerque, they passed through a succession of cultivated fields and
pastures, undoubtedly those of Atrisco, Armijo, Pajarito, and Los Padillas. Of the route near Atrisco, Kendall wrote, "After leaving Albuquerque, we continued our march through a succession of cultivated fields
and pastures until we reached a small rancho called Los Placeres, and
here we camped for the night"—a short distance from Albuquerque.[66]
By late evening of October 24, they had reached Valencia. Like other
settlers who lived along the Camino Real, atrisqueños approached the
prisoners and gave them corn, bread, and water.

The road to Mexico City was filled with death. Those who could not stand up and march were executed, the ears of the dead cut off as proof that they had not escaped. The lack of water and food and the desert heat took their toll on the Texans, especially after they left Socorro, as they were forced to march through the Jornada del Muerto before reaching El Paso. The Texans were brutally treated by their captors. Thirsty, starving, fatigued, beaten, they arrived in El Paso. As in the valley of Albuquerque and later in Ciudad Chihuahua, compassionate people came out to give them food and water. Finally, they made it to Mexico City, where many were released; a few, like Navarro, would be found guilty of sedition and treachery and sentenced to imprisonment in the dungeons of the Acordada in Mexico City or on the island fortress of San Juan de Ulloa in the harbor of Veracruz.

As for Governor Armijo, he emerged as a patriot for having dealt heroically with the invasion, limiting the loss of life for New Mexicans. Santa Fe Trail merchants kept away from the prisoners lest they be identified with the invaders. Within three weeks after the attempted Texan invasion, atrisqueños and other New Mexicans read a circular containing Armijo's proclamation of November 10, 1841. In it, he declared that it was necessary to confuse the Texans, apprehend them, and manipulate their surrender with minimal risk to New Mexicans and, in so doing, protect Mexico's honor. He emphasized that the nation's integrity had been challenged by Texans who wished to extend their claim to include New Mexico.[67] Then, and in all future relations, Armijo kept a wary watch on all foreigners. In 1889, Hubert Howe Bancroft wrote, "There can be no doubt that Governor Armijo was fully justified in seizing the Texan invaders, disarming them, confiscating their property, and sending them to Mexico as prisoners of war. He and his officers are accused, however, of having induced their victims to surrender by false assurances of friendship and false promises of welcome as traders, the giving-up of their arms being represented as a mere formality imposed on all vistors to Santa Fé."[68] In Santa Fe, however, Governor Armijo was greatly applauded. As a native of Albuquerque, he was doubtless looked on with pride by the citizens there and in the neighboring settlements between Bernalillo, Alameda, Atrisco, Pajarito, and Los Padillas. Armijo ruled New Mexico with an iron hand, but perhaps he did not deserve the historiographical legacy, begun with Kendall's writings, that would malign him in stereotypical terms. Still, Mexican authorities had long anticipated an invading army from Texas. They had issued warnings and reinforcements. When the invasion did occur in 1841, they praised Governor Armijo for the way he handled it.

Just prior to the occupation of New Mexico by the United States, a series of events took place that affected the distribution of land. Mexican law prohibited granting land within twenty leagues of an international border or ten leagues of a coastline without the consent of the central government in Mexico City.[69] No individual, furthermore, could receive more than eleven square leagues of land.[70] Especially during the 1840s, New Mexican officials used land grants to influence private enterprises and create defensive barriers against Indian, Texan, and Anglo-American intruders. New Mexicans were encouraged to settle lands in river valleys on the northeastern and eastern peripheries bordering the Republic of Texas.[71]

Governor Armijo, one of the more profligate grantors of land during the Mexican period in New Mexico, ostensibly gave away 16.5 million acres of the 31 million acres of land in New Mexico between 1837 and 1846.[72] In 1841, Guadalupe Miranda and Charles Beaubien requested and received lands from Armijo east of the Sangre de Cristo Mountains along the Cimarron and Canadian rivers. They planned to ranch, cultivate cotton and sugar beets, cut timber, and prospect for minerals. That grant later became the subject of one of the largest land grant claims when Beaubien's son-in-law, Lucien Maxwell, claimed nearly two million acres (2,680 square miles) in northeastern New Mexico and southeastern Colorado.[73]

Cautiously selecting land grant recipients to meet the defensive policies of New Mexico, Armijo generally chose foreign men who had either married Mexican women or lived in New Mexico since the 1820s. Most foreign grantees had New Mexican business partners. In 1845, for example, Gervasio Nolan, a French Canadian, and two New Mexican partners received land next to the Beaubien-Miranda grant on the Canadian River.[74] Charles Beaubien's thirteen-year-old son, Narciso, and a partner, Stephen Louis Lee, a fur trapper from St. Louis, received the Sangre de Cristo grant in the San Luis Valley, which straddled the border between the present New Mexico and Colorado.[75] Cerán St. Vrain and Cornelio Vigil received a grant along the Cucharas, Huerfano, and Apishapa rivers in eastern Colorado, known as the Animas grant, and John Scholly and his Mexican and Anglo-American partners received a grant northwest of Las Vegas, New Mexico.[76]

New Mexicans seemed to be alarmed by the amount of land granted to foreigners. One of Armijo's opponents was the celebrated cleric Father Antonio José Martínez of Taos. At the first opportunity, in February 1844, when interim governor Mariano Martínez had briefly replaced an ailing Armijo, Father Martínez urged him to annul the Beaubien-Miranda grant. Arguing that a law of March 11, 1842, permitted foreigners to acquire property anywhere in the Mexican Republic except in departments contiguous with other nations, which required special permission, Father Martínez persuaded the interim governor to oust Beaubien from his land in late spring 1844. Beaubien was a naturalized Mexican citizen but his partner in the land grant, Charles Bent, was a foreigner. Father Martínez's victory was short-lived, for the next governor, José Chaves, reinstated the rights of Beaubien, Bent, and St. Vrain, including the right to settle foreigners on the Beaubien-Miranda grant. In 1845, General Francisco García Conde, an inspector from the central government, ordered all foreigners in the Cimarron area to vacate their lands. Meanwhile, Manuel Armijo reassumed the governorship of New Mexico and encouraged foreigners to ignore the order. Motivated by his own one-fourth interest in the grant, Governor Armijo supported foreign settlers in their desire to remain on the Beaubien-Miranda land grant.[77]

Armijo's giveaway land grant policies attracted new immigrants into New Mexico, buoyed by the Mexican government's desire to colonize the northern frontier with anyone who would swear allegiance to the Mexican government, become a Roman Catholic, and promise to bring additional settlers into the area. Between 1821 and 1845, New Mexico's population grew from approximately forty-two thousand to approximately sixty-five thousand inhabitants.

The Mexican period was a time of mainly administrative change, proving the adaptability of New Mexicans to a new political system. In the short interval of twenty-seven years of Mexican rule, New Mexicans participated in the political system imposed by Mexico. Their initiation into Mexican politics prepared them for the next cycle of change. As regards the Atrisco land grant, Mexican legislation related to colonization had little, if any, effect on its status. Much of the business at Atrisco during that period revolved around conveyances among atrisqueños. The atrisqueños made no petitions for new lands during that period.

Great changes were in the wind by the middle 1840s. Between 1846 and 1848, atrisqueños and their fellow New Mexicans watched the outcome of the war between Mexico and the United States. As the Army of the West under General Stephen Watts Kearny occupied New Mexico, a new order was at hand. On September 18, 1846, Kearny addressed the people of New Mexico, but his words were no match for those of acting governor Juan Bautista Vigil y Alarid, whose words of acquiescence echoed with a certain *tristeza* throughout New Mexico. Standing in the Plaza de Santa Fe, Vigil y Alarid looked at Kearny and said,

> Do not find it strange if there has been no manifestation of joy and enthusiasm in seeing this city occupied by your military forces. To us, the

power of the Mexican Republic is dead. No matter what her condition, she was our mother. What child will not shed abundant tears at the tomb of his parents? . . . Today we belong to a great and powerful nation. . . . We know that we belong to the Republic that owes its origin to the immortal Washington, whom all civilized nations admire and respect.

With those poignant words, New Mexico slipped into the hands of the United States.

CHAPTER 11

The Treaty of Guadalupe Hidalgo

Hispanics and the Courts, 1849–1900

Mexicans . . . in the territories aforesaid . . . shall be incorporated into the Union of the United States and be admitted, at the proper time to be judged of by the Congress of the United States to the enjoyment of all the rights of citizens of the United States according to the principles of the Constitution; and in the mean time shall be maintained and protected in the free enjoyment of their liberty and property, and secured in the free exercise of their religion without restriction.

ARTICLE 9, TREATY OF GUADALUPE HIDALGO, 1848

The Constitution of the United States was ordained . . . by descendants of Englishmen, who inherited the traditions of English law and history; but it was made for an undefined and expanding future, and for a people gathered and to be gathered from many nations and of many tongues. And while we take just pride in the principles and institutions of the common law, we are not to forget that in lands where other systems of jurisprudence prevail, the ideas and processes of civil justice are also not unknown.

HURTADO V. CALIFORNIA (1884)

If atrisqueños and their fellow New Mexicans wondered how their land and citizenship rights would fare under the new government, that of the United States, they had only to witness the first few decades of the Anglo-American occupation of the Greater Southwest. Fortunately, their long experience with the legal traditions of Spain and Mexico had taught them how to defend themselves in court. The change in sovereignty, however, offered new challenges. In the first half-century following ratification of the 1848 Treaty of Guadalupe Hidalgo, hundreds of state, territorial, and federal legal entities produced a number of conflicting opinions and decisions in their interpretation of the provisions of the peace accord.

Citizenship rights seemingly guaranteed in Articles 8 and 9 of the treaty were not all they seemed.[1] Property rights of former Mexican citizens in Arizona, New Mexico, and Colorado proved vulnerable to interpretation by district and territorial courts. When Texas was granted statehood in 1845, Hispanics there had to defend their rights in the state court system. Within a generation, Mexican Americans who had been under the ostensible protection of the treaty learned to use the court system to challenge those who violated their rights. The Anglo-American judicial system, however, was administered by Anglo-American politicians, legislators, and judges, who usually worked against Mexican American interests. For nineteenth-century Hispanics, justice was not always served.

Early in the legal history of the Treaty of Guadalupe Hidalgo, Mexican Americans asserted their rights as citizens of their newly adopted country, the United States of America. In regard to land issues, a thousand claims had been filed by 1880, but only 150 had been considered by the federal government.[2]

This chapter discusses the efforts of Mexican Americans to gain recognition of the Treaty of Guadalupe Hidalgo in the courts, to assert citizenship rights under the U.S. Constitution, and to gain recognition of their land and water rights in conformity with the provisions of the treaty. Selected court cases in California and New Mexico during and after the territorial period as well as federal court litigation over lands ceded by Mexico to the United States under the treaty exemplify the issues.

The foremost issues affecting the lives of Mexican Americans living in the ceded territories, particularly between 1849 and 1900, revolved around Articles 8 and 9 of the treaty. These articles pertained to approximately a hundred thousand Mexicans, including a large number of Hispanicized and nomadic Indians living in the area encompassed by present-day New Mexico, Arizona, and California.[3] Texas was theoretically exempted from the treaty's provisions.

Article 8 of the treaty provided that persons living in the newly acquired territories had one year to elect Mexican or United States citizenship, or after one year they would automatically be considered U.S. citizens. According to the provision, they would be free to continue their residency in the ceded territory or move at any time to the Mexican Republic. Those who preferred to remain were given two options: to "retain the title and rights of Mexican citizens, or acquire those of citizens of the United

States." The provision specified that property, real or personal, belonging to Mexicans not living in the ceded territory would be inviolably respected. The owners and their heirs, and all Mexicans who would thereafter acquire property by contract in the United States, would be guaranteed rights to their property "equally ample as if the same belonged to citizens of the United States."

Article 9 further provided for the protection of property rights. It also reiterated that Mexicans who remained in the territories would "be incorporated into the Union of the United States and be admitted, at the proper time to be judged of by the Congress of the United States to the enjoyment of all the rights of citizens of the United States according to the principles of the Constitution; and in the mean time shall be maintained and protected in the free enjoyment of their liberty and property, and secured in the free exercise of their religion without restriction."

At the outset, the provisions of the treaty conferring citizenship rights on Mexicans living in the ceded territories seemed clear. The evolving practice of denying or suppressing those rights would prove otherwise. In the context of the United States in the nineteenth century, with its long history of nativism and racism vis-à-vis white-black relationships, Mexican Americans would have to fight for their rights. The struggle took on many forms, from armed resistance, to alienation from Anglo-American society, to direct involvement necessitating the intervention of the American court system.

Citizenship was at the crux of the provisions of the treaty. Mexican American citizenship in the ceded territory was challenged by Anglo-Americans who hoped to diminish Mexican American successes to advance their own interests in this newly acquired land. In 1869, for example, Pedro de la Guerra, a landholder who had been a signer of California's constitution, ran for district judge. His right to hold office was challenged on grounds that his citizenship had not been perfected, for he had only elected to become a citizen of the United States as provided by the treaty. His opponents argued that Mexican Americans were not yet citizens because Congress had not yet formally granted them citizenship.

In *People v. de la Guerra* (1870), the California Supreme Court ruled in de la Guerra's favor by declaring that the admission of California as a state of the United States conferred citizenship on former Mexican citizens who had remained within the territory as provided in the treaty.[4] The implied principle was that statehood, not the treaty, had with one broad sweep conferred on all legal residents full rights as citizens of the United States.

New Mexico was another story. Its status as a territory from 1848 to

1912 created a different environment. There, the franchise was limited to Anglo-American men only. New Mexicans attempted to broaden political rights by participating as members of the convention of 1849 aimed at drawing up an organic act to create the Territory of New Mexico as a step toward statehood. The majority of delegates were from old Hispano families. Regarding the issue of citizenship, they provided that citizenship should be limited to "free white male inhabitants residing within the limits of the United States, but who [had been residents] on the 2nd day of February 1848."[5] As a compromise, they agreed that former Mexican citizens would be required to take a court-approved oath of affirmation renouncing their allegiance to the Mexican Republic as a condition of citizenship in the Territory of New Mexico. The statement was approved by the U.S. Congress the following year.[6] In theory, the Treaty of Guadalupe Hidalgo had promised that they "in the mean time shall be maintained and protected in the free enjoyment of their liberty and property, and secured in the free exercise of their religion." But the territorial status of New Mexico relegated New Mexican Hispanics to second-class citizenship.

Efforts were made as early as 1848 to remind the general public that Hispanic New Mexicans were U.S. citizens. However, Acting Governor John M. Washington issued a controversial proclamation in April 1848 requiring New Mexican residents to declare publicly their intent to remain Mexican citizens, if that was their choice.[7]

> Whereas, I, John M. Washington, governor of the territory of New Mexico, do hereby ordain, that the clerks of the probate courts in the different counties of this territory shall immediately open, at the prefectures, records, which shall be handed as follows: "We elect to retain the character of Mexican citizens"; in which those of each county who shall so elect may personally record their names, and those who do not appear and sign said declaration, on or before the thirtieth day of May next, will be, in conformity with the treaty, considered citizens of the United States. Within six days after the thirtieth of May, the record shall be sent, with the certificates of the clerks of the prefectures of the several counties, to the secretary of the territory, that they may be published and distributed to the different tribunals of justice in the territory.
>
> Given under my hand and seal, at Santa Fe, the twenty-first day of April, 1848. (Signed) "J. M. Washington."[8]

It was generally agreed among jurists that such a public declaration was not necessary because the Treaty of Guadalupe Hidalgo had prescribed that permanence in the territory was sufficient. Governor Washington's proclamation on the subject was generally thought unnecessary because a voluntary, formal, but private, declaration before any court would have been enough.[9]

Others, as in *George Carter v. Territory of New Mexico* (1859) disagreed. They felt that "the filing of a declaration of intention to become a citizen of the United States by a Mexican who resided in this territory at the date of the treaty of Guadalupe Hidalgo, is not evidence that such Mexican had previously elected to retain his Mexican citizenship under that treaty." It was further argued that the mere signing of such a declaration was insufficient, especially in cases where the signatures had not been authenticated or certified in the absence of an appointed deputy.[10]

In 1858, George Carter had been indicted for assault with intent to kill and murder Juan Duro. Carter protested his indictment on grounds that the grand jury foreman, Anastacio Sandoval, was not a U.S. citizen.[11] Carter charged that his rights had been violated because he had not been properly indicted by a jury of his peers. At the time of his arraignment, Carter pleaded "that the territory of New Mexico ought not further to prosecute the said indictment against him, because he saith that Anastacio Sandoval, one of the grand jurors who found said indictment, was not at the time of finding said indictment a citizen of the United States, but was . . . a citizen of the republic of Mexico, etc. He prayed 'judgment' that he be discharged and dismissed from the premises in said indictment specified."[12] The attorney general agreed to tender the issue "to be tried by jury." Carter acquiesced to the process. In the ensuing arguments, the jury found the following verdict: "We, the jury, find the issue for the territory in this, that Anastacio Sandoval is a citizen of the United States."[13] Carter's assault case was then continued into the 1859 term.

At his arraignment in the new term, Carter pleaded not guilty to his indictment. In that trial, Carter was found guilty and fined sixty dollars as his punishment. Carter's lawyer then moved for a new trial on grounds that "the jury found against the law and the evidence in the trial of the issue upon the plea in abatement, and also upon the final issue of not guilty."[14] The motion was overruled, but the court allowed an appeal and granted Carter a stay of execution of the sentence.

It appeared that the court could have denied his appeal but preferred to give Carter the benefit of the doubt because "such shrinking . . . would be unworthy of the independence and dignity of an intelligent tribunal of justice. We may take judicial notice of the public and notorious acts which constituted a portion of the history of New Mexico during the past thirteen years, and in the midst of these the question of the retention of the character of Mexican citizenship has been exciting and disturbing. It is so now, and this fact imposes, in the investigation of this question on its legal merits, the greater labor and care."[15]

The case was reopened to allow the introduction of evidence to prove that Anastacio Sandoval, the grand jury foreman, had in fact retained the character of a Mexican citizen as stipulated in Article 8 of the Treaty of Guadalupe Hidalgo, and had "thereby established his Mexican citizenship and disqualification to serve as a juror."[16] It appeared that the court went to extraordinary lengths to serve justice and satisfy Carter's plea.

The court, indeed, undertook an exceptional position to demonstrate to Carter that he had been tried by a jury of his peers. In the best interests of justice, nevertheless, the ensuing arguments labored to indict or, at least, accuse New Mexican Hispanics of being disloyal to the United States, and affirm that Governor Washington had acted in the best interests of territorial security to weed out disloyal Mexicans.[17] Using the 1847 Taos Rebellion as the prime example to question the loyalty of New Mexican Hispanics, the argument was put forth in regard to Washington's proclamation that

> It was now after the peace confirming the conquest and its consequences and engendered among a people foreign in language, laws, customs, and religion, with the pride of kindred and race peculiar to all Spanish races, in the midst of those who had lately, as the Mexican cabinet council said, "risen against the government and the American name and blood in the country," and when risen, whose steps and deeds were marked with murder, robbery, and fiendish atrocity in the village of Taos, and who, as the counsel assert, though "their plans were discovered and disconcerted, their conspiracies frustrated, did not cease to conspire."[18]

The court argued that it was necessary to establish certain legal tests that would determine those persons of Mexican allegiance. In subdued, yet inflammatory, language, the judge stated that it was the "imperious duty of [Governor] Washington to allay the increasing excitement and tranquilize the inhabitants. . . . He has the power to call the excited Mexicans to pause, to consult more calmly and wisely their true interest, and let reason and judgment assume the control of passions and prejudices in the selection to be made between Mexico and the United States."[19]

Returning to the issue at hand—Sandoval's citizenship—the court attempted to ferret out the salient facts affecting his right to serve as foreman of the grand jury that had indicted Carter. The court stated:

> It must be borne in mind that the whole effort of the defense was to prove that Sandoval's Mexican citizenship resulted from his having elected to retain it under the treaty. If he was a resident of this territory, as was apparent at the time of the ratification of the treaty, and was so remained, and did not elect in favor of Mexico, then, with this explanation, neither

one nor a hundred declarations of intention in the district court would prove him a Mexican citizen, in fact and law. With such residence, the presumptions would be in favor of his citizenship to the United States, nor should he lose it or be deprived of it without the clearest proof. He may not have known his rights, or mistaken them, and had a fancy to make them doubly secure. The date at which he did that act, as it seems jointly with fifteen others, does not appear, but it is shown by the record that it was some time during the judicial administration of Chief Justice Deavenport. Sandoval was not defending his own rights of citizenship on the trial, and it is but a reasonable inference that he had perfected his naturalization, even if such in law be needed. The evidence was wholly insufficient to authorize the jury to find in the defendant's favor. They found rightly for the territory.[20]

The judge's gavel came down resoundingly, for Carter's conviction was upheld. The price, of course, was the revelation that some nineteenth-century Anglo-Americans in New Mexico harbored an intense disdain and distrust of Mexican Americans, and would continue to question Hispanic loyalty to the United States. That distrust would hamper Anglo-Hispanic relations and would affect the ability of Hispanics to progress in all aspects of American life.

Ironically, while the territorial court had argued that Mexicans had a choice, local authorities in territorial New Mexico between 1849 and 1850 did everything they could to discourage the out-migration of Mexicans because of the cost of moving them as well as financially disposing of or administering their property in the ceded territory. During that time, nine hundred New Mexicans petitioned the Mexican government to move to Chihuahua.[21] Hoping to convince them to remain in the territory, authorities argued that the move would result in great inconvenience, suffering, and misery. Additionally, their move would take place without the protection of either government against Apache raiders, because many New Mexicans lived in remote areas. Despite Governor Washington's proclamation, territorial officials "pressured Mexicans not to sign the lists."[22] Notwithstanding the provisions of the Treaty of Guadalupe Hidalgo and Governor Washington's proclamation, the effort to curb their out-migration demonstrated yet another force keeping New Mexicans within the territory.[23]

Still, it would take the rest of the century for courts in the ceded territory to admit, as it did in *Hurtado v. California* (1884), that

> the Constitution of the United States was ordained . . . by descendants of Englishmen, who inherited the traditions of English law and history; but it was made for an undefined and expanding future, and for a people

gathered and to be gathered from many nations and of many tongues. And while we take just pride in the principles and institutions of the common law, we are not to forget that in lands where other systems of jurisprudence prevail, the ideas and processes of civil justice are also not unknown. Due process of law, in spite of the absolutism of continental governments, is not alien to that code which survived the Roman Empire as the foundation of modern civilization in Europe.[24]

In the *Hurtado* case, the Fourteenth Amendment was the issue. Under this amendment to the Constitution, ratified in 1869, birth and residency in the United States were sufficient to determine citizenship. Its application in a California case meant only that California statehood had conferred upon Mexican Americans civil rights as citizens of the United States. In contrast, Mexican Americans who lived in territories such as New Mexico were denied full status as citizens of the United States until 1912, when New Mexico was admitted to the Union.

The question of the validity of the Treaty of Guadalupe Hidalgo in regard to full civil rights for Mexicans incorporated into the United States persisted throughout the nineteenth century. In *Albuquerque Land and Irrigation Company v. Gutierrez* (1900), the territorial court of New Mexico argued, on the basis of the maxim *qui facit per alium, facit per se,* that the doctrine of prior appropriation is the law governing water rights in New Mexico Territory; that is, a valid prior appropriation of waters of the Río Grande must be established. The validity of appropriation must include two factors: there must be a rightful diversion and there must be an application to some beneficial use.[25]

Quoting Articles 8 and 9 of the Treaty of Guadalupe Hidalgo, the territorial court disagreed with the logic of a district court judge in a prior decision of the case. That judge had opined:

Upon the allegation of defendants as to treaty rights, I am of the opinion that the lands of citizens of New Mexico since the cession, are subjects to the operation of the law of eminent domain under the laws of the United States, and the states and territories thereof, and not exempt therefrom by virtue of the treaty of Guadalupe Hidalgo. The appropriation and distribution of water must be governed by similar laws, inasmuch as the United States has adopted its own system of water rights and adjusted the system to the different sections of the country as necessity required, and the laws of the states and territories are in harmony therewith. Those laws must govern wherein they differ from the treaty provisions, and wherein they are harmonious, treaty provisions need not be considered. The laws of the United States and the states and territories are ample for the protection of the rights of appropriators of water in this territory, and remedies for impairment or destruction of such rights are adequate also.[26]

In contrast, the territorial court argued that the defendant, Gutierrez, did not dispute that the Mexican Cession was subject to all the laws of the United States resulting from provisions in the Constitution. His sole contention was that "rights recognized and guaranteed by the treaty are not subject to be impaired by acts of the territorial Legislature."[27] The territorial court recognized that Gutierrez's rights had also been curtailed by the district court.

The territorial court revisited the issue of Mexican American citizenship in the context of constitutional protections. In his statement on the issue, the territorial judge went out of his way to address the question of Mexican American disloyalty. Even if Gutierrez had been considered an alien enemy—the judge wrote—he would still have legal status:

> It is alleged that he was in the position of an alien enemy, and hence could have no locus standi in that forum. If assailed there, he could defend there. The liability and the right are inseparable. A different result would be a blot upon jurisprudence and civilization. We cannot hesitate or doubt on the subject. It would be contrary to the first principles of the social compact and of the right administration of justice.
>
> Whether the legal status of the plaintiff in error was, or was not, that of an alien enemy, is a point not necessary to be considered; because, apart from the views we have expressed, conceding the fact to be so, the consequences assumed would by no means follow. Whatever may be the extent of the disability of an alien enemy to sue in the courts of the hostile country, it is clear that he is liable to be sued, and this carries with it the right to use all means and appliances of defense. . . .
>
> Wherever one is assailed in his person or his property there he may defend, for the liability and the right are inseparable. There is a principle of natural justice, recognized as such by the common intelligence and conscience of all nations. A sentence of a court pronounced against a party without hearing him, or giving him an opportunity to be heard is not a judicial determination of his rights.
>
> A denial to a party of the benefit of a notice would be in affect to deny that he is entitled to notice at all, and the sham and the deceptive proceeding had better be omitted altogether. It would be like saying to a party, "Appear, and you shall be heard"; and, when he has appeared, saying, "Your appearance shall not be recognized and you shall not be heard."[28]

The territorial court's pronouncement in this case alludes to the unjust treatment of Mexican Americans in the district courts, where many of their complaints were dismissed by ethnocentric judges. Gutierrez sought to defend rights of Hispanics secured under the laws of Spain and Mexico, guaranteed under the Treaty of Guadalupe Hidalgo, saying that for "centuries, in some instances, their grantors and ancestors had used waters of the Rio Grande . . . to the full extent of the flow of said river during the planting and growing seasons."[29] As Gutierrez's land was downriver of the diversion constructed by the Albuquerque Land and Irrigation Company, the court ruled that it would not "consider the rights of all appropriators of water from the Rio Grande below the terminus,"[30] but "the complainant [Albuquerque Land and Irrigation Company] will not be allowed to destroy the present ditches or in any way diminish the flow of water lawfully diverted by or flowing through the old ditches. If, however, the canal can be constructed without injury to the present capacity of the old ditches, it may lawfully be done."[31]

The *Gutierrez* case demonstrated the reluctance of the territorial court of New Mexico to admit as a rule of law the governing articles of the Treaty of Guadalupe Hidalgo in regard to the citizenship rights of Mexican Americans. Even when rights of Hispanics were violated, such as in the district court's pronouncement in the *Gutierrez* complaint, the higher courts tended to apply legal precedents that had occurred in the legal tradition of the United States, further denying Hispanic traditions of law that established ownership and rights to land and water. In that regard, historian Daniel Tyler has concluded that "so long as the prior appropriation doctrine is not attacked, the state of New Mexico appears willing to recognize the legitimacy of customs in water litigation."[32] As in *Albuquerque Land and Irrigation Company v. Gutierrez,* cases were usually decided to benefit Anglo-American land corporations. Historian Richard Griswold del Castillo asserts that "a review of selected U.S. court cases shows that Anglo-American land corporations and the state and federal governments were the primary beneficiaries of the legal system's interpretation of the Treaty of Guadalupe Hidalgo. Although some Indians and Hispanics lodged lawsuits citing the treaty guarantees, the vast majority of them were unsuccessful in their efforts."[33]

Despite their assertive efforts to establish their citizenship rights under the Treaty of Guadalupe Hidalgo, Hispanic and Indian litigants were frequently on the losing end, for "defeats outnumbered victories by about two to one."[34] It may be erroneous to assume, as one historian has, that almost half of the major cases citing the Treaty of Guadalupe Hidalgo were tried before the Supreme Court.[35] It can be safely assumed that the majority of Spanish-Mexican land grant cases tried at the district court level never reached the territorial court, much less the Supreme Court.

As New Mexico remained a territory for sixty-four years, the civil rights of Hispanics there were deemed lesser than those of Hispanics in California, which had already become a state in 1850. Through precedents set by the Northwest Ordinances of 1787, the Louisiana Purchase Treaty of 1803, and the Wisconsin Organic Act of 1836, inhabitants of territories were considered a dependent people and not entitled to full participation in the political life of the United States. Hispanics of New Mexico did not acquire full rights as citizens of the United States until statehood in 1912.

CHAPTER 12

Atrisco, the Office of the Surveyor General, and the Court of Private Land Claims

Now, therefore it appearing to the satisfaction of the Court that all the requirements of the law have been complied with by the said petitioners and the Court being fully advised in the premises, it is ordered adjudged and decreed and the Court does hereby order, adjudge, and decree that prayer of the said petition be and the same is hereby granted that the owners and proprietors of the said respective land grants and real estate, the petitioners and their associates and successors be and are hereby created a body politic and corporation under the corporate name of the Town of Atrisco.

DECREE BY DISTRICT COURT, COUNTY OF
BERNALILLO, TERRITORY OF NEW MEXICO, 1892

Now upon this day come the parties to this cause and said cause having been argued by counsel . . . the court being now sufficiently advised in the premises, find that the said plaintiff and petitioner is the lawful successor in title and interest of the original grantees and owners of that . . . grant made . . . in the year one thousand six hundred and ninety-two . . . and also to that . . . other and additional grant . . . made to the . . . settlers of said town, community and settlement of Atrisco in . . . one thousand seven hundred and sixty-eight.

CHIEF JUSTICE JOSEPH R. REED, 1894

The failure of the U.S. government to adjudicate titles and ownership of many Spanish and Mexican land grants in the nineteenth century has proved to be one of the most shameful affairs in American history.

In the territorial period in New Mexico (1850–1912), Hispanic New Mexicans struggled to assert their rights in a system managed by unscrupulous, deceitful, and ethnocentric individuals. New Mexicans had seen their ilk before, but this time the stakes were high and the players, usually in the guise of Anglo-American lawyers with the deck stacked in their favor, played for keeps. If New Mexicans had learned anything from their legal experiences during the Spanish colonial and Mexican periods, it was to jealously guard historical documents proving their ownership of the land. This time, however, they confronted a system whose managers were dedicated not to seeking justice but to their own self-interest. The failure of the system eventually led to the creation of the Court of Private Land Claims, but not before havoc had been visited upon the civil rights of New Mexicans. Even then, the Court of Private Land Claims left much undone.[1]

The 1848 Treaty of Guadalupe Hidalgo had obligated Congress to recognize valid land claims, and the process of validation had begun as early as 1846. Under the "Kearney Code" of September 22, 1846, issued by Stephen Watts Kearny, commander of the Army of the West—which occupied New Mexico at that time—land grants had to be registered with the territorial secretary. The registration of grants created an abstract of land titles. But the process required that New Mexicans give up their original documentation, which meant that they were no longer available to their owners for future title investigations. Of that catastrophic loss, historian Richard Wells Bradfute writes, "Evidence exists that land titles were carted away and new ones created; at any rate, there was no assembling of titles in New Mexico as there was in California."[2] Land registration under the Kearney Code was repudiated by the New Mexico territorial legislative assembly in favor of an act to establish the offices of the Surveyor General of New Mexico, Kansas, and Nebraska, passed by the U.S. Congress on July 22, 1854.[3] Many members of the territorial assembly hoped that the surveyor general's office, charged with examining land claims and making recommendations to Congress, would fulfill the treaty obligations of the United States. That, however, was not the case.

For some forty years, from 1850 to 1890, the U.S. Congress vainly attempted to recognize legitimate titles to land grants that fell within the provisions of the Treaty of Guadalupe Hidalgo. In 1852, Congress created a commission to investigate and settle eligible claims in California. Owing to California's economic importance following the Gold Rush of 1849 and because California had become a state, the commission moved to confirm 618 of 813 claims, a process that took nearly thirty years.[4] However, Congress failed to act on grants in other areas of the ceded territory until 1854. That year, the office of the U.S. Surveyor General was created.

The legislation creating the office provided that land claimants could submit their claims to the surveyor general, who would then investigate the issues and make recommendations to Congress. Congress had the power to make the final determination or confirmation of a grant. Any land grant claim under consideration by Congress would in the meantime be reserved from the public domain until it was rejected or confirmed. Between 1854 and 1891, Congress confirmed grants one by one (which it preferred) and in groups. Congress made no other legislation or provision to deal with land grants during this period.[5]

Unfortunately, the inability of Congress to act decisively placed the land grants in limbo. Land grant syndicates such as the Santa Fe Ring attempted to gain as much control of grants as possible. Like the carpetbaggers of the Reconstruction South, these organizations controlled the territorial government of New Mexico. They were composed of politicians, lawyers, railroad administrators, and businessmen. It has long been suspected that territorial governor William A. Pile was a member of the Santa Fe Ring, as were at least three surveyors general and certain territorial delegates to Congress. So successful were these rings that the lawyers may have received as much as 80 percent of their fees in land grant property.[6] As they watched their landholdings dwindle, New Mexicans asked for reform.

On March 19, 1881, during the term of Surveyor General Henry M. Atkinson, heirs and legal representatives of the grant extending from Atrisco to the Río Puerco filed a petition for the confirmation of land that had once belonged to Joseph Hurtado de Mendoza and other settlers of the Town of Atrisco (see chapter 8). The petitioners presented Spanish colonial documents signed by Governor Pedro Fermín de Mendinueta. The file consisted of three instruments: the petition signed by Hurtado de Mendoza and his associates asking for a tract of land extending from the Bosque Grande in the Río Puerco to the Cerro Colorado; a granting decree dated April 28, 1768, citing the land boundaries; and the Act of Possession showing that on May 7, 1768, Francisco Trébol Navarro had given Hurtado de Mendoza and his associates the grant.[7]

After examining the file, Atkinson sought corroborating testimony. At issue were the boundaries: documentary and oral proof was required. The historical documents described the tract of Atrisco as being bounded

on the north, by the Barranca de Juan de Perea; on the east, by the Río

Grande; on the south, by the lands of Antonio Baca; and on the west, by the ceja of the Río Puerco.[8]

Similarly, the Río Puerco lands were bounded

on the north, by the Cerro Colorado which is located two leagues south of the San Francisco del Río Puerco; on the east, by the ceja of the Río Puerco Mountain; on the south, by a point three leagues south of the Cerro Colorado; and on the west, by the Río Puerco.[9]

The petitioners stated that Atrisco was already in existence when New Mexico was acquired by the United States. The heirs alleged that the original grant documents had been lost, but they presented a number of deeds demonstrating the activity in transactions and conveyances at Atrisco from a very early date as well as church records and oral testimony showing the continuous settlement of Atrisco and the Río Puerco lands. The atrisqueños hoped to convince Surveyor General Atkinson that they had been in possession of the grant since at least 1700.

In February 1884, the embattled heirs to the Atrisco grant met and complained about their need to protect themselves against Anglo-American squatters attempting to assume land owned by Hispanics through a process known as adverse possession. The grantees said they had been successful in running off squatters, but they knew time was against them. At the meeting, they formed a commission of six heirs to carry on the land grant claims of the Town of Atrisco and Ranchos de Atrisco before the territorial surveyor general. The atrisqueño commission retained two lawyers to represent them: Amado Chaves of San Mateo in Valencia County and Urbano Chacón of Santa Fe.[10]

They also formed a commission to help other embattled land-grant heirs in the Manzano Mountains. At a meeting held in February 1884, they appointed a two-member commission for Tajique to help Ramón Lucero reclaim his land from "*brincadores*" or squatters on his land. The atrisqueños wrote:

February 22, 1884. The below-signed citizens, owners of the property of the Sitio de Atrisco and Ranchos de Atrisco, today meeting in session, have commissioned in the names of all the below signatories, and by this means, empower the persons of Don Feliciano Sánchez and Don José María Herrera to proceed to the heart of Tajique to the house of Ramón Lucero and demand from him the land grant pertaining to the place— according to verified and legal information, we, the citizens, have notice that the said Mr. Lucero has it in writing that he is a legal heir of the said place to which we honorably call attention to Mr. Lucero so that he can join us to legalize the success of this poor pueblo—if he and the commission can show us his grant—in which today there are [Anglo] American squatters [brincadores] wanting to take possession of the said place, offering Mr. Lucero a very generous compensation for this pueblo.[11]

It was signed by the atrisqueños, who attended the meeting seeking similar justice for themselves against Anglo-American squatters.

In regard to the Atrisco land grant, lawyers Chaves and Chacón were unable to locate the original grant papers. Presenting the Atrisco claim in late December 1885, they noted that documents bearing the date 1768 referred to the second grant, that of Río Puerco. They were unable to find papers for the 1692 Atrisco grant, which they figured to be from around 1700. Offering those documents as evidence to initiate the history of the claim, they presented both the Atrisco lands and the Río Puerco grant as a consolidated claim to Surveyor General George W. Julian, who had replaced Atkinson.[12]

The surveyor general's decision was stalled for five years while an investigation took place. Finally, on January 28, 1886, Julian recommended to Congress that the circumstantial evidence presented by the heirs of the land at Atrisco indicated that a grant had been made in or about 1700. Furthermore, he declared that documents dated 1768 presented evidence that the Río Puerco grant was genuine. The land, reported Julian, covered an area of approximately seventy-two thousand acres measuring about eight miles from north to south and about fourteen miles from east to west. Julian recommended that Congress approve the Atrisco grant along with the Río Puerco claim. The people of Atrisco anticipated that the next step would be a survey of their land, prior to approval of their grant.

It appeared the atrisqueños had won a victory, but that was not the case. In May 1887, they learned that the commissioner of the General Land Office of the Department of the Interior had rejected their application for a survey of their land. The rejection was based on a lack of evidence proving the claim to the original grant on the Río Grande, the lack of boundary details, the incomplete list of legal heirs, and a lack of proof that the land had been continuously occupied. Amado Chaves learned of the decision on May 31, 1887. Shaking their heads in disappointment, the atrisqueños saw no recourse for this setback.

Four years later, luck favored their cause. On February 26, 1891, the territorial legislative assembly passed "An Act Relating to Community Land Grants, and for Other Purposes" (see appendix). This law provided for the incorporation of community land grants. As amended, section 38 provided that "this act shall not operate to divest any private rights or affect any private titles, but shall extend only to land grants made to a pueblo or colony or for the public use of a community."[13] The new law had broken the legal logjam in which Atrisco found itself. The definitions in section 2 of the act were directly applicable to Atrisco:

> Sec. 2. Any ten or more of the owners and proprietors of any such land grant or real estate so held in common as a colony community or town grant, as aforesaid, may within five years from and after the passage of this act, and not afterwards, file in the office of the clerk of the district court of the county in which such land grant or real estate (or the greater part thereof, if the same be situate in two or more counties) is situate, a petition setting forth the names and places of residence of all persons claiming or owning any interest in the said land grant or real estate who are known to the petitioners, a description of the said land grant or real estate by metes and bounds according to an actual survey thereof, if the boundaries of such land grant have been definitely fixed by an actual survey, but if no such survey has been made by the proper authority, then such land grant may be described by any other description which will reasonably designate the land grant and the name by which it is commonly known in the vicinity of its location, and the nature and extent of the title under and by virtue of which such land grant or real estate is held and claimed, and praying that the owners and proprietors of such land grant or real estate may be created a body politic and corporate under the provisions of this act.[14]

The people of Atrisco now saw a hopeful sign that their land grant could be recognized despite the lack of an authorized survey. Moreover, the provision to allow them to incorporate and form a body politic gave them the power to act in unison.

A few days later, on March 3, 1891, a congressional bill proposed the creation of the Court of Private Land Claims. The two actions proved significant, for they began the juridical process under which the people of Atrisco would gain permanent possession and official recognition of their ancestral lands stretching from the Río Grande to the Río Puerco.[15] On January 21, 1892, owners and proprietors of the land grant of Atrisco filed a petition with the office of the clerk of the District Court of the County of Bernalillo in behalf of 225 people who claimed an interest in the Atrisco grants. Their petition called for the incorporation of both grants into the Town of Atrisco. About ten months later, on November 7, 1892, the Town of Atrisco, now a municipal corporation, would file a suit in the Court of Private Land Claims against the City of Albuquerque and the United States.[16]

The creation of the Court of Private Land Claims had a history of its own. Appalled by the chaotic situation of land claims and in light of the increasing demand for a final determination of land grant titles by heirs and other interested persons, including the railroads and other commercial groups, New Mexico governor Edmund G. Ross sought a solution. He first suggested the creation of a land commission similar to that of California, but toward the end of his administration, he recommended the establishment of a court of private land claims.[17]

Grantees, businessmen, and settlers who needed land grant questions resolved had been clamoring for President Benjamin Harrison to hasten the adjudication of land grant issues in the ceded territory. Debate revolved around the kind of adjudication; should it be through a commission or a special judicial tribunal? President Harrison brought up the issue in his December 3, 1889, State of the Union presentation, but Congress did not take up the cause. Pressured by the Mexican government, which insisted that the rights of its former citizens be observed, Harrison urged Congress to act on the issue by writing:

> The United States owes a duty to Mexico to confirm to her citizens those valid grants that were saved by the treaty, and the long delay which has attended the discharge of this duty has given just cause of complaint.
>
> The entire community where these large claims exist, and indeed, all of our people, are interested in an early and final settlement of them. No greater incubus can rest upon the energies of a people in the development of a new country than that resulting from unsettled land titles.[18]

Harrison ended by expressing his hope that the present session of Congress would bring about the necessary legislation to resolve the issue.

A year later, Congress had not yet acted on Harrison's recommendations. Meanwhile, Antonio Joseph, the territorial delegate from New Mexico, along with several other senators and congressmen, presented a compromise bill.[19] The Act of March 3, 1891, created the land grant tribunal known as the Court of Private Land Claims. When all was said and done, the establishment of the Court of Private Land Claims responded to a need to reform a land claims process fraught with corruption on the part of territorial administrators. The enabling legislation for the Court of Private Land Claims repealed the Act of July 22, 1854, which had created the Office of the Surveyor General. Congress had finally taken a positive step toward resolving the land grant issues of Hispanics and others in the ceded territory. The Court of Private Land Claims was short-lived, lasting only thirteen years. Nevertheless, the court successfully quieted many land title claims against the United States, although it lacked the power to settle completely the land grant issues at hand.

Immediately signed by President Harrison, the act creating the Court of Private Land Claims provided for five justices—one chief justice and four associates—for the purpose of adjusting perfect and inchoate land claims in the ceded territory that had not yet been adjudicated. California was excepted from the act. With the exception of the first session, which required ninety days' notice to the people of the ceded territories, the court was instructed to publish announcements for all its sessions in English and Spanish. The announcements were to be published "once a week for two successive weeks" in one newspaper in the capital of the state or territory where the court presided.[20]

All claims of inchoate lands derived from Spain or Mexico within the ceded territory not filed by March 3, 1893, were forever barred.[21] Subsoil rights containing mineral wealth were also exempt, for such rights were vested in the U.S. government.[22] The United States quitclaimed its interest in surface estate only. Another limitation of the court was that it could not confirm inchoate claims exceeding eleven square leagues. Unfavorable decisions could be appealed directly to the U.S. Supreme Court.[23] Favorable decisions depended on a survey to be made by the commissioner of the General Land Office, who in turn would send the survey to the court for final approval.

The business of the court was twofold: to adjudicate the validity of land claims and to approve surveys made to confirm claims. The act provided that people who had been in actual and continuous adverse possession of land not exceeding 160 acres for twenty years were to be given patents following a survey of their land ordered by the court.[24] Persons making adverse claims, however, could not apply for lands to "any city lot, town lot, village lot, farm lot, or pasture lot held under a grant from any corporation or town the claim to which may fall within the provisions of section eleven of this act."[25]

The Court of Private Land Claims was originally chartered for five years to end on December 31, 1895, but its term was extended from time to time until it expired on June 30, 1904. The court originally convened for business in Denver, Colorado, on July 1, 1891. It relocated, however, to Santa Fe, New Mexico, for lack of a government building to house it in Denver. Nearly a year and a half later, on December 6, 1892, the Court of Private Land Claims began holding special sessions in Tucson and Phoenix, Arizona.In the course of thirteen years, the Court of Private Land Claims dealt with 290 claims covering an aggregate of 35,491,019 acres.[26] Two hundred twenty-eight cases were in New Mexico, 17 in Arizona, and 3 in Colorado. Of the totality, 158 cases were rejected. Only 21 cases were confirmed for the entire land claimed. In other cases, the court recognized titles, in whole or in part, covering a total of 2,051,525 acres, of which 116,539 were in New Mexico. A total of 33,439,494 acres of rejected claims reverted to the public domain. Some grants that exceeded the eleven-square-league limitation or were not as large as claimed were substantially reduced in size. Seventy-three cases, 58 in New Mexico and 15 in Arizona, were appealed to the U.S. Supreme Court. Of them, only 39 appeals were approved, of which 23 were upheld, 5 were reversed, and 11 were reversed or remanded. The U.S. government was the appellant in 26 cases. It was able to secure a reversal or a reversal and remand in 10 cases. Only one money payment, in the amount of $513.63, was made.[27] Thirteen years after its initiation, the Court of Private Land Claims had, according to Congress, discharged the obligations of the United States under the Treaty of Guadalupe Hidalgo (1848) and the Gadsden Purchase Treaty (1853).

During the thirteen-year existence of the Court of Private Land Claims, atrisqueños, like many other Hispanic land-grant heirs, had been busy defending the town's boundaries, just as they had during the administration of the Office of the Surveyor General. Before the court finished its business in 1905, its justices had learned much about the long history of the Atrisco land grant and its claim to additional land as far west as the Río Puerco. They knew about Pedro Durán y Chaves's occupation of lands in the Valle de Atrisco prior to the Pueblo Revolt of 1680. They had heard testimony about Fernando Durán y Chaves's 1692 grant of Atrisco and Angostura. They had read through translations of land transactions and conveyances between 1729 and 1772.

Poring over the ponderous documentary collection that formed the significant atrisqueño claim to land as far as the Río Puerco made by Joseph Hurtado de Mendoza in 1768, the justices learned about the Spanish legal system. The Court of Private Land Claim justices knew all about Joseph Hurtado de Mendoza's representation of Doña Efigenia Durán y Chaves in her attempt to gain possession of Las Ciruelas and Arbolito del Manzano. And they read all of the sordid details concerning Doña Efigenia's fight with Doña María over seven hundred head of sheep. In the end, they learned that the atrisqueño claim was longstanding.[28] Yet, like the surveyors general of the earlier period of land grant litigation, they seemed to have reservations about the grant. In their minds, to fulfill their duty it needed to be tested adversely.

The justices of the Court of Private Land Claims also reviewed the significant event of the creation of the Town of Atrisco under the Act Relating to Community Land Grants of February 26, 1891. The act provided that the people of Atrisco, claiming the two grants lying between two rivers, the Río Grande and the Río Puerco, should petition the District Court of the County of Bernalillo to incorporate their interests by creating a corporation with a body politic under the name of the Town of Atrisco. The justices were particularly interested in the provision of the law passed by the territorial assembly that provided that the district court could incorporate the owners of land grants if they filed a petition of incorporation along with proof that two-thirds of the grantees voted in favor. The justices of the Court of Private Land Claims were satisfied that the people of Atrisco had successfully called for a vote to incorporate.

Having conformed to all the requirements of the act, the atrisqueños petitioned the District Court of the County of Bernalillo for confirmation of the incorporation of Atrisco from the Río Grande to the Río Puerco. In affirming the legality of the actions taken by the people of Atrisco, the district court recognized that a legal and proper election had taken place in which two-thirds of the required voters had voted in favor of the petition to incorporate. On April 11, 1892, the court granted their request and declared the creation of the Town of Atrisco and the people there a duly constituted body politic. To that end, the District Court of the County of Bernalillo, Territory of New Mexico, decreed in 1892:

> Now, therefore, it appearing to the satisfaction of the Court that all the requirements of the law have been complied with by the said petitioners and the Court being fully advised in the premises, it is ordered adjudged and decreed and the Court does hereby order, adjudge, and decree that prayer of the said petition be and the same is hereby granted that the owners and proprietors of the said respective land grants and real estate, the petitioners and their associates and successors be and are hereby created a body politic and corporation under the corporate name of the Town of Atrisco.[29]

The town elected Manuel Antonio Jaramillo and José de la Luz Sánchez as president and secretary-treasurer, respectively, of the town's board of trustees.[30]

Barely had the atrisqueños incorporated as the Town of Atrisco when they were pulled into a new lawsuit. In early November 1892, the atrisqueños filed suit against the City of Albuquerque in the Court of Private Land Claims over boundary issues in the case of *Town of Atrisco v. the United States of America and the City of Albuquerque* (1892). The City of Albuquerque claimed that Atrisco fell within Albuquerque's municipal land grant. The Town of Atrisco retained the firm of Warren, Fergus-

son, and Bruner, which had represented them in earlier matters. The
defendant, the City of Albuquerque, was represented by E. W. Dobson,
attorney for the City of Albuquerque, and Matthew G. Reynolds, U.S.
attorney for the Court of Private Land Claims.

In their 1892 petition to the Court of Private Land Claims, the atrisqueños reminded the justices that the Town of Atrisco was a corporation duly organized and existing under the 1891 "Act Relating to Community Land Grants, and for Other Purposes." A lengthy discussion
followed concerning the historical boundaries of the Town of Atrisco;
the petitioners complained that a portion of their lands "was included
within the boundaries claimed by the City of Albuquerque."[31] The issue needed to be clarified. As part of its suit, the incorporated Town of
Atrisco also requested that the Court of Private Land Claims confirm
its two grants.

The plaintiffs asserted in the first paragraph of their petition that the
first grant of 1692 comprised 41,533 acres and the second grant of 1768
comprised approximately 26,958 acres.[32] They alleged that a portion
of the grant, approved in 1700, was improperly subsumed within the
boundary of the Town of Albuquerque:

> A portion of the said lands is included within a certain claim for a tract
> of four (4) square leagues of land, having for its center the center of the
> old Villa de Albuquerque (sic), by and on behalf of the City of Albuquer-
> que, a municipal corporation, created under the laws of the Territory of
> New Mexico, and situated in the County of Bernalillo, and which said
> claim was duly confirmed by this Honorable Court on April 26th, 1892,
> but without prejudice to the right of your petitioner to claim any por-
> tion of the said lands which lies on the west side of the Rio Grande. The
> portion of said lands so included within the boundaries claimed by the
> City of Albuquerque is claimed by your petitioner under and by virtue
> of said grant to the predecessors in title of your petitioner, made about
> the year 1700; and although the same is held and owned in severalty by
> persons owing the same, and the confirmation of the same under the
> said claim of the City of Albuquerque, will enure to the benefit of said
> individual owners, yet your petitioner claims title to the whole of said
> tract of land within the said boundaries thereof, hereinbefore set forth,
> adversely to any claim thereto on the part of the City of Albuquerque.[33]

The atrisqueños contended that Atrisco should prevail, as it predated Albuquerque.

In their statement, the atrisqueños elaborated that the recent history
of the grant included their petition to Surveyor General Julian, who

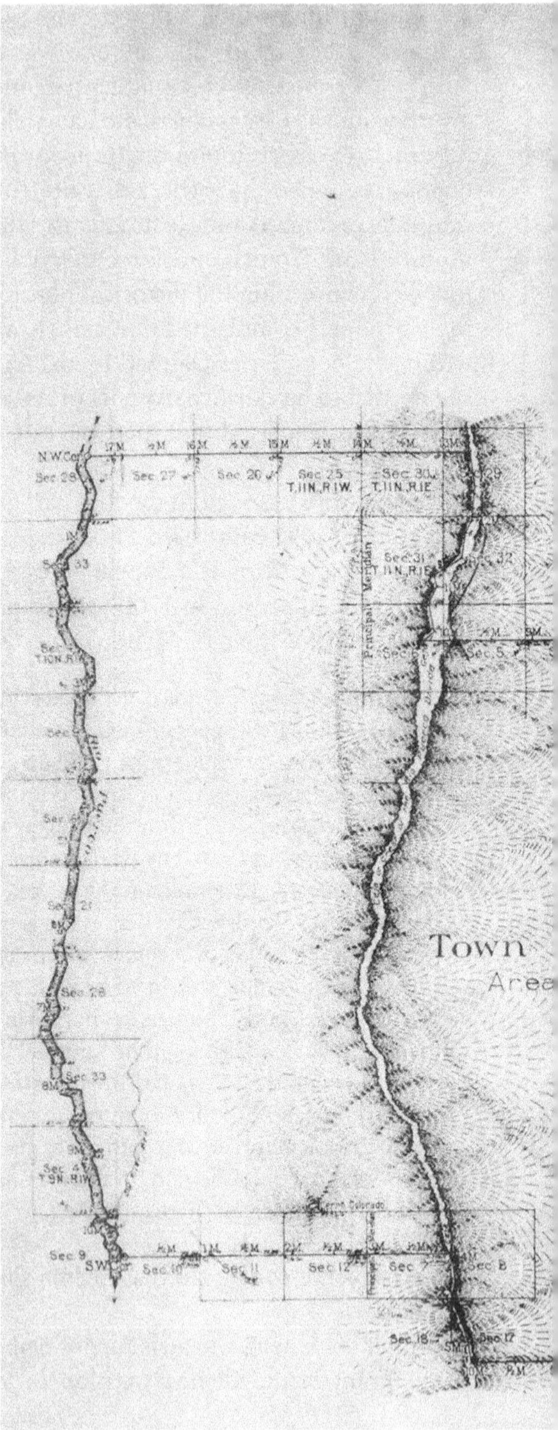

Map 3. Map of the Surveyor General showing the Atrisco Land Grant between the Río Grande and the Río Puerco.
COURT OF PRIVATE LAND CLAIMS, 1892, AND ATRISCO HERITAGE FOUNDATION, ALBUQUERQUE

Plat of the

wn of Atrisco Grant
in
NEW MEXICO.
surveyed Oct. 8ᵗʰ to Oct. 26ᵗʰ, 1896 by
Geo. H. Pradt. U.S.Dep. Sur.
Contract No. 301, dated May 21ˢᵗ, 1896
and
Special Instructions, dated Nov. 17ᵗʰ, 1897

Scale. 80 Chs. to 1 Inch.
(Scale of Original Plat, 40 Chs.=1 Inch)

isco Grant

.72 Acres.

Albuquerque Grent

West Bdy. Albuquerque Grant

Atrisco

Ranches of
Atrisco.

5M. South Bdy. 4 M.Albuquerque 3 M.Grant

Sec.36
T.10N.R.2E.

Ranches

Sec. I
T.9N.R.2E.

Sec.12
T.9N.R.2E.

S.E.Cor. & Beg. Cor.
Lat. 35° bo.N.
Long. 106° 41' W.

Pajarito Grant

had written his decision and recommendation in his report to Congress approving both grants on January 28, 1886. Congress had taken no action, and therefore "the said claim has not been heretofore submitted to any authorities constituted by law for the adjustment of land titles within the limits of the said Territory."[34] In other words, no survey had been granted or made of Atrisco at that time. The atrisqueños included maps of both grants to show the area of their claim.

The terse response by the City of Albuquerque, predictably, refuted the claim by the Town of Atrisco. Albuquerque said:

> That it denies that at any time subsequent to the year of our Lord 1692 and prior to the year 1768, or at any other time, there was duly and lawfully made by the then Governor and Captain General of the Kingdom and province of New Mexico under the Crown of Spain, to the inhabitants and settlers of the Town of Atrisco a grant of a tract of land situated and bounded as set forth in the first paragraph of said petition; and it denies that there was in existence at the date of said supposed grant as set forth in said paragraph of said petition any town known and called the Town of Atrisco.[35]

The City of Albuquerque alleged that, by admission of the atrisqueños, no documentary record existed for either the 1692 or 1768 grant. With impunity, the City of Albuquerque stated:

> This defendant further denies that after the making of the said supposed grant about the year 1700, the settlers of the Town of Atrisco possessed or occupied, or improved, or cultivated, as grantees, the said first mentioned tract, but admits that from and after the date of the grant made in 1768, the grantees under the said grant, possessed, occupied, improved and cultivated, as grantees, the said tract therein described.[36]

The City of Albuquerque continued:

> This defendant avers that whatever possession or right any person or persons may have had to the lands included within the description set forth in the first paragraph of said petition have been under and in subordination to the jurisdiction, authority and title of the Villa de Albuquerque (sic), in the same manner and to the same extent as other persons holding, possessing and owning lands within the limits of the grant of said Villa de Albuquerque (sic) as already recognized and confirmed by this Honorable Court.[37]

The City of Albuquerque reminded the Court of Private Land Claims that the court had already settled the matter on April 16, 1892, without prejudice to the right of the Town of Atrisco to claim any portion of lands lying on the west side of the Río Grande. To that end, the City of Albuquerque appended the ruling stemming from an earlier adjudicated case, *City of Albuquerque v. United States* (1892). At that time, the City of Albuquerque had sought to define its boundaries based on its Spanish land grant. It had claimed that since its founding, it had been entitled to four square Spanish leagues of land measuring from the center of the plaza to each of the four cardinal points of the compass. The findings, it claimed, were confirmed and based on Spanish law contained in the *Recopilación de las leyes de los Reynos de las Indias*, Book 4, titles 5, 7, 12, and 13. In that regard, the Court of Private Land Claims declared

> that the said four square Spanish leagues of land are situated in the County of Bernalillo in the Territory of New Mexico, on both sides of the Rio Grande, and have for their center the center of the plaza or public square of the Villa or Old Town of Albuquerque, and are bounded on the north by the lands of the Diego Montoya grant, sometimes known as the Grant of the Ranchos de Albuquerque, on the east and south by the public domain, and on the west by the grant made to the people of Atrisco and containing 17,361.06 acres.
>
> It is therefore ordered, adjudged and decreed that the claim of said petition for four square Spanish leagues of land situate, bounded and described as hereinbefore set forth be and the same is hereby confirmed, and that this confirmation to said City of Albuquerque is in trust for the use and benefit of the lot holders under grants from the Villa of Albuquerque (*sic*) or other competent authority, and as to any residue, in trust for the use and benefit of the inhabitants and owners of the whole tract.
>
> It is further ordered, adjudged and decreed by the Court that this decree is to be taken and considered as made without prejudice to the right of the Town of Atrisco in a proper proceeding instituted in its own name in this court, to claim any portion of this decree may, upon the conclusion of such proceeding in the name of the town of Atrisco, be modified as the court may then deem just and proper so as to exclude any portion of said lands which the said town of Atrisco may, to the satisfaction of the Court, prove it is entitled to have confirmed it.[38]

At that point, the City of Albuquerque had considered the issue of their boundaries resolved. The atrisqueños thought differently.

The atrisqueños were puzzled over the government's contention that a grant had never been made to Atrisco in or about 1700, and that no documents existed to support the Town of Atrisco's claim. The atrisqueño response came quickly. When they wrote their petition to the Court of Private Land Claims, the atrisqueños had already collected a number of much-needed documents dating to the end of the seventeenth century related to Atrisco, which the City of Albuquerque had failed to notice.

The Atrisco plaintiffs argued that the grant given to Don Fernando was a community grant, not one given to an individual. The government argued the contrary: even if a grant had been given to Don Fernando, it was to him as an individual, and the people of Atrisco had no interest in the claim. Still, no document demonstrating that investiture had been given to Don Fernando had yet been located.

The atrisqueños clarified their understanding of the dates in question.

> At some time subsequent to the Year of our Lord 1692 and prior to the year 1768, and as your petitioner believes and states during or shortly subsequent to the year 1700, there was duly and lawfully made by the then Governor and Captain General of the Kingdom and Province of New Mexico, under the Crown of Spain, to the inhabitants and settlers of the Town of Atrisco a grant of a tract of land.[39]

The government argued that the 1768 grant (to Joseph Hurtado de Mendoza and others) was made to fifteen individuals. In other words, the Río Puerco claim was not a grant, but a life estate or license in favor of Hurtado de Mendoza and his associates.

In the midst of the debate between the Town of Atrisco and the City of Albuquerque, the Atlantic and Pacific Railroad Company asked for a dismissal of the claims made by the atrisqueños. The railroad based its interest on the fact that on March 12, 1872, it had filed a map with the General Land Office designating its railroad tracks. In 1881, it had constructed its line through the counties of Bernalillo and Valencia in the Territory of New Mexico. Furthermore, when the Atlantic and Pacific Railroad was incorporated by Congress in 1866, it had been granted odd-numbered sections of public land in New Mexico. The railroad argued that their right-of-way was "within a distance of forty miles on each side of the line of railroad constructed by it; and that the land, the title to which is sought to be confirmed by plaintiff [Town of Atrisco] in this section lies within the fifty mile limit." The railroad company further alleged that when it filed its map, "no proceedings were had any where or in any way preventing the rights granted to this defendant by said Act of Congress, from attaching to any of the real estate described in plaintiff's petition, to which they could attach under the terms of its said grant." Therefore, "this defendant prays that the plaintiff's petition be dismissed as to all of the odd-numbered portions."[40]

The U.S. attorney next took his turn at discrediting the Town of Atrisco in the ongoing case. His supplemental arguments, entered in the August term of 1894, basically followed those of the City of Albuquerque, especially in stating that the atrisqueños did not have any record or documentary evidence supporting the grant. His strongly worded argument alleged that if "any such grant was ever made to said Fernando Duran y Chaves, the same was surrendered or annulled prior to the year 1700; and the heirs and representatives of said supposed grantee have never claimed and do not now claim any title or interest whatever adverse to or in conflict with the said title by your petitioner and its predecessors in interest, under and by virtue of the said two grants to the inhabitants and settlers of the town of Atrisco."[41]

The attorney for the United States stated that his office had undertaken its own research and had indeed found a document supporting that a 1692 grant had been made to Fernando Durán y Chaves, as alleged by the atrisqueños, but there was no evidence that Don Fernando had ever been placed in possession of the land in Atrisco. As the grant was made to an individual, he argued, it was not a community grant. He concluded that, as the grant was made to an individual, it therefore could not, "under the laws of New Mexico, be incorporated as a community grant, and therefore this suit cannot be maintained by this plaintiff."[42]

The Court of Private Land Claims had already read through the original Spanish documents at the Office of the Surveyor General for New Mexico. Eusebio Chacón, the official translator for the Court, had certified that the translations had been compared and accepted.[43]

The court tried to establish the historical continuity between the incorporators of the Town of Atrisco and the original grantees of the Atrisco land grant. Four of the incorporators were able to trace their lineage back to the original grantees. Antonio José Chaves proved that he was the descendant of Efigenia Chaves on his paternal side and of Tomás García, another original grantee, on his maternal side. Juan Baca also descended from Tomás García. Juan Sánchez traced his lineage to Pedro Sánchez, an original grantee. José de la Luz Sánchez traced his lineage to José Sánchez, another original grantee (see chapter 8).[44]

On September 4, 1894, the court confirmed that a grant held under Spain covering a large tract of land issued to a number of individual heads of families and occupied by their heirs over two centuries was clearly a community grant. Chief Justice of the Court of Private Land Claims Joseph R. Reed, in acknowledging the community grant characteristics of the Atrisco grant made in 1692, included the Río Puerco grant of 1768 as if it were one large grant. In recognizing the Atrisco and Río Puerco grants as one, he pronounced in 1894:

> Now upon this day come the parties to this cause and said cause having been argued by counsel . . . the court being now sufficiently advised in the premises, find that the said plaintiff and petitioner is the lawful successor in title and interest of the original grantees and owners of that . . . grant made by the Government of Spain in the year one thousand six hundred and ninety-two. . . . and also to that certain other and additional grant . . . made to the . . . settlers of said town, community and settlement of Atrisco in . . . one thousand seven hundred and sixty-eight.[45]

Thus, Chief Justice Reed confirmed the contention of the atrisqueños that Atrisco was indeed a community grant. He continued: "It is therefore ordered, adjudged and decreed by the court that the claim of the said plaintiff and petitioner to and for the said original and additional grants as aforesaid. . . . is hereby established and confirmed to said petitioner, The Town of Atrisco, in trust for the use and benefit of the inhabitants of said original and additional grants as their respective interests may appear, the said land so confirmed as aforesaid."[46]

As for the interest held by the City of Albuquerque, the court decreed its claim to the Atrisco land as void. The atrisqueños had not only validated their boundaries, but gained title to both grants between two rivers. Their grant to the Town of Atrisco was confirmed "in trust and for the use and benefit of the inhabitants of said original and additional grants may appear, the said land so confirmed as aforesaid being in width from north to south, three leagues, more or less, for the entire length, thereof from the Rio Grande to the said Rio Puerco."[47] The Town of Atrisco had prevailed. Both the Atlantic and Pacific Railroad Company and the U.S. government appealed the decision in 1895, but their time of sixty days to appeal had expired. In 1897, the United States again objected, this time to the validity of the survey, claiming that the boundaries in all directions, north, east, south, and west, did not conform to the decree of confirmation.[48]

Nonetheless, as prescribed by procedure, the grant was surveyed by the surveyor general's office prior to final approval. Atrisco was surveyed by deputy surveyor George H. Pradt. The survey showed that the two tracts covered a total area of 82,728.72 acres. The cost of the Atrisco survey was $813.59. This cost, along with fees incurred in clearing the title with the Court of Private Land Claims, resulted in a "peculiar trustee arrangement in late 1898" in which the Town of Atrisco lost twelve thousand acres of its common lands.[49] The trust deed agreed upon by the president and secretary of the corporation of the Town of Atrisco provided for a special trustee to hold twelve thousand acres as security for the $1,000 owed for the survey cost and fees for clearing the land titles of the Town of Atrisco. The corporation failed to pay the fees by the deadline of September 12, 1899. As required, the trustee auctioned the land to the highest bidder after posting proper notice in an Albuquerque newspaper. From the proceeds, the trustee paid off the costs of the sale, amortized the debt with interest for payment, collected his fee of $50.00, and gave the balance to the corporation. Fortunately, the commissioners of the Town of Atrisco were allowed to bid at the auction of their land. Thus, at the auction, twelve thousand acres, or nearly half of the 1768 grant, "passed into the hands of private interests, mostly heirs and officials of the Atrisco grant."[50]

Just before the auction, however, in 1898, the southern boundary of Atrisco was adjusted to make it congruent with the northern boundary of Pajarito. The Court of Private Land Claims ordered a survey for an area "commencing at a point three chains west of the 10 mile corner on said north boundary of the ceja of the Rio Puerco to a point due east of the northwest corner of said survey of the Pajarito grant; thence west to said northwest corner of said survey of the Pajarito grant on the Rio Puerco."[51]

On May 5, 1905, President Theodore Roosevelt signed the U.S. patent confirming the lands approved by the Court of Private Land Claims along with the survey for the Town of Atrisco. The patent was issued "in trust for the use and benefit of the inhabitants of said original and additional grants as their respective interests may appear, and to their successors in interest and assigns forever."[52]

Atrisco's ability to weather the change to American governance appears remarkable, in contrast to other land grant heirs throughout the ceded territory, who did not fare as well. Their legal internship during the Spanish colonial period had trained them well to conserve their documents, for when they needed them, they made the difference between victory and defeat. It was during the period of the Court of Private Land Claims that the atrisqueños learned the value of preparation, both through legal and historical research. In the end, history vindicated their claim and saved them from oblivion.

CHAPTER 13

The Last Will of
Jesús Armijo y Jaramillo,
1895–1903

It is further ordered, adjudged and decreed by the court that the said deed of conveyance made by the said Jesús Armijo y Jaramillo to the defendant Policarpio Armijo on the 17th day of July, 1896, and recorded in Book 26, page 454 in the records of deeds of the Recorder's office of Bernalillo County, New Mexico, be and the same is hereby cancelled and set aside, and the cloud upon the title to the property hereinbefore described created thereby be and the same is hereby removed, and the title to said property freed therefrom.

JOSÉ MARÍA ROMERO V. MANUEL
ANTONIO JARAMILLO, NEW MEXICO
TERRITORIAL SUPREME COURT, 1903

As the owners of the evolving Atrisco land grant faced down outside challengers, they also defended their terrain against fellow insiders—in life as in death. As often happened throughout New Mexico, bequests of property sometimes resulted in a series of legal fights within extended families. Last wills and testaments— certified in New Mexico since the Spanish colonial period—often had a story behind them. Inherited real and personal property was not only a source of wealth; it symbolized a kind of inclusion that could only come from one's association with the deceased. A bequest from a probated will might stand for many things—from certified proof of a relationship or kinship with the deceased, to entitlement, acknowledgement, closure, and sometimes, vindication.

One example of a probated will from early twentieth-century Atrisco reveals relationships and issues among atrisqueños in their cultural setting. On January 12, 1901, Jesús Armijo y Jaramillo dictated his last will and testament. "Being sick in bed," he wrote, "[I] hereby order and command this my last will to be made."[1] He died sometime in January 1901, and his will was quickly probated on February 12. In his will, he declared that he was married to Trinidad Lucero de Armijo, with whom he had no children. He did have children from a previous marriage to Altagracia Lucero: a daughter, Sofía Armijo de Romero, and two minor sons, Miguel Antonio Armijo and Telésfor Armijo. Had the will involved only them, the process could have been confined; but Jesús Armijo y Jaramillo had many ties to those around him.

After he signed his will, it was witnessed by Severo Sánchez and José Saavedra y Jaramillo and notarized by J. B. Lucero. A few months later on April 1, 1901, his will went through the probate court of Bernalillo County and was officially signed by the deputy probate clerk, T. Werner. It seemed then that all the executor needed to do was to attend to Armijo y Jaramillo's last wishes.

José María Romero read the will to the family. The deceased had bequeathed all real and personal property to his two sons with the stipulation that all his debts be paid first. Much to the disappointment of his daughter, Sofía, he declared that "I do not devise or bequeath anything" to her.[2] He explained that she had already received a life insurance policy valued at three thousand dollars. In addition, Armijo y Jaramillo stated that he had paid for a store "kept by her and her husband in [the] new town of Albuquerque, and numberless many other things which amount to more than four thousand dollars."[3]

Armijo y Jaramillo had kept careful records of what he owed others as well as what was owed to him. Policarpio Armijo, for example, owed him $3,500 on a mortgage he held on all of his property.[4] Jesús ordered that it be collected. Santiago Baca and Melitón Chávez owed him $4,000. Additionally, Baca owed him $700 for five thousand pounds of wool, and $600 that Armijo y Jaramillo had paid to Jesús Candelaria on Baca's behalf. Librado C. de Baca of Peña Blanca owed him $150; Ramón López of Arizona owed him $400. Jesús had turned the debts over to attorney N. B. Field for collection.[5]

Aware of the proceedings, the family of another woman named Trinidad R. de Jaramillo, who had died sometime before Armijo y Jaramillo, reviewed the holdings of her estate. It appeared that she and Armijo y Jaramillo had gone through some litigation in 1895 resulting in a judgment against him for $2,746 which he had not paid.[6] The debt to Trinidad was not acknowledged in his will.

The estate of Trinidad R. de Jaramillo sued the estate of Jesús Armijo y Jaramillo. The crux of the matter was aptly explained in the summary by E. W. Dobson, attorney for the estate of Trinidad R. de Jaramillo.

Affiant further states that the estate of Jesus Armijo y Jaramillo is justly indebted unto ... said estate of Trinidad de Jaramillo, in the sum of Four Thousand five hundred and eighty Dollars, for on account of a certain judgment rendered in the district court of the second judicial district of the Territory of New Mexico, within and for the County of Bernalillo, in favor Trinidad R. de Jaramillo, in her lifetime, and against the said Jesus Armijo y Jaramillo in his lifetime; which said judgment was rendered on the 24th day of October 1895, for the sum of $2735.82, together with the costs amounting to $10.90, and said judgment bears interest at the rate of one per-cent per month from the date of its rendition, and the same is recorded in Book "I" page 89 in the records of the Clerk of said District Court.

Affiant further states that none of said indebtedness has been paid, but the whole amount thereof is still due and unpaid.[7]

The first action in the litigation against the estate of Jesús Armijo y Jaramillo began in November 1901, when Bernalillo County Sheriff J. A. Hubbell served a summons from the district court to all parties concerned. Hubbell documented his actions as follows:

I, Sheriff of Bernalillo Co., N.M., certify that I have served this summons, by delivering a copy of the same in the said County of Bernalillo, to Policarpio Armijo, and a copy to Policarpio Armijo, as administrator of the estate of Jesus Armijo y Jaramillo, deceased, on the 18th day of November 1901; by delivering a copy of the same to Trinidad Lucero de Armijo, administrator of the estate of Jesus Armijo y Jaramillo, deceased, on the 25th day of Nov. 1901; by delivering a copy of the same to Miguel Antonio Armijo, and a copy to Telesfor Armijo on the 25th day of Nov. 1901; by delivering a copy of the same to Mrs. Manuel Antonio Jaramillo, a free person over the age of fifteen years, residing at the usual place of abode of the within named Manuel Antonio Jaramillo, (the said Manuel Antonio Jaramillo being then absent); on the 25th day of Nov. 1901; and by delivering a copy of the same to the within named Sofia Armijo de Romero, on the 26th day of Nov. 1901.

Fees:—Service & return, $6.50   Mileage, 12 mi., 1.50 $8.00[8]

The record indeed demonstrated that Jesús Armijo y Jaramillo had become indebted to Trinidad R. de Jaramillo six years earlier and had not paid her. As proof, Romero introduced the "Transcript of Judgment Docket" in *Trinidad R. de Jaramillo v. Jesús Armijo y Jaramillo,* a case filed on November 26, 1895. In order to be paid, Trinidad had attempted to attach the proceeds of a sale of land between Jesús and Policarpio Armijo, which would have covered the amount owed her. It appeared that when Jesús had sold Policarpio some of his land, Trinidad expected to be paid from the proceeds. Such was not the case.

The "Transcript of Judgment Docket" showed that on July 17, 1896, Jesús Armijo y Jaramillo had sold Policarpio Armijo a piece of land in Atrisco. Both atrisqueños agreed that a fair price for the land was $3,000. Jesús then signed over the deed to Policarpio.[9]

The transaction actually involved several pieces of land. One piece consisted of Jesús's ranch and home in Precinct 28, Bernalillo County. The first property was described as

> being a strip of land running from the Arenal Pedregoso on the east some Eleven hundred yards more or less to Las Lomas de Atrisco on the west, and being about One hundred and fifty-three (153) yards wide on the east of the main road to the Arenal, and about One hundred and eighty-three (183) yards wide from north to south on the west of the main road to said Lomas or hills, and there being excepted from this sale, a small square of land about 150 by 150 yards square that this grantor heretofore sold to Roman Romero, which is located on the west end of this tract near the foot of the Lomas or hills, this tract being bounded on the north by lands of Salvador Herrera, and on the south by lands of Manuel Antonio Jaramillo, and containing the house, corrals, outhouses, stables, orchards and vineyards etc., of this grantor.[10]

The second was a tract of land about a mile south of the tract last described, which measured about three hundred yards from east to west, and about the same number of yards from north to south. It was bounded "on the north by land formerly known as of Plácida Saavedra, on the east by land formerly known as of Miguel Saavedra, on the south by the main road running west towards Laguna, and on the west by lands of Vivian Saavedra."[11]

The third was a tract of land "just south of and across the said main road from the last described, which measures Nine hundred (900) yards in length from east to west, and varying in width from Three hundred (300) yards on the west and Four hundred (400) yards on the east end, from north to south, and being bounded on the north by said main road running east and west, on the east by the acequia madre of Atrisco, on the south by land of José María Jaramillo and on the west by land of Anastasio Saavedra."[12]

The fourth tract of land was "situated about one hundred yards south of the tract last above described, which measures Five hundred (500) yards more or less in length from east to west, and One hundred and ninety-four (194) yards more or less in width from north to south, and being bounded on the north by lands of José María Jaramillo, and the acequia madre that turns around there from the north line, and by the tract of land next below described."[13]

The fifth tract of land lay "west of and across the acequia madre from the tract last described, measuring Six hundred (600) yards more or less in length from north to south, and Four hundred and fifty (450) yards more or less in width from east to west, and being bounded on the north by lands of Anastasio Saavedra, on the east by the acequia madre and lands of Francisco Armijo y Otero, on the south by lands of Aban Montoya, and on the west by lands of Rafael Armijo."[14]

The land had been deeded on March 15, 1876, to Jesús Armijo y Jaramillo by Salvador Armijo and his wife. The right, title, interest, claim, and demand to the land had been legally conveyed to him as he was "entitled to in and to the Atrisco Land Grant, the Bernardo Montaño Land Grant, and the Luis Jaramillo Land Grant in Bernalillo County, N.M., as the same are known and designated in the archives of said Territory in the Surveyor General's office thereof."[15] Thus signed and sealed by Jesús Armijo y Jaramillo, the entire sale to Policarpio Armijo was legally accomplished before the world. On July 18, 1896, Jesús had appeared before B. S. Rodey, notary public, Bernalillo County, and signed a statement acknowledging that the sale of land was done of his own free will.[16] Thus the land belonged to Policarpio Armijo, pending, of course, payment of the mortgage.

The suit against the Jesús Armijo y Jaramillo estate in 1901 revolved around the attempt of the plaintiff—the estate of Trinidad R. de Jaramillo, represented by José María Romero—to set aside the deed of conveyance made to Policarpio Armijo so that the debt to her estate could be satisfied. By filing the suit, a lien against the land sold to Policarpio was created, thus placing a cloud over his ownership. In the view of the defendants, the suit should have been made against the estate of Policarpio Armijo, not the estate of Jesús Armijo y Jaramillo.

In the "Demurrer," E. V. Chávez, attorney for the estate of Jesús Armijo y Jaramillo, took exception to the suit. He argued that the complaint ought be dismissed because José María Romero was not the proper plaintiff, for he had "no legal capacity to sue in said action." Chávez further argued that the administrators of the estate of Jesús Armijo y Jaramillo were not defective as alleged and that Sofía Armijo de Romero, Miguel Antonio Armijo, and Telésfor Armijo were not proper parties to the suit. Chávez went on to explain that "in said action plaintiff seeks to set aside a deed of conveyance, shown by said Complaint to have been executed to the Defendant Policarpio Armijo, and in which none of the other Defendants are shown to have any interest or claim, but who are utter strangers to said action." Moreover, Chávez pointed out that the plaintiff, Trinidad, had not waited "for one year from the time of the appointment of the administrators in the Jesús Armijo y Jaramillo estate for the collection of said claim against said estate, as required by law."[17]

Such sandbagging maneuvers did not sit well with José María Romero, who responded that the debt was not the responsibility of Policarpio Armijo's estate, but that of Jesús Armijo, who had in his lifetime owed money to Trinidad R. de Jaramillo.

In the complaint, Romero alleged that executions were issued upon the judgments on November 13, 1895; June 2, 1896; and January 8, 1897; commanding that "the goods and chattels, lands, and tenements of the said Jesus Armijo y Jaramillo be caused to be made the amount of said judgment, interest, and costs." All of the executions were returned *nulla bona*.[18] Even so, the plaintiff argued that the inventory of the estate listed in probate court was not enough property to pay the debt. Given that Trinidad's rights and interests were superior to those of Policarpio Armijo, the plaintiff demanded that the lien be foreclosed and sold under the direction of the court in order to satisfy the debt. On April 23, 1902, the district court rendered judgment in favor of the plaintiffs. Administrator José María Romero and the family of Trinidad R. de Jaramillo had won their case. Their victory party would have to wait, however, as Manuel Antonio Jaramillo would appeal the case to the Supreme Court of the Territory of New Mexico. Attorney E. V. Chávez lost little time in requesting the appeal, and by January 16, 1903, it had been granted.[19]

Quickly reviewing the proceedings of the district court, territorial supreme court justice B. S. Baker rendered a "Final Judgment and Decree" on March 28, 1903. Addressing each issue, Justice Baker checked if the lower court had followed a proper procedure in its adjudication of the case.

To the first issue, Justice Baker noticed that the demurrer interposed by E. V. Chávez had been overruled. However, it had allowed his clients, the Jesús Armijo y Jaramillo estate, time to plead to the complaints. Justice Baker observed that they had failed to do so in a timely fashion required by law. He pointed out that E. W. Dobson, representing the estate of Trinidad R. de Jaramillo, had presented proofs in support of the allegations contained in their complaints, which were the same ones now considered by the territorial supreme court.[20] Taking each issue, Justice Baker formed his opinion.

The documentary proof for the first issue clearly supported that Trinidad R. de Jaramillo had a superior claim and interest against the estate of Jesús Armijo y Jaramillo. The text of the "Transcript of Judgment Docket" of 1895 demonstrated that Trinidad had prevailed against Jesús. Because the judgment was yet unpaid, it continued to accrue interest at the rate of twelve percent annually. By January 1903, the debt had risen to $4,842.40.

Regarding the appropriateness of having filed the judgment of 1895 in probate court, Justice Baker ruled that it had been proper in order to establish a lien against the property in question. In regard to the authorized role of the executor, José María Romero, which was questioned in the demurrer, Justice Baker recognized him as the "duly appointed qualified and acting administrator of the estate of Trinidad R. de Jaramillo, and that Manuel Antonio Jaramillo, Policarpio Jaramillo, and Trinidad Lucero de Armijo [widow of Jesús]" similarly were the executors of the estate of Jesús Armijo y Jaramillo.

Having established certain truths in the matter, Justice Baker turned to the issue of the ownership of the land deeded to Policarpio Armijo. Trinidad had requested four times that the amount of judgment be collected through the sheriff of Bernalillo County, but none of the efforts were successful. Therefore, the court found that Trinidad's claim was the first and paramount lien on the property and deed issued to Policarpio Armijo. Justice Baker pronounced:

> Therefore, the premises considered, it is ordered, adjudged, and decreed by the court that the plaintiff José María Romero, administrator of the estate of Trinidad R. de Jaramillo have and recover from the defendants Manuel Antonio Jaramillo, Policarpio Armijo and Trinidad Lucero de Armijo as executors of the estate of Jesús Armijo y Jaramillo, the sum of four thousand eight hundred fifty dollars and 95 cents, and that said indebtedness is hereby decreed a first lien upon the following described tract, pieces and parcels of the land and real estate, situate in the County of Bernalillo and Territory of New Mexico.[21]

The court's description of the property covered all of the lands deeded earlier to Policarpio Armijo.

Before the final gavel, Justice Baker issued additional instructions:

> It is further ordered, adjudged and decreed by the court that the said deed of conveyance made by the said Jesus Armijo y Jaramillo to the defendant Policarpio Armijo on the 17th day of July, 1896, and recorded in Book 26, page 454 in the records of deeds of the Recorder's office of Bernalillo County, New Mexico, be and the same is hereby cancelled and set aside, and the cloud upon the title to the property hereinbefore described created thereby be and the same is hereby removed, and the title to said property freed therefrom.
>
> It is further ordered, adjudged and decreed by the court that upon the failure of the said defendant Manuel Antonio Jaramillo, Policarpio Armijo and Trinidad Lucero de Armijo, as the executors of the estate of Jesus Armijo y Jaramillo to pay said indebtedness hereinbefore found to be due and owing, or any other persons for or on their behalf, that the real estate

hereinbefore described or so much thereof as may be necessary, be sold at public auction for the purpose of satisfying said judgment and indebtedness and W. E. Dawe, be and is hereby appointed special master for the purpose of executing this judgment and decree, and upon failure of said defendants, or any of them, to pay said indebtedness, said special master shall cause said property to be advertised in some newspaper, printed and published in the County of Bernalillo, New Mexico, the length of time required by law, notifying all whom it may concern that said real estate hereinbefore described will be sold at public auction to the highest bidder for cash, at a certain time and place in said notice to be therein inserted, and upon the day of sale said special master shall sell the same to the highest and best bidder for cash and out of the proceeds received therefrom shall pay first, the costs of this suit, including compensation for himself for his services as special master in making such sale, and next he shall apply the proceeds received, or so much thereof as may be necessary, to the satisfaction and payment of this indebtedness together with interest thereon, at the rate which the same bears.[22]

Dawes was instructed to report his doings to the court and to confirm the sale and account for costs and revenues from the land in the estate of Jesús Armijo y Jaramillo.

As for Sofía Armijo de Romero, Miguel Antonio Armijo, and Telésfor Armijo, the children of Jesús, they were "barred and estopped from having or claiming any right, title or interest, prior, superior, paramount or adverse to plaintiff's lien upon the property hereinbefore described." As the gavel sounded in the courtroom, justice had been served in the long-drawn-out case affecting the estates of three atrisqueños: Trinidad, Jesús, and Policarpio.

The story behind Jesús Armijo y Jaramillo's last will and testament represents a capsulized social history of Atrisco. Indeed, Armijo y Jaramillo's story is one of an examined life with many complicated relationships. The fertile minds of atrisqueños seemed never to be without excitement, for there was always a negotiation to be haggled over or a profit to be gained. At Atrisco, there was invariably a winner and a loser. It has always been so.

Epilogue

This heir is willing to give up everything . . . to fight this battle. I hope others will join me to save our Atrisco Land Grant—our center.

JEROME A. PADILLA, CONCERNED HEIRS OF ATRISCO

Our heritage comes from within. This is just land.

ABAN LUCERO

I wouldn't like to speculate on what motivates shareholders to support or oppose the plan. I certainly can understand where both sides of this are coming from. The money is good for some people who could use it. I can also see the attachment to the land and the herencia of Atrisco. It's not an easy decision.

RORY MCCLANNAHAN, ALBUQUERQUE JOURNAL

We are pleased that Westland's shareholders have ratified the board's recommendation to approve the SunCal transaction.

SOSIMO PADILLA, WESTLAND BOARD OF DIRECTORS

As the twentieth century unfolded, Atrisco emerged in one piece. Atrisqueños had made the right choices in defense of their land and proved that they could protect themselves against any rivals. Three hundred years of ownership were solidly bolstered by a comparable span of legal experience in three cultures: Spanish colonial, Mexican, and Anglo-American. The only unconquered foe atrisqueños faced in the early years of the twentieth century was that within.

After the incorporation of the land grant as the Town of Atrisco, atrisqueños faced a series of tests. Joseph V. Metzgar, historian and heir to Atrisco lands, identifies a common thread throughout the early decades of the modern history of Atrisco:

The twentieth century brought rapid economic change and Atrisqueños had to adopt new ways of gaining benefits from their common lands. Meanwhile, a constant problem was that of preventing "inside" interests from gaining rewards and acreage for themselves without regard to the interests of all heirs. Indeed, the corporation failed seriously in several respects. First, it did not establish definitive and complete heirship listings. Second, it did not keep secured and adequate records of all land transactions. Third, it did not provide official accounting of funds. Finally, it did not maintain a record of the minutes of trustee meetings. That kind of free and easy organization fostered wheeling and dealing of acreage, monies, and influence among "inside" politicos, and often most uninformed and busy heirs, struggling to make a living, felt powerless to do anything to stop the machinations. Considering the circumstances, it seems surprising that so much of the common lands remained intact and integrated. Yet there was concern and honest leadership within and without the inner circle which helped regain integrity and beneficial communal development.[1]

During the first half of the twentieth century, atrisqueños wrestled once more with the phantom power of astute insiders, just as they had in the eighteenth century. In 1968, the Atrisco land grant yielded to Westland Development Company (composed of atrisqueño land-grant heirs) to manage the land and its extensive holdings.

Farming and ranching at Atrisco had diminished and, in many cases, had become untenable. After 1890, New Mexicans who depended on rural industries such as grazing and agriculture saw their economies steadily decline in the valley of Albuquerque as the nation transformed itself from rural to urban. After 1890, for example, the amount of usable open range shrank as government land management, conservation programs, privatization of watering places, fencing, and homesteading became widespread trends. The close of the open range brought about a decrease in grazing capacity in New Mexico. In turn, livestock raising declined to nearly 60 percent of former levels between 1890 and 1920. By the 1930s, drought and overgrazing had depleted range vegetation by nearly 60 percent.[2] Not only had settlements along the Río Puerco been abandoned by the 1930s, but the extensive grazing of sheep on Atrisco's common lands was virtually over.

Similarly, agriculture declined. Records of the State of New Mexico Middle Río Grande Conservancy District identify the number of acres irrigated in 1894, 1895, and 1896. The acequias or ditches of Ranchos de Atrisco along the Río Grande, for example, released 420 acre-feet of water in 1894, 560 acre-feet of water in 1895, and 280 acre-feet of water in 1896.[3] By 1928, the same acequias were only watering 140 acre-feet.

Irrigated acreage overall in the Middle Río Grande Conservancy District fell from 125,000 in 1880 to 40,000 in 1925.[4]

Other factors spawned in the world theater touched Atrisco. By the 1930s, war and economic downturns affected New Mexicans. The Great Depression profoundly influenced the future of Atrisco. As both livestock grazing and agriculture declined, atrisqueños were forced to seek jobs in Albuquerque and beyond. During the period preceding World War II, economic and environmental factors accelerated the move from farm to city.

During this period, the Town of Atrisco board of trustees embarked on some daring and foresighted enterprises. In 1920 it signed its first lease ever to an outside interest for the exploration and development of any gas and oil resources found in its jurisdiction. In 1926 the Town of Atrisco negotiated another lease to the Albuquerque firm of Cegelsky, Avery, and Preston for the mining of volcanic ash. One of the board's most far-reaching decisions involved the lease for the construction of an airport that became the Cutter-Carr Airport and Cutter-Carr Flying Service. In the 1930s, the board of trustees signed right-of-way easements for telephone and telegraph lines and quitclaimed five-acre plots to some heirs who sold them for the construction of Highway 66, along which modern Interstate 40 extends west of Albuquerque.[5]

The new trend of leasing land to outside interests drew objections from some Atrisco heirs. In October 1935, James M. Hubbell filed suit (*James M. Hubbell v. Town of Atrisco*), asking the court to identify all legal heirs entitled to share in profits and benefits of the Town of Atrisco. One criterion used was the list of original owners and incorporators of the Town of Atrisco in 1892; the second criterion required that direct descendants of those atrisqueños named on the 1892 list document their relationships. The presiding district court judge, Fred E. Wilson, approved the list. Other heirship petitions were subsequently presented to the court, resulting in an amended list. The last heirship petition related to the *Hubbell* case was made in 1952.[6]

Antonio J. Carbajal and other atrisqueños sued the Board of Trustees of the Town of Atrisco in district court in 1940. The plaintiffs were concerned about common lands being sold or alienated without the approval of heirs. They charged mismanagement and the violation of state law regarding the sale of land grants, and they demanded the removal of trustees involved in illegal practices as well as an accounting of the Town of Atrisco's monies and budget. Anticipating a judicial order, the president and secretary-treasurer resigned on the day before the court made its pronouncement. In January 1941, Judge George W. Hay ordered all corporation funds impounded and any new business barred until a new board could be elected.[7]

In the balloting, David J. Armijo was elected president and Jake Armijo was elected secretary. The court maintained general supervisory control over the Town of Atrisco's business dealings. The president of the board was required to post a surety bond of one thousand dollars, maintain a set of books, record minutes of all board meetings, and file an annual audit report by a certified public accountant.[8] The court appointed an attorney, Gilberto Espinosa, to investigate illegal disbursements and misappropriations originally cited in the 1940 *Carbajal* suit. Finally, the court ordered that no common lands belonging to the Town of Atrisco could be sold or alienated without the approval of the court.[9] The Town of Atrisco would remain under that court order for the remainder of its existence as a corporation.   Atrisco's tax-exempt status was another problem area that eventually went before the New Mexico Supreme Court. In *Town of Atrisco v. Monahan, et al.* (1952), the court entertained whether the municipality could claim *res judicata*, thus dismissing the case, and whether the Town of Atrisco could permanently stop or prohibit the taxation of its common lands. Finding no basis for Atrisco's tax exemption, the court ruled negatively on both issues. Historian Metzgar wrote of the case: "this decision by the New Mexico Supreme Court in 1952 settled once and for all the question of the Atrisco grant's tax status and stimulated a more determined search by *atrisqueños* for more monetarily advantageous policies in using their common lands."[10]

Meanwhile, Albuquerque's west side had begun to expand. The rapid construction of homes caused atrisqueños to rethink how the development of the area could benefit or harm them. Hoping to redefine their proprietary status, Alfredo Armijo filed suit in district court against the Town of Atrisco in 1952. The case (*Armijo v. Town of Atrisco*) went to the Supreme Court of New Mexico on appeal. The issue revolved around the age-old question, did the heirs own the grant lands in fee simple (that is, with the right to sell or give them to anyone) as tenants in common? Or did the Town of Atrisco hold the lands in trust for them? If the first question was affirmative, then the parties to the suit hoped that the lands could be divided among them so that they could dispose of them as they wished.

In *Armijo v. Town of Atrisco* (1952), the New Mexico Supreme Court reviewed the entire history of the Atrisco land grant from its earliest times to define whether it was a community land grant. As decided by the Court of Private Land Claims in 1894, and as shown by the patent of 1905, the historical grant had been declared a community grant that would be in-

corporated under the Town of Atrisco. The court recognized the authority of the corporation to form "a body politic and corporation under the
corporate name to the Town of Atrisco" with all power and authority to
administer, convey, lease, mortgage, or otherwise dispose of its real estate.[11] In its conclusions, the court declared:

> The plaintiffs claim that they either own the lands in question in fee
> simple as tenants in common or that the Town of Atrisco has been hold-
> ing said lands in trust for them and that the lands should now be di-
> vided among them. It is my opinion, however, that title to said lands has
> been vested in The Town of Atrisco for over fifty years in fee simple and
> that the plaintiffs have no interest in said lands except that they do have
> the right as set forth in our State Statutes to participate in the affairs of
> the corporation, as they and their predecessors have been doing for fifty
> years.[12]

Thus, the New Mexico Supreme Court upheld the decision of the lower
court. The decision, in effect, prevented individual ownership of the land
administered by the Board of Trustees of the Town of Atrisco. The quest
continued, nevertheless, to allow commercial development of the land in a
way that would be equitable and profitable for the atrisqueños.

A new plan emerged. In 1953, John N. Brunacini, attorney for the
Town of Atrisco, asked the district court to distribute ten thousand
acres of land to certain Atrisco heirs. Brunacini noted that in the past,
boards of trustees had distributed land to certain heirs and had caused
an inequitable circumstance for those not favored. The district court
approved the plan. However, Jake Armijo and other heirs asked the district court for a stay of proceedings. They then appealed to a higher
court. Meanwhile, seventy tracts of land had already been distributed
under the plan.

Four years later, Brunacini stood before the New Mexico Supreme
Court explaining the proposal once again. The court asked Brunacini
to affirm his understanding of the proposal as follows:

> [The trustees] will sell to each heir who applies ten acres of land, at $10
> per acre except those heirs who previously received five-acre allotments
> and to them they will sell only five acres; that before the sale is consum-
> mated, the Board wishes to quiet title to approximately 10,000 acres and
> give each person title according to that survey, after application is ap-
> proved. Approved applicants will be matched each to the surveyed tract
> on the basis of a jury wheel or similar to a rotary system, is that your
> plan in substance?[13]

Brunacini acknowledged that it was. Assignment of land in terms of its location would be made by lottery from the amended list of names determined by the *Hubbell* case of 1935. Brunacini advertised the plan and reported that 2,134 people had applied for the lottery, of whom 1,800 had been approved.[14]

After discussing the plan further, the supreme court better understood the proposal. Thus, to the court's understanding, the plan was as follows:

> The Trustees of the Atrisco Grant want to sell ten acres of land to each heir; except those heirs who have already received five acres, to those heirs, the Grant will sell only five acres; and to those heirs who have already received ten acres, they will not receive any additional land. Now, the Grant wants to sell this land to the heirs for $10 an acre—that is, a ten-acre tract would cost an heir $100. The trustees have worked out a plan, in principle at least, with the aid of Mr. Coker and Mr. Walker. If one of the heirs is entitled to ten acres and he is too poor to pay the $100, then the Trustees of the Grant will let him borrow the $100 to buy his ten acres. All of the details of the plan have not been worked out, but the plan in general is to distribute 10,000 acres, more or less, of the lands of the Atrisco Grant among about 2,000 heirs of the Grant who have applied or will apply for the land. The details of this plan, to make it fair for everyone and to correct any mistakes as to who the heirs actually are, have not been all worked out. If the Court works out these plans, on the suggestion of Mr. Coker, in his words, in accordance with the principle of law, the guiding light of the Court will be to avoid fraud, to avoid graft, and to avoid excessive fees.
>
> Now, it has been explained to the Court that this fee of $10 an acre—this sale price of $10 an acre—is necessary. They will have to charge this so that the land can be surveyed and the title quieted by a proceeding in the Court, so that when ten acres is sold to an heir, he will know what land he is receiving and he will get a good title to it. He will not have to go to his own lawyer and spend $300 to $400 of his own money to have this done.[15]

With that clarification, the supreme court was ready to proceed; and, on May 29, 1957, it rendered a decision reversing the decision of the lower court. The Town of Atrisco had prevailed.

Writing for the supreme court, Justice Sadler pointed out that the means to distribute the land violated state law prohibiting lotteries; that the distribution of land would result in the dissipation of the Town of Atrisco's assets, also a violation of state law regarding land grants; and that the plan ignored elemental concepts of due process under the Fourteenth Amendment of the Constitution. Sadler also observed that many heirs ("in excess of 2,000") were not heard before the court. With Justice Sadler's words, "reversed and remanded," the Town of Atrisco narrowly escaped placing itself on the road to oblivion.

Meanwhile, Albuquerque's expansion to the west continued to bring tempting opportunities to atrisqueños. Under approval of the district court in 1959, Hoffman Homes bought four thousand acres in the subdivision known as Westgate. It was the first major housing development on the west mesa. Of the event—in which the land was purchased for $1,250,000—Metzgar writes, "most heirs, however, gained no direct benefit from the transaction."[16]

In the meantime, atrisqueños sought the remedy Justice Sadler had recommended in his 1957 decision. He had suggested that change could be achieved through the legislature. Lobbyists had been hard at work to achieve that change. They focused on laws permitting corporations established under the 1891 Act Relating to Community Land Grants to reorganize under the general corporation laws of New Mexico. In 1967, a law permitted community land-grant corporations to change their legal status to one of domestic stock corporation. The law not only allowed flexibility in land transactions with non-Atrisco interests, it also permitted heirs to receive stock dividends.

To that end, in July 1967, a number of lawful owners and heirs submitted articles of incorporation leading to the creation of the Westland Development Company. By 1969, the Westland Development Company had supplanted the Town of Atrisco. Through a court order, District Judge Edwin L. Swope ordered the Board of Trustees of the Town of Atrisco to transfer all books, records, and land to Westland. On November 15, 1969, the Town of Atrisco trustees executed a quitclaim deed to the Westland Development Company. With that, Atrisco quietly entered into a new era. Like the Roman god Janus, who looked to both past and future, Westland, keeping an eye toward the future, was keenly aware that its past was its refuge.

As Albuquerque's west side expanded, developers and property owners clashed with Westland's land and management policies and practices. Issues continued to exist concerning the special type of exception known as *terrenos en común*—lands held in common—and water rights. In principle, the Laws of the Indies and the Plan de Pitic posit that lands held in common within a land grant cannot be conveyed or alienated by any of the landholders.[17] Lands held in common include a number of uses such as farming, grazing, easements, cemeteries, and the main irrigation ditches known as acequias madres. The river that borders the land grant is also used in common (for irrigation purposes, watering of stock, human consumption, and so forth). Even though *tierra y agua* are essential provisions of all Spanish and Mexican land grants, the state of New Mexico is loath to adjudicate cases that deal with both. Instead, water is treated as a separate issue.

History provides part of the answer to the issue of common lands. Nineteenth-century courts acknowledged the historical documentation that resulted in the deed for the Town of Atrisco in 1905. The deed to Atrisco conveyed title to lands within the boundary between the Río Grande and a point on the bluff and lands beyond it to the Río Puerco. The land between the high bluff and the bank of the Río Grande, as well as the river itself, however, have always been treated by Atrisco as *terrenos en común* and reserved for the joint use of the people of Atrisco.

Water, too, was held in common and its use regulated through an acequia association.[18] Along with pasturage and wooded areas for firewood and building materials, water was a requirement for all land grants. Obstruction of rights-of-way for water was not permitted, as demonstrated in the 1786 case in which Governor Juan Bautista de Anza decreed that atrisqueños were free to traverse unobstructed to the river (see chapter 9). If history offers any consolation to atrisqueños, it is that the defense of their land followed the prescribed logic of legal processes within the Laws of the Indies, the traditional uses of land and water, and the terms stipulated in the land grant.

Although modern litigation has followed a strict interpretation of historical legal processes, there is one other way to test the intent of language in land grants in New Mexico. Comparative studies should be made of historical land grants outside of New Mexico, such as those in the northern states of Mexico, which can provide insights into the practice of Spanish colonial and Mexican period law and justice. In any case, the Town of Atrisco could not give a deed to an individual for any of the common lands in the bosque east of the high bluff. The simple reason is that individual ownership of any part or all of the bosque, pasturage, and river conflicts with the common-land usage by settlers within the land grant. It is clear in the historical documents that the bosque and land along the river were held in common so that all landholders and their assigns could utilize them in order to meet basic needs of living. In the twentieth century, the creation of Westland Development Company was indeed a bold, innovative, and collaborative effort among the atrisqueños to decide how to manage and protect their interests to the common lands.

Although Westland Development Company remained firmly in control of the fate of the Atrisco land grant after 1968, it was not without opposition from some atrisqueños, who formed the Atrisco Land Rights Council. Among other issues, they continually questioned whether Westland had the right to speak for all Atrisco land grant heirs.[19] One of the leaders of the Atrisco Land Rights Council, Jaime Chávez, a former executive director of the council, also argued that while Hispanic culture should be safeguarded, the cultural heritage of Atrisco included a much-ignored Native American component.

Atrisco had never been without its adversaries. Soon its fears would be realized. Throughout 2005, atrisqueños became increasingly disturbed by rumors that Westland Development Company intended to sell its holdings, thus ending the historical land tenure of Atrisco. How the plan to divest came about is not clear. The announcement was made in July 2005 after Westland submitted its master plan for the area called Zacate. The *Albuquerque Journal* reported on August 31, 2006, that "not long after the master plan was submitted to the county, Westland became the target of a buyer bid, which has not been settled."[20] Almost immediately, a new group emerged opposing any sale of the land. One member of the group, Concerned Heirs of Atrisco, declared, "this heir is willing to give up everything . . . to fight this battle. I hope others will join me to save our Atrisco Land Grant—our center."[21] By 2006, opposition to the sale flared into open protests as Westland's officers debated the proposal to sell its lands. A developer from Las Vegas, Nevada, supposedly offered $311 a share for the land. Later, SunCal Companies of Irvine, California, offered "$315 for each of the 794,927 Westland shares, or $250 million total" for more than 55,000 acres.[22] Beyond that, as part of the sale, SunCal promised "to promote and preserve the ancestral and cultural heritage of the shareholders of Westland" via the creation of a foundation.[23] David Soyka, director of marketing for SunCal, said, "the culture of the land will change, but it will be honored."[24] Upon approval of the sale, the bidder offered to fund the foundation at the rate of "$1 million a year for 100 years."[25]

Amid the rumors, atrisqueños raised myriad questions. They ranged from concerns regarding the destruction of their heritage to the value of stocks controlled by Westland. One person asked about the promised donation to the educational heritage foundation—"or will they just build a $100 million monument to the foundation?"[26] Specifics from Westland about the cultural foundation were vague pending the results of the sale and future planning.

Other questions revolved around whether the land contained oil and gas. As part of the sale, SunCal would agree to create a limited liability company in New Mexico called Atrisco Oil and Gas LLC. In return, Westland would agree to assign its entitled 100 percent of all rents, royalties, and other benefits and 50 percent of its future oil and gas revenue to Atrisco Oil.[27]

In the twentieth century, oil and gas exploration companies on the Atrisco land grant indicated that the land could possibly yield as much as five hundred million barrels total. Atrisqueño sentiment was divided over the likelihood of such bounty. The *Albuquerque Journal* reported that "state records show that oil companies have been drilling test wells since at least the 1940s. No production has occurred there."[28] In September 2006, Tecton, a Texas-based energy exploration company, began drilling on leased land from Westland Development Company.[29]

Other questions concerned the aftermath of the sale. What would developers do with the land in terms of community planning? Would the development be residential, commercial, mixed housing? What would become of the master plan for the development called Zacate?

The master plan for Zacate was submitted to the Bernalillo County Planning Commission in July 2005 but the commission deferred it for September. Westland needed time to conduct studies of traffic, water availability, impacts on schools, and a host of other details. Decisions on the master plan were postponed for an additional six months pending completion of required studies.[30]

The proposed Zacate master plan encompassed over 14,000 acres south of Interstate 40 and would take nearly forty years to develop. The plan designated 850 acres to industrial purposes, 450 acres to commercial office space, and 780 acres to commercial retail space. Additionally, 450 acres would be assigned for institutional purposes such as schools, and 4,200 acres would be designated as open space with parks and trails. The remaining 7,300 acres would be residential, with 38,000 houses built, creating eight "villages" on the land.[31] All such questions about the master plan could be summed up in one answer: it would be "up to whomever owns the property."[32] That statement was more than a declaration of fact, it was a prediction. In early January 2007, SunCal's land acquisition manager, Will Steadman, announced that "SunCal would reassess all of Westland's current and future development projects."[33]

Despite the controversy surrounding SunCal's offer, on July 19, 2006, Westland's board of directors voted unanimously to accept SunCal's offer to buy Westland and its assets. At that meeting, the board of directors announced that the shareholder meeting to vote on SunCal's proposal would be held on November 6, 2006, at 10:00 A.M. at the Kiva Auditorium in the Albuquerque Convention Center. They instructed Westland's staff to mail out proxy statements and detailed information about the sale to the company's shareholders so that they could prepare their votes. Time was needed to air out the contents of the deal.

Atrisqueños searched for solutions to the conundrum posed by the proposed sale of Westland. One query raised hope against hope. Rudy Gonzales asked, "Has Westland ever thought of turning it back to [the]

'Town of Atrisco'?" While some atrisqueños opposed the sale to SunCal, others supported it.

In the midst of the consternation, Richard Chávez proposed to buy the shares of other minor shareholders for $325 each. He hoped to acquire as many shares as possible to increase his ability to control the vote against the sale. Although well-intentioned, he was accused of "trying to buy an election and take over the land grant successor, Westland Development Co." Chávez replied that even though he was not an heir, his only motivation was "to protect the Atrisco Land Grant." Chávez owned 1,300 shares of Westland stock. His plan was to vote against the offers made to Westland Company.[34] Chávez's proposal further stipulated that he would buy anyone's shares, and he offered to "pay 5 percent of the $325 per share sale price of the stock before the Nov. 6 shareholder meeting. In return, shareholders would give up their proxies for Chávez to vote. The shareholders selling to Chávez would not give up their stock certificates until after the Nov. 6 vote."[35] Chávez announced the caveat that the offer was only good if the sale did not go through.

In another line of opposition to the sale, María Elena Rael filed a lawsuit in March 2006 over Westland's plans to sell the company and more than 55,000 acres. In early November 2006, Second District Chief Judge William F. Lang filed a dismissal of the suit, citing that "the court specifically finds that each and every ground stated by defendants warrant dismissal of the action."[36] Despite the hopes and schemes of atrisqueños, history's clock could not be turned back.

On November 6, 2006, shareholders of the Westland Development Company took their historic vote and, despite last-minute efforts by opponents to the sale, chose to sell their shares and land to SunCal. Amid clamor that "the vote was fixed," SunCal claimed that "69 percent of the proxy votes favored the buyout."[37] In the election, one share represented one vote; for example, anyone holding one hundred shares would have one hundred votes. Some members held shares numbering in the thousands. On the appointed day, about 500 of more than 6,100 Westland shareholders gathered at the Albuquerque Convention Center to vote. Others not in attendance, who had earlier submitted proxy votes, were allowed to change their vote if they wished. After forty-five minutes, Westland officials announced a preliminary count indicating that the vote favored the sale. The final vote count, which included the votes taken in the meeting and the proxy votes, was given to Moss Adams LLP, a Seattle accounting firm with offices located in Albuquerque. Representatives of the firm took the ballot boxes containing all of the votes for a final tabulation. The results were not known for nearly two weeks.

On November 21, 2006, Westland Development Company announced that "72.4 percent of the 794,927 common stock shareholders voted in favor of the sale and 97.75 percent of the 85,100 Class B stock voted for approval."[38] The Class B stock had been issued only to present and former Westland board members. SunCal Companies' offer to buy 794,927 Westland shares at $315 per share totaling $250 million had been accepted. The amount of land included in the sale was 55,000 acres associated with the 1768 Río Puerco unit of the land grant. In a news release, Sosimo Padilla, chairman of Westland's board, said, "this has been a long process for the board, management and our shareholders, and we look forward to concluding our transaction with SunCal. We are pleased that Westland's shareholders have ratified the board's recommendation to approve the SunCal transaction." The only requirement left to complete the sale was that the New Mexico Securities Division and the Delaware Secretary of State sign off on the sale (Delaware was where SCC Acquisitions LLC, the corporation SunCal created to buy Westland, was incorporated).[39]

Opponents and supporters of the sale voiced their opinions. The Concerned Heirs of Atrisco vowed to continue the fight against the sale of the land. Opponents of the sale demonstrated that they were not yet ready to give up their fight by filing at least four lawsuits in district and federal courts.[40] Those who favored the sale argued that the decision to sell provided an opportunity to people who would otherwise never have benefited from Westland's ability to develop the land. Meanwhile, questions about the demise of Atrisco's rich heritage continued to surface. Aban Lucero put it in a nutshell: "Our heritage comes from within. This is just land."[41]

SunCal issued a news release on December 9, 2006, stating that "Westland is now a wholly owned subsidiary of SunCal Companies."[42] Three items were left on the agenda of the sale. The first item was that Westland shareholders would receive shares in the newly created Atrisco Oil and Gas LLC. The second was that they would receive instructions on how to cash in their old Westland shares. The third was that SunCal would start funding the Atrisco Heritage Foundation at the rate of $1 million every year for the next hundred years.[43]

The future of Atrisco had once more teetered in the balance. This time appeared to be the last. The historical process had finally revealed Atrisco's fate. Atrisqueños, like their ancestors, had taken on all challenges by outsiders and insiders. If history holds true, both sides of the story of the vote will continue to be told as long as atrisqueños remember the debates leading to and immediately following November 6, 2006. There were, after all, loose ends that spelled the beginnings of a new struggle for the cultural survival of the people of Atrisco. All atrisqueños can look on their past with pride, for they, like their cousins in other land grants, are truly history's children. As the story of the Atrisco land grant came to an end, a cool fall breeze swept across the Valle de Atrisco, just as it had many times before the coming of the early Spanish settlers. At the end of 2006, the Valle de Atrisco stood on the threshold of a new era.

Appendix

CHAPTER LXXXVI.

AN ACT RELATING TO COMMUNITY LAND GRANTS, AND FOR
OTHER PURPOSES. H. B. 48; APPROVED FEBRUARY 26, 1891.

CONTENTS.

SEC. 25.	All officers shall serve without pay, and shall not be interested in any contract with said corporation.
SEC. 26.	Trustees no power over land claimed in private ownership. Except, etc.
SEC. 27.	Suits in ejectment against adverse claimants or owners.
SEC. 28.	Suits in trespass.
SEC. 29–30.	Of titles to persons claiming in private ownership.
SEC. 31.	When money may be applied to public schools.
SEC. 32.	Disposition of land in good faith. Corporation shall be valid.
SEC. 33.	Fees of clerk of district court.
SEC. 34.	Meaning of the words, "owners" and "proprietors," defined.
SEC. 35.	Legal and equitable title to vest in the corporation.
SEC. 36–38.	Not applicable to any grant other than community, town or municipality.

BE it enacted by the Legislative Assembly of the Territory of New Mexico.

SECTION 1. The owners or proprietors of any tract or grant of land in this Territory, ceded or granted by the governments of Mexico or Spain to any colony, community or town or to any person or persons, for the benefit of any town or colony community who shall within five years next after the passage of this act accept the benefits of the provisions of this act in the manner hereinafter designated, shall become a body corporate and politic, with all the powers hereinafter granted and for the purposes hereinafter mentioned, and shall have perpetual succession.

SEC. 2. Any ten or more of the owners and proprietors of any such land grant or real estate so held in common as a colony community or town grant, as aforesaid, may within five years from and after the passage of this act, and not afterwards, file in the office of the clerk of the district court of the county in which such land grant or real estate (or the greater part thereof, if the same be situate in two or more counties) is situate, a petition setting forth the names and places of residence of all persons claiming or owning any interest in the said land grant or real estate who are known to the petitioners, a description of the said land grant or real estate by metes and bounds according to an actual survey thereof, if the boundaries of such land grant have been definitely fixed by an actual survey, but if no such survey has been made by the proper authority, then such land grant may be described by any other description which will reasonably designate the land grant and the name by which it is commonly known in the vicinity of its location, and the nature and extent of the title under and by virtue of which such land grant or real estate is held and claimed, and praying that the owners and proprietors of such land grant or real estate may be created a body politic and corporate, under the provisions of this act.

SEC. 3. Upon the filing of such petition it shall be the duty of the clerk of the district court to cause to be printed notices to the owners and proprietors of the land grant or real estate described in said petition, which said notice shall describe the said land grant or real estate by the name by which it is commonly known in the vicinity of its location, setting forth the filing and object of such petition, the name of the petitioners, and that on a day and at a place to be named in said notice an application will be made to the judge of said district court to grant the prayer of such petition.

SEC. 4. Two copies of the notices provided for in the foregoing section, one in Spanish and one in the English language, shall be forthwith mailed by the clerk of the district court to each of the persons named in said petition as owning or claiming any interest in the said land grant, to the post office nearest to the place of residence of such person as alleged in the said petition, providing that it shall not be necessary to mail any copy of such notice to any person who shall join in such petition as a petitioner.

SEC. 5. Five copies of such notice in the English language and five copies of the same in the Spanish language shall be posted in public and conspicuous places on the said land grant or real estate for at least sixty days next before the application shall be made to the judge of the district court to grant the prayer of the said petition, and no such application shall be heard by any such district judge until there shall be filed in the record satisfactory evidence of such posting.

SEC. 6. Within thirty days after the filing of such petition, if it shall satisfactorily appear to the judge of the district court that the notices have been mailed as required by section 4 of this act, and that the notices remain posted upon the land grant or Real estate as required by section 5 of this act, it shall be the duty of the judge of the district court, upon request of the petitioners, to appoint three well qualified householders, residing upon and having an interest in the said land or real estate, to ascertain how many of such persons are in favor of the granting of the prayer of such petition, and how many are opposed thereto.

SEC. 7. Every person owning or claiming to own any interest in the said land grant or real estate shall be entitled to vote at the said election: *Provided*, That if the right of any such person to so vote be challenged at the time the vote is taken, and a memorandum of such challenge is made at the time upon the poll book, and it shall appear upon the hearing before the judge of the district court that the allowance or disallowance of such challenges all taken together, may affect the result of any such election, it shall be incumbent upon every person whose vote is so challenged to prove that at the time of such election he was the owner of some interest in such land grant or real estate, and in default of such proof it shall be the duty of such judge to reject such vote.

SEC. 8. The vote at any such election shall be cast by ballot, and it shall be the duty of each person casting a ballot to write his name on the back of such ballot: *Provided,* That if the voter is unable to write, his name may be written by another, if attested by two witnesses who shall each sign as witnesses on such ballot.

SEC. 9. It shall be the duty of the persons so appointed by the judge of the district court to hold an election at some central and convenient point on the said land grant or real estate, for the purposes of this act, and to give notice of the time and place of such election by posting notices thereof in both the English and Spanish languages, for at least thirty days, in five public and conspicuous places on said land grant or real estate, and to certify the result of such election to the judge of the district court within five days after the holding of such election, such persons shall also return to the clerk of the district court the original poll book and all ballots cast at any such election.

SEC. 10. If it shall appear by the certificate of the persons appointed to hold such election that two-thirds of all voters voting at such election voted in favor of granting the prayer of the petition, the judge of the district court shall, on the day named in the notice issued by the clerk of said court, proceed to hear any objections that may be interposed in writing by any person to the fairness of such election, or the right of any person voting to vote thereat, and shall continue such hearing from day to day and from time to time until the same is completed.

SEC. 11. If no objections be made on the day of such hearing, or if the objections made are found by the judge of district court to be not well taken, and it appears that two-thirds or more of the qualified voters voting at such election voted in favor of the granting of the prayer of said petition, the judge of the district court shall enter up a decree granting such prayer and setting forth that the petitioners and their associates and successors are by the said decree created a body politic and corporate under a name to be therein stated.

SEC. 12. If less than two-thirds of the qualified voters voting at any such election shall have voted in favor of the granting of the prayer of such petition, the same shall be dismissed at the cost of the petitioners.

SEC. 13. Upon the entry of the decree of the district court granting the prayer of any such petition, the petitioners, their associates and successors, shall thereby be and become a body corporate and politic, under the name designated in the said decree, and shall have and possess the following powers:

First. To sue and to be sued in their corporate name.

Second. To sell, convey, lease, mortgage or otherwise dispose of so much of the land grant or real estate described the said petition as is held in common by the owners and proprietors.

Third. To make such rules and regulations not in conflict with the constitution and laws of the United States or the laws of the Territory as may be necessary to the protection and improvement of such common lands and real estate and the use and enjoyment thereof, and of the common waters thereon.

Fourth. To assess against the owners and proprietors thereof such taxes and other assessments as may be necessary to defray the expenses of conducting the business of said corporation and to enforce the payment thereof by such owners and proprietors.

Fifth. To have a common seal and to alter and amend the same at pleasure.

Sixth. To determine the number of animals that may be permitted to graze upon the common lands aforesaid, and the price which shall be paid by any owner or proprietor for the privilege of grazing thereon: *Provided,* Such price shall be uniform as to all owners and proprietors.

SEC. 14. The corporate powers of such corporation shall be exercised by a board of nine trustees, who shall be owners and proprietors, reside upon the land grant or real estate, and be heads of families. Such board of trustees shall be elected by the owners and proprietors of such land grant or real estate, and the first election for members of such board of trustees shall be held within sixty days after the entry of such decree, by the persons appointed by the district judge to hold the election provided for in section 9 of this act, who shall give notice of such election in the same manner as is provided in said section for the notice of election therein referred to: *Provided,* That if any one of such persons shall be for any reason disqualified or shall refuse to act, the remaining two may hold such election, and if two or more of such persons shall be for any reason disqualified or refuse to act, the judge of the district court shall designate other qualified persons to act in their stead: *And provided further,* That the persons receiving the highest number of votes at such first election shall respectively hold their offices until the election and qualification of their successors, as hereinafter provided.

SEC. 15. A majority of such board of trustees and of their successors shall constitute a quorum for the transaction of business, and their corporation shall be in all respects bound by the acts of the majority of its board of trustees, done in pursuance of the provisions of this act, within the scope thereof.

SEC. 16. The board of trustees of every corporation created under the provisions of this act shall hold four meetings in each and every year, on the first Saturdays in the months of January, April, July and October, for the transaction of all business of the corporation, of which meetings all persons shall be required to take notice; but the corporation shall not be bound by any sale, mortgage, conveyance, lease or other disposition of its common property, unless the same be made and executed in pursuance of a resolution of such board passed by the affirmative vote of all of the members present at any of the stated meetings of said board, and duly entered upon the record of such meetings and attested by the president of said board.

SEC. 17. The said board of trustees may hold special sessions at such times as the business of the corporation shall render necessary, but at such special meetings the only business transacted shall be such as may be necessary to protect said land grant or real estate from trespassers, the levying of taxes or other assessments for special purposes, and such other business as shall relat only to the general routine of the corporation, and shall not dispose in any way of any part of the said common lands.

SEC. 18. Each board of trustees elected under the provisions of this act shall, at the first meeting held after such election, select one of its members to be president of said board, and another of its members to be secretary and treasurer thereof, and shall adopt rules for the government of such corporation and the use of the common lands of such corporation and the common waters thereon; and such rules so adopted shall be uniform as to all the inhabitants thereon. The secretary shall reduce to writing, in a book to be kept for that purpose, minutes of the business transacted at each special meeting of the board.

SEC. 19. No sale, mortgage, lease, or other disposition of the common property of any corporation created under the provisions of this act, shall take effect or become operative until the regular meeting of the board of trustees held next after the meeting at which the resolution authorizing the sale is passed as provided by section 16 of this act, at which time, if such resolution is not objected to in writing, as provided in the next succeeding section of this act, it shall be the duty of the president and secretary of such board of trustees, in the name of and under the seal of such corporation, to execute all necessary documents to carry the same into effect; and such documents when so executed shall operate to bind all persons interested in such common property to the same extent as if each of such persons had separately signed, sealed and executed the same.

SEC. 20. Every person interested in the common lands of such corporation who shall be dissatisfied with any sale, mortgage, lease or other disposition of any such common property so made by any such board of trustees held next after the meeting at which any resolution for any such sale, mortgage, lease or other disposition shall have been passed, file with such board of trustees a protest in writing against the carrying out of such resolution, and if a majority of the parties in interest shall so file a written protest against such action within the time aforesaid, such resolution shall be rescinded by such board of trustees and become void and of no effect.

sec. 21. On the first Saturday in December next after rendition of any decree as provided for in this act, and every three years thereafter, there shall be chosen by ballot, by the owners and proprietors of such common lands, a board of trustees, having the qualifications and possessing the powers provided for in this act.

sec. 22. The election provided for in section 21 of this act shall be held by three persons having all the qualifications prescribed by section 6 of this act for the persons appointed to hold the first election provided for in this act. Such persons shall be appointed by the justice of the peace of the precinct in which such land grant or real estate is situate; if such land grant or real estate shall be situate in more than one precinct, then such persons shall be appointed by the justices of the peace of the several precincts in which such land grant or real estate is situate: *Provided, however,* That if such justices of the peace can not agree upon the persons to be appointed, such justices of the peace, or a majority of them if there be more than two, shall hold such election and certify the results thereof.

sec. 23. The nine persons receiving the highest number of legal votes cast at any such election for trustees shall be declared elected, and shall receive from the persons holding such election, a certificate of election which shall authorize them respectively to discharge the duties of such board of trustees for the term of three years and until the election and qualification of their successors.

sec. 24. If a vacancy shall occur in any such board of trustees, the qualified members thereof remaining shall fill such vacancy by appointment to be made at the regular meeting of such board, and the persons or persons so appointed shall hold their office until the next general election for members of such board and until the election and qualification of a successor or successors.

sec. 25. All officers of any corporation created under this act shall serve without pay or emolument of any kind, and no officer during his term of office shall make any contract with or be interested in any contract made with such corporation.

sec. 26. The board of trustees of any corporation created under this act shall have no power or control over the lands within the exterior boundaries of any such grant which are held or claimed in private ownership, except hereinafter provided.

SEC. 27. If any person or persons shall hold in possession or claim in private ownership within the exterior boundaries of any such land grant or real estate, any tract, piece or parcel, or any tracts, pieces or parcels of land, when in the opinion of any such board of trustees such person or persons had no right to hold the same, such board of trustees may institute in the name of the corporation an action of ejectment against such person or persons, and if upon the trial of any such action, it shall appear that the possession or claim of any such person or persons is without right, judgment shall be entered in favor of such corporation for the possession of such tract, piece or parcel of land, and for such damages as may be proven to have been sustained by such corporation by the wrongful detention thereof..

SEC. 28. The several courts of this Territory exercising chancery jurisdiction shall, under the practice of courts of chancery, entertain bills of complaint, filed by any such board of trustees to prevent trespassers upon the common lands and common waters of any such corporation, if it shall appear that the complainants are without a plain, speedy and adequate remedy at law, or that the persons committing such trespasses are insolvent or unable to respond in damages to such corporation for the injury alleged.

SEC. 29. Any person or persons who have not an unquestioned paper title holding or claiming in private ownership any tract or tracts, piece or pieces, parcel or parcels of land within the exterior boundaries of any such land grant or real estate may, within two years after the election of the first board of trustees of any corporation created under the provisions of this act, file with such board of trustees a petition in writing, setting forth a description of such land according to an actual survey thereof, and the nature and source of his title, and praying that such land may be conveyed and confirmed to him by such board of trustees, and thereupon it shall be the duty of such board of trustees to examine such petition, and the evidence offered in support thereof, and if the claim or claims of such person or persons shall, in the opinion of the majority of such board of trustees be sustained by the evidence, such board of trustees shall immediately convey to such person or persons and his or their heirs and assigns the land described in such petition, or so much thereof as is shown by the evidence to belong to such person or persons: *Provided, however,* That if such board of trustees shall fail or refuse for any reason to make such conveyance, such person or persons shall have the right to file in the district court of the proper county a bill of complaint in chancery against such corporation, praying that such person and his heirs and assigns the property so claimed and held in private ownership, and if upon the hearing of such cause it shall appear that such person or his grantors is entitled, under the law, usage or custom of Spain, Mexico, the Territory of New Mexico or the United States, to such land, a decree shall be entered in such cause requiring such board of trustees to convey and confirm the same to such person, his heirs and assigns.

SEC. 30. Any conveyance made in pursuance of the provisions of this act shall operate to conclude [include] all persons claiming the lands described therein by, through or under the original title upon which the owners or proprietors of any such land grant or real estate base their claim thereto.

SEC. 31. The moneys arising from the sale, lease or other disposition of the common land of any such corporation, after defraying the expenses of such corporation, may be by the board of trustees of any such corporation applied to the support and maintenance of free, non-sectarian public schools within the limits of any such land grant or real estate.

SEC. 32. Nothing contained in this act shall be construed as in any manner affecting any sale, mortgage conveyance lease or other disposition of any common lands heretofore made by any person or persons claiming or pretending to act on behalf of any owners or proprietors of any common lands within the Territory, but all such sales, mortgages, leases and other disposition of any such common lands shall be construed and acted upon as if this act had never been passed: *Provided, however,* That any body of persons heretofore claiming to exercise corporate powers in the disposition of common lands of the character described in this act may perfect their organization under the terms and provisions of this act, and after the entry of a decree by the district court creating such corporation, all acts done in good faith by such persons under pretense of such corporate authority before the passage of this act, shall thereby be and become valid and binding upon such corporation in all respects, as if the same had been done and performed in strict accordance with this act.

SEC. 33. The clerk of the district court shall receive, for all services required to be performed by him under the provisions of the first twelve sections of this act, the actual cost of the printing, stationery and postage necessary to be expended by him under the provisions of said sections, and the further sum of ten dollars, and no more, all of which shall be paid at the time of filing such petition by the petitioners; for all services rendered in any action or proceeding by the clerk of the district court under the provisions of sections 27, 28 and 29 of this act, such clerk shall be entitled to demand and receive five dollars, and not more, to be paid at the time of the institution of such action or proceedings by the party instituting the same.

SEC. 34. That whenever the words, "owners" and "proprietors," or equivalent expressions occur in the foregoing act, they shall in all cases be construed to mean the members of the colony community or town to which said grant was originally made, or their successors, including all persons residing within the exterior boundaries of such grant, and who shall have been in occupation and adverse possession of any part or portion of said grant for a period of not less than two years prior to the passage of this act, and all persons who shall have improved any portion [of] said grant and paid taxes on the same for two years prior to the passage of this act.

SEC. 35. That in all cases when the judge of the district court shall by his decree create a body politic and corporate under the provisions of this act, such action shall be final and conclusive and shall operate to vest in the said corporation and body politic the legal and equitable title to all the land within the exterior boundaries of such grant to which such town or colony community is entitled at the time of the passage of this act, and such corporation shall have full power and authority to obtain and hold all evidences of title to such lands, and manage and dispose of any and all of such lands in accordance with the foregoing provisions of this act.

SEC. 36. This act shall not be held or construed to affect any grant of land is not strictly a colony community grant or a grant to a town or municipal corporation, and when there shall arise the question as to whether the grant which it may be claimed comes under the provisions, does so or not, such questions shall be decided by the district court, subject to review in the Supreme Court in an appropriate proceeding, and no proceedings under the provisions of this will be held or construed to affect any grant or land or part or portion thereof where the same was made to an individual right, or where the same has been confirmed or patent issued for the same to any individual or individuals or his or their heirs or assigns or any or all of them.

SEC. 37. Where the words, "common property" or "common lands," are used or mentioned in this act, or where property or land is herein referred to as held or owned in common, or words of the same import are used in this act, they shall be construed and held to be, mean and intend only such lands as have been granted heretofore to a colony, community or town, and which under the terms of this act shall be vested in a corporation hereby authorized to be formed; but when any real property may be held authorized to be formed; but when any real property may be held or claimed to be held by any individual or individuals in trust, expressed or implied, for the use or benefit of any colony community or town, and which under the terms of this act shall be vested in a corporation hereby authorized to be formed; but when any real property may be held or claimed to be held by any individual or individuals in trust, expressed or implied, for the use or benefit of any colony community or town, such fact shall not prevent the organization of a corporation under this act, but such corporation may be formed and organized on such facts being made to appear to the district judge or district court, and such corporation shall then be authorized to commence proceedings in the district court to have such trust declared, and divested, and such property or land decreed to be held by the corporation, free and discharged from such trust, and the court shall be authorized to enter such decree if justified by the law and facts of the case.

SEC. 38. This act shall apply to all grants of land, except those grants which were made to the petitioners for the same for the exclusive use of such petitioners, their heirs and assigns.

SEC. 39. This act shall take effect and be in force from and after its passage.

CHAPTER LXXXVII.

AN ACT TO AMEND SECTION 38 OF AN ACT OF THE 29TH LEGISLATIVE ASSEMBLY OF THE TERRITORY OF NEW MEXICO, ENTITLED "AN ACT RELATING TO COMMUNITY LAND GRANTS, AND FOR OTHER PURPOSES." II. B. 200;

Approved February 26, 1891.

CONTENTS.

SECTION 1. Incorporation shall extend only to grants made to a pueblo or colony for public use.

Be it enacted by the Legislative Assembly
of the Territory of New Mexico:

SECTION 1. That section 38 of an act of the 29th Legislative Assembly of the Territory of New Mexico, entitled "An Act relating to community land grants, and for other purposes," be and the same is hereby repealed, and the following is hereby substituted therefor:

"SECTION 38. This act shall not operate to divest any private rights or affect any private titles, but shall extend only to land grants made to a pueblo or colony or for the public use of a community."

SEC. 2. All acts and parts OF acts in conflict herewith are hereby repealed, and this act shall be in force and take effect from and after its passage.

Notes

Abbreviations

AGI	Archivo General de Indias, Sevilla
AGN	Archivo General de la Nación, Mexico City
BNM	Biblioteca Nacional de Madrid
CPLC	Court of Private Land Claims
MANM	Mexican Archives of New Mexico
SANM	Spanish Archives of New Mexico, New Mexico State Records Center and Archives, Santa Fe
SG	Records of the Surveyor General
SMLL	Spanish and Mexican Land Laws: New Spain and Mexico. St. Louis, Mo.: Buxton and Skinner Stationery, 1895.

Preface

1. The Records of the Surveyor General and the files of the Court of Private Land Claims are microfilmed and may be found in the Center for Southwest Research at the Zimmerman Library of the University of New Mexico, Albuquerque, or in the State of New Mexico Records Center and Archives, Santa Fe. For a complete review of land grants in New Mexico, see U.S. General Accounting Office (GAO), *Treaty of Guadalpe Hidalgo: Findings and Possible Options Regarding Longstanding Community Land Grant Claims in New Mexico* (June 2004). See also a Spanish-language version translated by Joseph P. Sánchez, Jerry Gurulé, and Mario Milliones, *El Tratado de Guadalupe Hidalgo: Hallazgos y opciones posibles con respecto a los reclamos de larga duración de mercedes de tierras comunitarias en Nuevo México.*

Introduction

1. Río Puerco land grant conceded to the settlers of Atrisco, signed by Governor Pedro Fermín de Mendinueta, 1768, Villa de Santa Fe, Records of the Surveyor General (hereinafter SG) 145, no. 1042. Translated by Joseph P. Sánchez.

2. Ibid.

3. Ralph Emerson Twitchell, ed., The Spanish Archives of New Mexico (Cedar Rapids: Torch Press, 1914), 1:141–42.

4. Joseph P. Sánchez, Explorers, Traders, and Slavers: Forging the Old Spanish Trail, 1678–1859 (Salt Lake City: University of Utah Press, 1997), 107–108.

5. Ibid., 114–15.

6. Adrian Bustamante and Marc Simmons, trans. and eds., The Exposition on the Province of New Mexico by Don Pedro Baptista Pino (Santa Fe: Rancho de las

Golondrinas, and Albuquerque, University of New Mexico Press, 1995), 11.

7. See William H. Dusenberry, The Mexican Mesta: The Administration of Ranching in Colonial Mexico (Urbana: University of Illinois Press, 1963).

Chapter 1

1. Frances Karttunen, An Analytical Dictionary of Nahuatl (Norman: University of Oklahoma Press, 1983), 15. Karttunen defines Atlixco as "(literally 'surface of a body of water') / encima del agua, o en la superficie." Also, Atlixca-tl is a person from Atlixco. Also see A-tl possessed form: "-Auh water, liquid; crown of the head / agua, orines, guerra, o la mollera de la cabeza . . . there has also been a confusion of the possessed form of A-tl 'water' with Spanish agua, and this confusion has spread to the 'crown of the head' sense" (p. 12). See also ix-tli which means "face, surface, eye / la haz o la cara, o el nudo de la caña, faz, rostro, por ext. ojo" (p. 121).

2. Peter Gerhard, A Guide to the Historical Geography of New Spain: A Revised Edition (Norman: University of Oklahoma Press, 1993), 56.

3. Gilberto Espinosa and Tibo J. Chavez, El Rio Abajo (Belen, N.Mex.: Bishop Publishing, n.d.), 12.

4. Joaquín F. Pacheco, Francisco de Cárdenas, and Luis Torres de Mendoza, eds., Colección de documentos inéditos relativos al descubrimiento, conquista y organización de las antiguas posesiones españolas de América y Oceanía (Madrid: M. B. de Quirós 1864–65), 3:511–13. See also George P. Hammond and Agapito Rey, trans., Narratives of the Coronado Expedition, 1540–1542 (Albuquerque: University of New Mexico Press, 1940), 182–84. The history of the Coronado expedition is recounted in Herbert E. Bolton, Coronado: Knight of Pueblos and Plains (Albuquerque: University of New Mexico Press, 1949). See also Joseph P. Sánchez, The Río Abajo Frontier, 1540–1692: A History of Early Colonial New Mexico (Albuquerque: Albuquerque Museum, 1987), 1.

5. Hernán Gallegos, Relación, Archivo General de Indias (hereinafter AGI), Sección Patronato 22; George P. Hammond and Agapito Rey, eds. and trans., The Rediscovery of New Mexico, 1580–1594 (Albuquerque: University of New Mexico Press, 1966), 83.

6. Joseph P. Sánchez, Río Abajo, 31.

7. Hammond and Rey, Rediscovery of New Mexico, 84.

8. Ibid., 177.

9. Sánchez, Río Abajo, 37.

10. Primera Audiencia de Don Bernardo López de Mendizábal, Año de 1663, Archivo General de la Nación (hereinafter AGN) Inquisición 594, capítulo 172.

11. Ibid.

12. Ibid.

13. Testimony by Diego Peñalosa, Hearing of December 11, 1665, in Charles Wilson Hackett, ed., Historical Documents Relating to New Mexico, Nueva Vizcaya, and Approaches Thereto, to 1773 (Washington, D.C.: Carnegie Institution of Washington, 1937), 3:265. Brackets in original.

14. Richard E. Greenleaf, "Atrisco and Las Ciruelas," New Mexico Historical Review 42 (January 1967): 5.

15. Joseph P. Sánchez, "Twelve Days in August: The Pueblo Revolt in Santa Fe," in David Grant Noble, ed., Santa Fe: History of an Ancient City (Santa Fe, N.Mex.: School of American Research, 1989), 19–52.

16. Juan Domínguez de Mendoza, along with his brother Thomé, Francisco Gómez Robledo, and Diego de Trujillo, were among the officers under Otermín who directed the abandonment of Santa Fe on August 21, 1680, during the first days of the Pueblo Revolt (Stanley M. Hordes, To the End of the Earth: A History of the Crypto-Jews of New Mexico [New York: Columbia University Press, 2005], 180). Hordes establishes the existence of Crypto-Jews among the early Spanish settlers in New Mexico.

17. Statement signed by Juan de Echeverria, Joseph de Ugartte, etc., December 13, 1680, AGN Provincias Internas 34.

18. Ibid. Translated by Joseph P. Sánchez.

19. Juan Domínguez de Mendoza was a native of Mexico City. In spring 1680 he gave his age as 46, but in 1681 he claimed to be 52 years old (Fray Angélico Chávez, Origins of New Mexico Families in the Spanish Colonial Period [Santa Fe, N.M.: William Gannon, 1975], 25). He married Isabel, the daughter of Pedro Durán y Chaves (Chávez, Origins of New Mexico Families, 19). During the administration of Governor Bernardo López de Mendizábal (1659–62), he was placed in charge of defense of the Río Abajo (Testimony of Nicolás de Freitas, January 24, 1661, and Letter of García de San Francisco, January 22, 1661, in Hackett, Historical Documents, 3:156–62). In 1667, following a revolt against Spaniards by Manso Indians, Domínguez de Mendoza was sent to the El Paso area to pacify Apaches led by Chiquito and El Chilmo, which he accomplished (Letter of Governor Fernando de Villanueva, February 10, 1667, Biblioteca Nacional de Madrid [hereinafter BNM], Ms. 19258). In late 1669, Domínguez de Mendoza led campaigns to retaliate against Apaches from Siete Ríos who had raided the Tompiros of the pueblo at Las Humanas (Report of Juan de Miranda, July 27, 1671, BNM, Ms. 19258). See also Declaration of Pedro de Leiva, October 20, 1681, in Hackett, ed., Revolt of the Pueblo Indians of New Mexico, and Otermín's Attempted Reconquest, 1680–1682, trans. Charmion Clair Shelby, 2 vols. (Albuquerque: University of New Mexico Press, 1942), 2:168. By May 1670, Domínguez de Mendoza had been appointed one of the encomenderos of Las Humanas (Letter of Governor Juan de Medrano y Mesía, May 1, 1669, BNM, Ms. 19258). As encomendero, Domínguez de Mendoza was entitled to collect tribute of one manta or blanket and one fanega of corn from each household in the pueblos under his encomienda. The Apaches retaliated, attacking Las Humanas and killing eleven Tompiros and capturing thirty-one others. The church was desecrated and religious paraphernalia destroyed (Letters of Governor Juan de Medrano y Mesía dated June 5 and September 11, 1670, BNM, Ms. 19258). In December 1680, Domínguez de Mendoza was part of the reconnaissance led by Governor Antonio de Otermín in which the destruction and extent of the Pueblo Revolt of 1680 were surveyed. In 1684, Governor Domingo

Jironza Petris de Cruzate ordered Domínguez de Mendoza to lead an expedition to reconnoiter the Río de las Perlas (the present Colorado River in Texas). The expedition traveled south from El Paso to the Junta de los Ríos (confluence of the Pecos and Río Grande). From there, they traveled northwest along the Pecos to a village they called "Jediondos" near present Fort Stockton, where Apache raiders ran off most of the Spanish horses. They finally reached the confluence of the Concho and Colorado rivers, where the expedition turned around (Letter of Governor Domingo Jironza, November 29, 1683, BNM, Ms. 19258). See also "Diary of Juan Domínguez de Mendoza" in Herbert E. Bolton, Spanish Exploration in the Southwest, 1542–1706 (New York: Barnes and Noble, 1952), 320–42; "Diario del viaje que hizo a Jumanas el maestre de campo Juan Dominguez de Mendoza," AGN Historia 299; Letter of Fray Nicolás López to the Viceroy, 1686, in Hackett, Historical Documents, 3:361–62. In 1685, Domínguez de Mendoza fled El Paso after being involved in a plot to desert the refugee camp there. In March 1689, his son Baltasar received permission to leave El Paso for New Spain. He was accompanied by his mother, Isabel Durán y Chaves, and their servants. Later, Juan and his son left for Spain to seek royal favor. Their ship wrecked, but they survived. Juan Domínguez de Mendoza died shortly after in a hospital in Madrid, Spain (Chávez, Origins of New Mexico Families, 25–26). In an effort to win favor from Spanish officials, Domínguez de Mendoza or one of his relatives appears to have forged documents about his merits and services to the crown, casting doubt about the authenticity of his career. With some exceptions, the facts presented above are verifiable events mentioned in the allegedly forged documents.

20. Declaration of the lieutenant general of the cavalry, Place of the Río del Norte, December 20, 1681, in Hackett, Revolt of the Pueblo Indians, 2:258.

21. Sánchez, Río Abajo, 138.

22. Ibid., 141.

Chapter 2

1. Chávez, Origins of New Mexico Families, 19.

2. Fray Francisco Pérez Huerta, Relación Verdadera, AGN Inquisición 316. See also Joseph P. Sánchez, "The Peralta-Ordóñez Affair and the Founding of Santa Fe," in Noble, Santa Fe (1989), 27–38.

3. Chávez, Origins of New Mexico Families, 19.

4. Ibid., 20.

5. Ibid.

6. El Capítan Don Luis de Guzman que nuevamente aproveydo por governador de las provincias dela Nueva Mexico, AGN Hacienda, Tomo 472.

7. "Los Catorce Soldados que an de yr haziendo escolta a los Carros de su Majestad que este pressente año de 1646 se despachan alas provincias de la Nueva Mexico con el socorro hordinario delos Religiossos que asisten en ellas = Chichimecas y Nueva Mexico." Firmado por Don Phelipe Moran dela Cerda, Mexico, October 31, 1646, AGN Hacienda 472. The document, "Lista delos soldados que van ala Nueva Mexico," describes each of the soldiers as follows:

Francisco Hurtado, son of Francisco, 29 years old from Sevilla. Swarthy with a thick nose and his brows were joined. He had a scar on the middle finger of his left hand.

Don Fernando Durán y Chaves, son of Pedro. He was 31 years old from the Villa de Santa Fe. (If so, he was born in 1615. Fray Angélico Cháves, Origins of New Mexico Families, p. 20, speculates that he was born in 1617. Chávez writes: "in 1660, he gave his age as forty-three, so that, if born in 1617, he was the son of Isabel de Bohórquez." Chávez also writes that in 1644, Don Fernando claimed to be 35 years old. If so, he would have been born in 1609.) Well-built and robust with a short beard.

Don Agustín de Chaves, 20 years old, son of Pedro. He, too, was from Santa Fe, tall, swarthy, with a mole on his face. (Chávez, Origins of New Mexico Families, 20, writes that Don Fernando "and his son, Don Agustín de Chaves, were in the soldier-escort that brought a new governor, Don Luis de Guzmán, from Mexico City to Santa Fe." However, Agustín is listed as "son of Pedro" in the escolta list. If so, that would make him Fernando's brother or nephew.)

Pedro de Montoya, son of Tomas. He was from Villa de Madrid, 40 years old. He was of medium build with a short nose, black beard and hair. He had a scar over his left brow.

Lorenzo de Solís, son of Don Francisco de Solís. He was 20 years old from Mexico. Tall, swarthy with black beard and hair. He bore a scar on the palm of his right hand.

Agustín de Ynojosa, son of Fernando. He was 33 years old from Santa Fe, well-built, swarthy with black hair and beard.

Lucas de Cubía Pacheco, son of Juan. He was 35 years old from Durango in Mexico. Medium build, short beard. No wounds.

Francisco de Aragón, son of Francisco. He was 32 years old, from Mexico, tall and slim with a wide forehead and a scar on his forehead.

Andrés López de Gracia, son of Bentura. He was 30 years old from the Ciudad de los Angeles (Puebla), tall, slim, swarthy. He had a scar on the left side of his forehead near the hairline.

Pedro de Bentura de Gracia, son of Andrés Jurado. He was 22 years old, from Puebla de los Angeles. He was tall and thin, with a scar on his forehead.

Francisco Domínguez, son of Captain Tomas Domínguez. He was 26 years old, from Puebla de los Angeles. He was tall, swarthy, with a small wound on his forehead.

Andrés de Loaysa, son of Andrés. Medium build. He was from Puebla de los Angeles, swarthy, black hair, facial pock scars from smallpox.

Manuel Suárez, son of Manuel. He was 26 years old from San Luis de la Paz, well-built, swarthy, thick, black hair, large eyes, pointed nose, no scars visible.

Captain Francisco López Palomino, son of Blas. He was 34 years old from the Villa de Culiacan in Nueva Galicia. He was tall with a short beard and had a small scar in the middle of his forehead.

8. Autos delos Oficiales Reales, AGN Hacienda 472.

9. Chávez, Origins of New Mexico Families, 20–21.

10. Chávez, "Don Fernando Durán y Chávez," El Palacio 55 (April 1948), 114.

11. Ibid.

12. Certified Copy, Court of Private Land Claims (hereinafter CPLC), Case 45, 730, p. 1. Durán y Chaves establishes his right to petition the governor for a grant by offering the proper justification:

> To the Governor and Captain General—Fernando Duran y Chaves resident of these Provinces of New Mexico asking that all the privileges allowed by law be given him, appears before Your Excellency and says: That in the year ninety-two General Don Diego de Vargas entered this Kingdom, and on that occasion I came at my own expense and mention with my arms and horses to do this duty and without expense to the King of a single real and it was a long campaign with many hardships and much more so to one who came at his own expense as I did, and after having traveled over the whole Kingdom and baptized more than two thousand babies and as we were leaving the estate called Mejia, I presented a petition praying a new grant to the two tracts claiming a right to the said tract because of its having belonged to my father, to which the said general replied to me on that occasion that no one could claim a right to anything that it was a new conquest which the King made at this expense and that I might petition as a conqueror, and Father Cristoval Barrosa and Francisco Miguel Munis being present he made me the grant in the name of the King.

13. Certified Copy, CPLC, Case 45, 733, p. 1. Mejia is believed to be the present Barelas, an area southwest of downtown Albuquerque.

14. Certified Copy, CPLC, Case 45, 727, p. 1.

15. Chávez, Origins of New Mexico Families, 87.

16. Certified Copy, CPLC, Case 45, 727, p. 1. See also CPLC, Case 45, 733, p. 1.

17. Certified Copy, CPLC, Case 45, 734, p. 2.

18. Certified Copy, CPLC, Case 45, 729, p. 3.

19. Chávez, Origins of New Mexico Families, 20–21.

20. Chávez, "Don Fernando," 114.

21. Certified Copy, CPLC, Case 45, 730, pp. 1–2.

22. Hackett, Historical Documents 3:351.

23. Chávez, "Don Fernando," 115.

24. Ibid., 118.

25. Certified Copy, Case 45, 735, p. 4.

26. Decree of October 19, 1701, signed in Santa Fe by Governor Pedro Rodríguez Cubero and witnessed by Pedro Morales, Civil and Military Secretary, CPLC, Case 45, 735. Governor Rodríguez Cubero's use of the words "pocesion real" indicates that Don Fernando was given possession of the land by authority vested in the sovereign with all attendant titles and privileges of ownership.

27. "Noticias que da Juan Candelaria vecino de esta villa de San Francisco Xavier de Albuquerque de edad de 84 años; nació el año de 1692," New Mexico Historical Review 4 (1929): 278–79.

28. Chávez, Origins of New Mexico Families, 155–56.

29. Twitchell, Spanish Archives, 1:141–42.

Chapter 3

1. Petition of Santa Fe residents to the cabildo, November 5, 1704, Spanish Archives of New Mexico (hereinafter SANM), New Mexico State Archives and Record Center, Santa Fe.

2. Ovidio Casado-Fuente, Don Francisco Cuerbo y Valdés, Gobernador de Nuevo México, fundador de la Ciudad de Alburquerque (Oviedo, Spain: Principado de Asturias, Instituto de Estudios Asturianos, 1983), 34.

3. Governor Cuervo y Valdés, Santa Fe, August 25, 1705, SANM I.

4. Muestra General, signed by Cuerbo y Valdés, SANM II, no. 110.

5. Chávez, Origins of New Mexico Families, 236.

6. Ibid., 141. Chávez states that in 1699 Baca gave his age as forty.

7. Ibid., 198.

8. Ibid., 189.

9. Hackett, Historical Documents, 3:379. See also Certificación, Audiencia de Guadalajara, AGI, 116; and transcription by Casado-Fuente, Don Francisco Cuerbo y Valdés, 98.

10. Hubert Howe Bancroft, History of Arizona and New Mexico, 1530–1888 (San Francisco: History Company, 1889), 17:228.

11. Casado-Fuente, Don Francisco Cuerbo y Valdés, 103.

12. Ibid., 99.

13. Ibid., 98.

14. Chávez, "Don Fernando," 118–19.

15. Ibid., 119.

16. Greenleaf, "Atrisco and Las Ciruelas," 6.

17. Twitchell, Spanish Archives, 1:351.

18. Ibid., 1:352.

19. Ibid.

20. Ibid.

21. Hackett, Historical Documents, 3:464.

22. "Noticias que da Juan Candelaria," 274–76.

23. Chávez, Origins of New Mexico Families, 189.

24. Eric Louis Palladini. "Don Fernando's Legacy: A Microhistory of Atrisco, New Mexico, 1692–1821" (Master's thesis, Tulane University, 1990), 19.

25. Chávez, "Don Fernando," 116; Chávez, Origins of New Mexico Families, 189; Palladini, "Don Fernando's Legacy," 19.

26. Chávez, "Don Fernando," 116; Palladini, "Don Fernando's Legacy," 20.

27. Ibid.

28. Chaves, "Don Fernando," 116; Palladini, "Don Fernando's Legacy," 21.

29. Eleanor B. Adams, ed., Bishop Tamaron's Visitation of New Mexico, 1760 (Albuquerque: Historical Society of New Mexico: 1954), 43–44.

Chapter 4

1. The people of Atrisco were among the larger sheep ranchers in New Mexico in the eighteenth century. Hordes, To the End of the Earth, 197, writes that by the end of the Mexican period, "the Pereas were one of five families (along with the Armijos, Chaveses, Oteros, and Yrizarris) who controlled the sheep trade."

2. See chapter 12 for the historical arguments defining the Atrisco land grant as a community grant. See also chapter 9 for a continuation of the history of Atrisco's evolving communal character.

3. Virginia Langham Olmstead, transcriber, Spanish and Mexican Censuses of New Mexico: 1750–1830 (Albuquerque: New Mexico Genealogical Society, 1981), 133–34.

4. Sánchez, Fr. William, "Descendants of Francisco Muñoz," Legacy, January 14, 2007.

5. Compadrazgo is generally a compaternity or sponsorship sanctioned by canon law that is a spiritual affinity or a connection contracted by the parents of a child in baptism or by the bride and groom in matrimony.

6. AGN Tierras 934.

7. Conveyance of Land at Sitio de Atrisco by Leonor Montaño and her daughter María Antonia de Chaves to Antonio de Chaves, September 9, 1729, SANM I, microfilm roll 1, frames 1250–52.

8. Twitchell, Spanish Archives, 1:71, no. 178.

9. Town of Atrisco v. The United States of America and the City of Albuquerque, 1892, CPLC, Case 45, translation of Exhibit 10 offered by the Petitioner, 758. A vara is equal to 32.5 inches.

10. Conveyance of Land in the Puesto de Atrisco from Pedro Gómes de Chaves to Bernabe Baca, Villa de San Phelipe de Alburquerque, March 26, 1732, SANM I, microfilm roll 1, frames 632–33. Translated by Joseph P. Sánchez.

11. Conveyance of lands in the Puesto de Atrisco between Francisco Xavier de Miranda and Francisco Antonio Gonzales, March 25, 1735, SANM I, microfilm roll 2, frames 707–708. Translated by Joseph P. Sánchez.

12. Twitchell, Spanish Archives, 1:71.

13. Ibid., 70–71.

14. Petición de Quitería Chaves sobre el repartimiento de unas tierras a sus Hijos naturales en defecto de no tenerlos legítimos, Año de 1764, no. 871, SANM I, microfilm roll 1, frame 1386.

15. Quitería Chaves, petition to divide her estate among her natural children, Atrisco, 1764, SANM I, microfilm roll 1, frame 1381.

Chapter 5

1. William J. Parish, The Charles Ilfeld Company: A Study of the Rise and Decline of Mercantile Capitalism in New Mexico (Cambridge, Mass.: Harvard University Press, 1961), 150–51. See also John O. Baxter, Las Carneradas: Sheep Trade in New Mexico, 1700–1800 (Albuquerque: University of New Mexico Press, 1987), 28–29.

2. Statement addressed to Governor Pedro Fermín Mendinueta, signed by María Ignacia Lucero [1768], AGN Tierras 934, exp. 7, ramo 10, f. 1. This chapter follows the counts of sheep, ewes, and rams in the original documents in order to remain true to what the protagonists were saying at the moment when they were writing their statements. Perhaps the math does not work out to us, but somehow it did to them.

3. Declaración de Loreto [Lorenzo] Santillanes, May 11, 1768, Santa Fe, AGN Tierras 934, expediente 7, ramo 10, f. 2.

4. Ibid.

5. Comisión al Alcalde mayor Don Francisco Trébol Nabarro, May 11, 1768, AGN Tierras 934, expediente 7, ramo 10, f. 2v.

6. Notificación, June 4, 1768, signed by Francisco Trébol Navarro, AGN Tierras 934, exp. 7, ramo 10, f. 3.

7. Chávez, Origins of New Mexico Families, 197.

8. Ibid.

9. Statement signed by Joseph Hurtado de Mendoza, n.d., AGN Tierras 934, exp. 10, ramo 7, f. 4.

10. Ibid.

11. Ibid.

12. Ibid.

13. Ibid.

14. Ibid.

15. Auto para el reconocimiento de señales, signed by Governor Pedro Fermín de Mendinueta, June 14, 1768, Santa Fe, AGN Tierras 934, exp. 10, ramo 7, f. 4v.

16. Notificación, July 20, 1768, signed by Francisco Trébol Navarro, AGN Tierras 934, exp. 10, ramo 7, ff. 5–6.

17. Auto de citación a Loreto [Lorenzo] Santillanes, July 20, 1768, AGN Tierras 934, exp. 10, ramo 7, f. 6.

18. Declaración de Loreto [Lorenzo] Santillan[es], July 20, 1768, Puesto de San Isidro de Pajarito, AGN Tierras 934, exp. 10, ramo 7, f. 6.

19. Ibid.

20. Ibid.

21. Declaración de Antonio Alberto Aragón, July 20, 1768, AGN Tierras 934, exp. 10, ramo 7, f. 7.

22. Declaración de Bernardo Mirabal, May 19, 1769, Puesto de San Isidro de Pajarito, AGN Tierras 934, exp. 10, ramo 7, f. 6r.

23. Declaración de Ignacio Jaramillo, May 23, 1769, AGN Tierras 934, exp. 10,

ramo 7, ff. 8v–9r.

24. Auto de Remisión al Señor Governador, signed by Francisco Trébol Navarro, June 3, 1769, Puesto de San Isidro de Pajarito, AGN Tierras 934, exp. 10, ramo 7, f. 9.

25. Ibid., ff. 9r–9v.

26. Auto de Traslado, signed by Governor Pedro Fermín de Mendinueta, June 15, 1769, Santa Fe, AGN Tierras 934, exp. 10, ramo 7, f. 9v.

27. Traslado a Doña María Lucero, signed by Francisco Trébol Navarro, June 19, 1769, Puesto de San Isidro de Pajarito, AGN Tierras 934, exp. 10, ramo 7, f. 10.

28. Respuesta, signed by Manuel Sanz Garbizu, n.d., AGN Tierras 934, exp. 10, ramo 7, ff. 11–13.

29. Traslado dado a Don Joseph Hurtado de Mendoza, signed by Francisco Trébol Navarro, July 1, 1769, San Isidro de Pajarito, AGN Tierras 934, exp. 10, ramo 7, f. 13.

30. Respuesta de Joseph Hurtado de Mendoza, n.d., AGN Tierras 934, exp. 10, ramo 7, f. 12v.

31. Ibid., f. 13.

32. Declaración firmado por Diego Antonio Durán y Chaves, Pedro de Chaves, Juan Antonio Durán y Chaves, a ruego de Ignacio Chaves, and Bernardina Lena Durán y Chaves, June 9, 1768, Puesto de Atrisco, AGN Tierras 934, exp. 10, ramo 7, f. 14.

33. Auto de Remisión al Señor Gobernador, signed by Francisco Trébol Navarro, July 5, 1769, San Isidro de Pajarito, AGN Tierras 934, exp. 10, ramo 7, f. 15.

34. Sentencia Definitiva, signed by Governor Pedro Fermín de Mendinueta, July 11, 1767, Villa de Santa Fe, AGN Tierras 934, exp. 10, ramo 7, ff. 15r–16v.

35. Ibid., f. 15r.

36. Ibid.

37. Ibid.

38. Ibid., f. 16r. Translated by Joseph P. Sánchez.

39. Ibid.

40. Ibid., f. 16v.

41. Auto de citación de las partes, signed by Francisco Trébol Navarro, July 14, 1769, Puesto de San Isidro de Pajarito, AGN Tierras 934, exp. 10, ramo 7, f. 17r.

42. Notificacion de la Sentencia, signed by Francisco Trébol Navarro, July 14, 1769, Puesto de San Isidro de Pajarito, AGN Tierras 934, exp. 10, ramo 7, f. 17r.

43. Segunda notificación a Doña Efigenia Chaves, signed by Francisco Trébol Navarro, July 14, 1769, AGN Tierras 934, exp. 10, ramo 7, f. 17v.

44. Tercera notificación a Doña Efigenia Chaves, signed by Francisco Trébol Navarro, July 20, 1769, Puesto de San Isidro de Pajarito, AGN Tierras 934, exp. 10, ramo 7, f. 18.

45. Entrega del Ganado, signed by Francisco Trébol Navarro, July 23, 1769, Puesto de San Isidro de Pajarito, AGN Tierras 934, exp. 10, ramo 7, f. 18r.

46. Respuesta signed by Joseph Hurtado de Mendoza, July 17, 1769, Villa de Santa Fe, AGN Tierras 934, exp. 10, ramo 7, f. 19.

47. Statement signed by Francisco Trébol Navarro, July 28, 1769, Puesto de San Isidro de Pajarito, AGN Tierras 934, exp. 10, ramo 7, f. 21.

48. Statement by Francisco Trébol Navarro, August 3, 1769, Puesto de San Isidro de Pajarito, AGN Tierras 934, exp. 10, ramo 7, f. 20v.

49. Auto de remisión, signed by Francisco Trébol Navarro, September 4, 1769, Puesto de San Isidro de Pajarito, AGN Tierras 934, exp. 10, ramo 7, ff. 21–22.

Chapter 6

1. Greenleaf, "Atrisco and Las Ciruelas," 8.

2. Chávez, Origins of New Mexico Families, 163.

3. Greenleaf, "Atrisco and Las Ciruelas," 8.

4. Autos seguidos entre Yfigenia Duran y Chabes y Andres Antonio Romero en nombre de su madre sobre un pedazo de tierra en Atrisco, 1769, AGN Tierras 934. Translated by Joseph P. Sánchez.

5. AGN Tierras 934, exp. 7, ramo 2; Greenleaf, "Atrisco and Las Ciruelas," 8.

6. Autos seguidos entre Yfigenia Duran y Chabes, Atrisco, 1769, AGN Tierras 934, f. 96. See also Greenleaf, "Atrisco and Las Ciruelas," 8.

7. Autos seguidos entre Yfigenia Duran y Chabes, Atrisco, 1769, AGN Tierras 934. Translated by Joseph P. Sánchez.

8. Ibid., f. 26. Translated by Joseph P. Sánchez.

9. Ibid. Translated by Joseph P. Sánchez.

10. Ibid. Translated by Joseph P. Sánchez.

11. Greenleaf, "Atrisco and Las Ciruelas," 9.

12. Autos seguidos entre Yfigenia Duran y Chabes, Atrisco, 1769, AGN Tierras 934, f. 35v. Translated by Joseph P. Sánchez.

13. Citaciones y Vista de Ojos, Puesto de Atrisco, April 13, 1769, signed by Francisco Trebol Nabarro, Pedro Duran y Chabes, Santiago Duran y Chaves, surrogate signer for Bernardo Chaves, Joseph de Chaves, witnessed by Antonio Baca, in Autos seguidos entre Yfigenia Duran y Chabes, Atrisco, 1769, AGN Tierras 934. Translated by Joseph P. Sánchez.

14. Nota: Estando poniendo el auto que antesede dijo la dicha Doña Ana Chabes a Don Pedro Duran y Chabes, alias, Gomes, que el era firmado por testigo, en Autos seguidos entre Yfigenia Duran y Chabes, Atrisco, 1769, AGN Tierras 934, f. 99.

15. Statement of Alfonso Rael de Aguilar, 1722. Translated by Joseph P. Sánchez.

16. AGN Tierras 934. Translated by Joseph P. Sánchez.

17. Autos seguidos entre Yfigenia Duran y Chabes, Atrisco, 1769, AGN Tierras 934, f. 99.

18. Letter to Excelentíssimo Governador y Capitán General signed by Joseph Hurtado Mendoza, April 19, 1769, Villa de Santa Fe, in Autos seguidos entre Yfigenia Duran y Chabes, Atrisco, 1769, AGN Tierras 934.

19. Villa de Santa Fe, April 19, 1769, signed by Pedro Fermín de Mendinueta, AGN Tierras 934.

20. Auto de Comisión, April 29, 1769, Santa Fe, AGN Tierras 934, f. 102. See also Notificación, En San Ysidro de Pajarito en cinco dias del mes de mayo de 1769, signed by Francisco Trébol Navarro, AGN Tierras 934.

21. Statement by Andrés Antonio Romero, n.d., AGN Tierras 934.

22. Ibid. Translated by Joseph P. Sánchez.

23. The statement was already admitted as a factor to consider before alcalde mayor Trébol Navarro; see Citaciones y Vista de Ojos, Puesto de Atrisco, April 3, 1769, AGN Tierras 934.

24. Statement by Andrés Antonio Romero, n.d., AGN Tierras 934.

25. Ibid. Translated by Joseph P. Sánchez.

26. Ibid. Translated by Joseph P. Sánchez.

27. Nota: Estando poniendo el auto que antesede dijo la dicha Doña Ana Chabes a Don Pedro Duran y Chabes, alias, Gomes, que el era firmado por testigo, en Autos seguidos entre Yfigenia Duran y Chabes, Atrisco, 1769, AGN Tierras 934, f. 99.

28. Yntterrogatorio de Preguntas, AGN Tierras 934, f. 107. Translated by Joseph P. Sánchez.

29. Ynterrogatorio de Preguntas, AGN Tierras 934, f. 107. Translated by Joseph P. Sánchez.

30. Declaracion de Don Joseph Chaves, May 9, 1769, Puesto de San Isidro de Pajarito, AGN Tierras 934.

31. Ibid.

32. Ibid.

33. Ibid.

34. Ibid.

35. Declaración de Bernardo de Chaves, May 13, 1769, Puesto de San Isidro de Pajarito, AGN Tierras 934.

36. Declaración firmada por Doña Antonia Baca, n.d., AGN Tierras 934, f. 111.

37. Declaración de Pedro Gomes, May 18, 1767, Tome, Primera Pregunta, AGN Tierras 934, f. 111.

38. Ibid., Segunda Pregunta, AGN Tierras 934, f. 112.

39. Ibid., Sexta Pregunta, AGN Tierras 934, f. 112v.

40. Ibid., Octava Pregunta, AGN Tierras 934, f. 112v.

41. Ibid., Novena Pregunta, AGN Tierras 934, f. 113.

42. Declaración de Antonio Chaves, May 29, 1767, Puesto de San Isidro de Pajarito, AGN Tierras 934, ff. 113v–114v.

43. Statement by Joseph Hurtado de Mendoza, n.d., AGN Tierras 934, f. 115.

44. Auto signed by Francisco Trébol Navarro, May 29, 1767, Puesto de San Isidro de Pajarito, AGN Tierras 934, ff. 115v–116.

Chapter 7

1. Respuesta de Andrés Antonio Romero, AGN Tierras 934, f. 25.
2. Ibid.
3. Ibid.
4. Ibid. By calling him a "genízaro," Andrés means Antonio is a half-blood who has been raised as a Spaniard.
5. Ibid.
6. Ibid., f. 25.
7. Statement signed by Isidro Sánchez Vañares Tagle, June 6, 1769, Santa Fe, AGN Tierras 934, f. 26.
8. Ibid.
9. Diligencia signed by Francisco Trébol Navarro, June 8, 1769, Puesto de San Isidro de Pajarito, AGN Tierras 934, f. 27.
10. Ibid., ff. 27–27v.
11. Declaración de Don Diego Antonio Chaves, June 8, 1769, Puesto de San Isidro de Pajarito, AGN Tierras 934, ff. 27v–28.
12. Ibid.
13. Declaración de Ignacio Chaves, June 8, 1769, Puesto de San Isidro de Pajarito, AGN Tierras 934, ff. 28v–29.
14. Response by Joseph Hurtado de Mendoza, n.d., AGN Tierras 934, ff. 30r–30v.
15. Ibid.
16. Auto signed by Trébol Navarro, June 12, 1767, Puesto de San Isidro de Pajarito, AGN Tierras 934.
17. Declaraciones de Don Diego Antonio Chaves and Don Joseph Chaves, June 12, 1767, Puesto de San Isidro, AGN Tierras 934, ff. 31r–31v.
18. Ibid.
19. Ibid.
20. Declaración de Ignacio Chaves, June 12, 1769, Puesto de San Isidro de Pajarito, AGN Tierras 934, f. 34.
21. Notation signed by Francisco Trébol Navarro, June 12, 1769, AGN Tierras 934, f. 33v.
22. Declaración de Juan Candelaria, June 14, 1769, Villa de Alburquerque, AGN Tierras 934, ff. 34r–35v.
23. Traslado a Andrés Romero, June 16, 1769, Puesto de San Isidro de Pajarito, AGN Tierras 934, f. 35r.
24. Response by Andrés Romero to Don Francisco Trébol Navarro, n.d., AGN Tierras 934, ff. 37r–38v.
25. Pedro Fermín de Mendinueta, July 5, 1769, Santa Fe, AGN Tierras 934, f. 39.
26. Obedecimiento, July 5, 1767, signed by Francisco Trébol Navarro, AGN Tierras 934, f. 39v.

27. Joseph Hurtado de Mendoza to Señor Alcalde Mayor y Capitán a Guerra, n.d., AGN Tierras 934, f. 41.

28. Sentencia definitiva, signed by Governor Pedro Fermín de Mendinueta, August 11, 1769, Santa Fe, AGN Tierras 934, ff. 42r–43v.

29. Ibid., f. 42v.

30. Notificación de la Sentencia, August 22, 1769, Puesto de Atrisco, signed by Francisco Trébol Navarro, AGN Tierras 934, ff. 44–45.

31. Attached note signed by Governor Mendinueta, n.d., AGN Tierras 934, f. 45.

Chapter 8

1. Petition by Joseph Hurtado de Mendoza et al. to Governor Pedro Fermín de Mendinueta, 1768, SG 145, no. 1037. Translated by Joseph P. Sánchez.

2. Ibid.

3. Twitchell, Spanish Archives, 1:91.

4. Ibid., 1:141–42.

5. Statement by Agustín Gallegos, teniente, 1759, Población de Nuestra Señora de la Luz de San Fernando y San Blas, SANM I, microfilm roll 1, frame 810.

6. Statement by Governor Francisco Antonio Marín del Valle, February 21, 1759, Villa de Santa Fe, SANM I, microfilm roll 1, frame 811.

7. Ibid.

8. Statement by Miguel Tenorio, August 11, 1764 (copied from the original during the administration of Governor Pedro Fermín de Mendinueta), SANM I, microfilm roll 1, frame 812.

9. Statement signed by Juan Bautista Montaño, Bernardo de Mirabal, Antonio Durán, Joseph Mariano Barela, Tomás Gurulé, Joseph de Jesús Montaño, Juan Antonio Grole [Gurulé], Y[g]nacio Jaramillo, Antonio Mariano Gallegos, a ruego Agustín Gallegos, a ruego Martín Gallegos, a ruego Antonio Candelaria, a ruego Antonio Montaño, a ruego Juan Candelaria, y a ruego Marcos Baca, SANM I, microfilm roll 1, frame 814.

10. Ibid.

11. Decision of Governor Tomás Vélez Cachupín, July 17, 1766, Villa de Santa Fe, SANM I, microfilm roll 2, frame 816.

12. Ibid.

13. Ibid.

14. Petition by Joseph Hurtado de Mendoza et al. to Governor Pedro Fermín de Mendinueta, 1768, SG 145, no. 1037.

15. Joseph V. Metzgar, "The Atrisco Land Grant, 1692–1977," New Mexico Historical Review 52 (October 1977): 272.

16. Ibid.

17. Petition by Joseph Hurtado de Mendoza et al. to Governor Pedro Fermín de Mendinueta, 1768, SG 145, no. 1037. Translated by Joseph P. Sánchez.

18. Ibid., no. 1038. Translated by Joseph P. Sánchez.

19. Río Puerco Land Grant conceded to the settlers of Atrisco, signed by Governor Pedro Fermín de Mendinueta, 1768, Villa de Santa Fe, SG 145, no. 1042. Translated by Joseph P. Sánchez.

20. Auto signed by Francisco Trébol Navarro, May 6, 1768, Puesto de San Isidro de Pajarito, SG 145, no. 1043; and Citación signed by Francisco Trébol Navarro, May 8, 1768, Puesto de la Población de San Fernando, SG 145, no. 1044.

21. Statement signed by Francisco Trébol Navarro, May 9, 1768, Población de San Fernando en el Río Puerco, SG 145, no. 1045. Translated by Joseph P. Sánchez.

22. Ibid.

23. Ibid.

24. Ibid.

25. Statement signed by Francisco Trébol Navarro, May 9, 1768, Población de San Fernando en el Río Puerco, SG 145, no. 1046. Translated by Joseph P. Sánchez.

26. Ibid.

27. Ibid., no. 1046–47.

28. Ibid., no. 1047. Translated by Joseph P. Sánchez.

29. Ibid.

30. Ibid., no. 1048. Translated by Joseph P. Sánchez.

31. In present-day terms, it is roughly ten miles from Las Barrancas (the bluffs seen as one drives west on Interstate 40 across the Río Grande bridge) to the Río Puerco. A red, ferrous hill on the left as one descends on Interstate 40 to the Río Puerco is Cerro Colorado.

32. Petition of the Settlers of San Fernando, 1767, SANM I, microfilm roll 4, frames 623–43. See also Twitchell, Spanish Archives, 1, no. 692.

33. Petition of the Settlers of San Fernando, 1767, SANM I, microfilm roll 4, frames 623–43.

34. Ibid., frames 625–35.

35. Ibid., frame 628.

36. Ibid.

37. Ibid.

38. Petition signed by Juan Bautista Montaño, Antonio Joseph Castillo, Antonio Montaño, Ignacio Jaramillo, Antonio Candelaria, Agustín Gallegos, María Gallegos, Pedro Montaño, Tomás Gurulé, Joseph de Jesús Montaño, Mateo Antonio Durán signed for Antonio Durán, 1770, SANM I, microfilm roll 5, frames 1466–69. See also Twitchell, Spanish Archives, 1, no. 1083.

39. Petition signed by Juan Bautista Montaño et al., 1770, SANM I, microfilm roll 5, frame 1467.

40. Ibid., frames 1466–67.

41. Antonio Baca to Governor Pedro Fermín de Mendinueta, May 31, 1770, Villa de Santa Fe, SANM I, microfilm roll 5, frame 1470.

42. Ibid.

43. Statement signed by Governor Pedro Fermín de Mendinueta, May 31, 1770,

Villa de Santa Fe, SANM I, microfilm roll 5, frames 1470–72. Translated by Joseph P. Sánchez.

44. Twitchell, Spanish Archives, 1:91

45. Statement signed by Governor Pedro Fermín de Mendinueta, May 31, 1770, Villa de Santa Fe, SANM I, microfilm roll 5, frame 1472. Translated by Joseph P. Sánchez.

46. Statement signed by Juan Bautista Montaño to Governor Pedro Fermín de Mendinueta, n.d., SANM I, microfilm roll 5, frame 1466.

47. Statement signed by Carlos Mirabal, June 20, 1770, Puesto de Nuestra Señora de la Luz, SANM I, microfilm roll 5, frame 1474.

48. Statement by Carlos Mirabal, June 20, 1770, Paraje de Nuestra Señora de la Luz del Río Puerco, SANM I, microfilm roll 5, frame 1475.

49. Statement signed by Carlos Mirabal, June 20, 1770, Puesto de Nuestra Señora de la Luz, SANM I, microfilm roll 5, frame 1475.

50. Notification signed by Governor Pedro Fermín de Mendinueta, July 1, 1770, Villa de Santa Fe, SANM I, microfilm roll 5, frame 1479. See also frames 1477–79.

51. Twitchell, Spanish Archives, 1:90–91.

52. Ibid., 1:92.

53. Statement signed by Bernabel Manuel Montaño de Cuéllar, March 3, 1772, Puesto de Nuestra Señora de la Luz de San Fernando y San Blas, SANM I, microfilm roll 2, frame 479.

54. Ibid.

55. Concuerda signed by Governor Pedro Fermín de Mendinueta, n.d., SANM I, microfilm roll 5, frame 482.

Chapter 9

1. Ted J. Warner, ed., and Fray Angélico Chávez, trans., The Domínguez-Escalante Journal: Their Expedition through Colorado, Utah, Arizona, and New Mexico in 1776 (Salt Lake City: University of Utah Press, 1995), 142, n. 472.

2. Palladini, "Don Fernando's Legacy," 52.

3. Ibid., 53.

4. Ibid., 61.

5. Ibid., 56.

6. Ibid., 58.

7. Ibid., 59.

8. Twitchell, Spanish Archives, 241, no. 878.

9. Ibid., 266, no. 887.

10. Ibid., 316, no. 1064.

11. Ibid., 266, no. 889.

12. Ibid., 46, no. 130.

13. Conveyance of Land by Doña Tomasa Tenorio, February 3, 1782, Puesto de Atrisco, SG 145, no. 1171. Translated by Surveyor General. A second, but incomplete, copy of the conveyance can be found in Thomasa Tenorio, widow of Salva-

dor Jaramillo, to Miguel Jaramillo, son, February 3, 1782. Yrisarri Family Papers, Conveyances, Atrisco, New Mexico State Records Center and Archives, Santa Fe.

14. Conveyance of Land by Doña Tomasa Tenorio, February 3, 1782, Puesto de Atrisco, SG 145, no. 1171.

15. Ibid.

16. Ibid.

17. Presentation of Francisco Antonio Chaves and Bartolomé Montoya against Diego Antonio Chaves on damages and boundaries, Year 1786, No. 3, CPLC 45, no. 739. Translated by Court of Private Land Claims. For a copy of the Spanish document of the same proceedings, see "Francisco Antonio Chabes and Bartolomé Montoya, Proceeding against Diego Antonio Chaves for access to their lands, 1786, Atrisco. SANM I, roll 1, frames 1404–1408.

18. Presentation of Francisco Antonio Chaves and Bartolomé Montoya against Diego Antonio Chaves on damages and boundaries, Year 1786, No. 3, CPLC 45, no. 740. Translated by Court of Private Land Claims.

19. Decision by Governor Juan Bautista de Anza, May 16, 1786, Villa de Santa Fe, CPLC 45, no. 741. Translated by Court of Private Land Claims.

20. Ibid.

21. Notification presented by Alcalde Mayor of the Jurisdiction of Alburquerque, Manuel de Arteaga, April 17, 1786, San Agustín de Isleta, CPLC 45, no. 742.

22. Notification of Sale signed by Alcalde Mayor Manuel de Arteaga, October 5, 1798, Plaza de San Andrés de Los Padillas, SG 145, no. 1124. Translated by Office of the Surveyor General.

23. Ibid., no. 1125.

24. Ibid.

25. Ibid., no. 1126.

26. Ibid., no. 1127.

27. Conveyance of Sale signed by Alcalde Mayor Manuel de Arteaga, May 9, 1804, San Andrés de Pajarito, SG 145, no. 1135. Translated by Will M. Tipton, U. S. Surveyor General's Office, March 30, 1886.

28. Ibid., no. 1136.

29. Ibid.

30. Ibid., no. 1137.

31. Ibid., no. 1137–38.

32. Ibid., no. 1138.

33. Notarized Notification of Sale signed by Marcos Lobato, Justice of the Peace, and witnesses Juan Antonio Sarracino and José Antonio Chaves, n.d., SG 145, no. 1139.

34. Conveyance of Land by Don Francisco Antonio Chaves, January 23, 1815, San Felipe de Neri de Alburquerque, SG 145, no. 1114. Translated by Will M. Tipton, Surveyor General's Office, March 30, 1886, Santa Fe, New Mexico Territory.

35. Conveyance of Land by Don Francisco Antonio Chaves, January 23, 1815, San Felipe de Neri de Alburquerque, SG 145, no. 1114.

36. Ibid., no. 1115.

37. Ibid., no. 1116–17.

38. Ibid., no. 1116.

39. Ibid., no. 1115.

40. Marc Simmons, The Little Lion of the Southwest: A Life of Manuel Antonio Chaves (Chicago: Swallow Press, 1973), 11.

41. Simmons, Little Lion of the Southwest, 1.

42. Ibid., 24.

43. Willa Cather, Death Comes for the Archbishop (New York: Vintage Books, [1927]1971), 183.

44. Diario, signed by Juan Armijo, October 23, 1821, Mexican Archives of New Mexico (hereinafter MANM), microfilm roll 1, frames 273–79.

45. Ibid.

46. Ibid.

47. Ibid.

48. Ibid.

49. Ibid.

50. Ibid.

51. Ibid.

Chapter 10

1. David J. Weber, ed., "An Unforgettable Day: Facundo Melgares on Independence," New Mexico Historical Review 48 (1973), 27. See also Joseph P. Sánchez and Janet LeCompte, "When Santa Fe Was a Mexican Town," in Santa Fe: A History of an Ancient City, ed. David Grant Noble (Santa Fe, N.Mex.: School of American Research, rev. ed. 2008), 79–96.

2. Weber, "Unforgettable Day," 32. See also Sánchez and LeCompte, "When Santa Fe Was a Mexican Town."

3. Weber, "Unforgettable Day," 39. See also Sánchez and LeCompte, "When Santa Fe Was a Mexican Town."

4. Ibid.

5. Weber, "Unforgettable Day," 38.

6. Ibid., 33. See also Sánchez and LeCompte, "When Santa Fe Was a Mexican Town."

7. Marc Simmons, Spanish Government in New Mexico (Albuquerque: University of New Mexico Press, 1968), 219.

8. En la plaza de los ranchos de Atrisco, February 2, 1833, signed by Toribio Sedillo, presidente, and secretaries Tránsito Román Sánchez, Matías Castillo, and José Baca, MANM, microfilm roll 16, frame 694.

9. A transcribed and annotated copy of the Plan de Pitic is published in Joseph P. Sánchez, "El Plan de Pitic de 1789 y las nuevas poblaciones proyectadas en las provincias internas de la Nueva España," Colonial Latin American Historical Review 2, no. 4 (Fall 1993): 449–67. See also Iris H. W. Engstrand, "A Note on the Plan of Pitic, Colonial Latin American Historical Review 3, no. 1 (Winter 1994): 78. For

a brief view of the historical precedent of the Plan de Pitic see Jane C. Sánchez, "The Plan of Pitic: Galindo Navarro's Letter to Teodoro de Croix, Comandante General de las Provincias Internas," Colonial Latin American Historical Review 3, no. 1 (Winter 1994): 79–89. Jane Sánchez writes, p. 79:

> The correspondence . . . discusses the need for formation of the Plan of Pitic for an area in which the laws of the Recopilación de Indias de 1680 could not be applied in toto. The correspondence also contains many suggestions about what should be included in the plan, most of which were implemented. Like many legal papers of the period, it draws an accurate picture of the legal values of the colonial culture. Toward the end of the Spanish period, the Plan de Pitic of 1789 reiterated the legal usage of propios in the establishment of the town of Pitic (present Hermosillo). Later, the Plan de Pitic was applied to the establishment of towns in Alta California in the eighteenth century as well as to other areas in New Spain's northern frontier. Indeed, the Plan de Pitic was a short, ready-to-use reference of the Laws of the Indies that related to land tenure.

Historian Iris W. H. Engstrand emphasizes the importance of the Plan de Pitic in regard to town founding throughout the frontier provinces of New Spain. She observes:

> Although the Plan of Pitic was formally adopted after the first two pueblos in Alta California were founded (San José in 1777 and Los Angeles in 1781), it was used as a guideline for founding the Villa de Branciforte between Monterey and San Francisco in the mid-1790s. The Plan, because it restated the municipal ordinance contained in the Laws of the Indies, and embodied the regulations used for town founding throughout the frontier provinces of New Spain, is a key document to be studied in understanding Spain's well-established rules for civilian settlement.

10. J. J. Bowden, "Private Land Claims in the Southwest" (LLM thesis, Southern Methodist University, 1969), 71.

11. Ibid., 74.

12. Ibid., 76.

13. Ibid., 82.

14. Last Will and Testament of Miguel Jaramillo, March 30, 1823, Alburquerque, SG 143, no. 1153.

15. Last Will and Testament of Miguel Jaramillo, March 30, 1823, Alburquerque, SG 145.

16. Ibid.

17. Ibid.

18. Ibid.

19. Decree of January 1824, SMLL, 116. The Constitutive Act reads:

> Art.1. The Mexican Nation is composed of the provinces comprised

in the viceroyalty formerly called New Spain in what was called the Captaincy General of Yucatan and in the Commandancies General of the Internal Provinces of the East and of the West. . . .

#7. The States of the Federation for the present are the following: Guanajuato; the Internal State of the West, composed of the Provinces of Sonora and Sinaloa; the Internal State of the East, composed of the Provinces of Coahuila, New Leon and Texas; the Internal [State] of the North, composed of the Provinces of Chihuahua, Durango and New Mexico; Mexico; Michoacan; Oaxaca; Puebla de los Angeles; Quereta-ro; San Luis Potosi; New Santander, which shall be called Tamaulipas; Tlaxcala; Vera Cruz; Jalisco, Yucatan; the Californias, etc.

20. Decree of July 6, 1824, SMLL, 117. "The Sovereign General Constituent Congress has seen fit to decree: Art. 4. The Province of New Mexico remains a Territory of the Federation."

21. Law of March 20, 1837, SMLL, 211–21.

22. Decree of June 13, 1843, SMLL, p. 243. It should be noted that as the War between the United States and Mexico began in May 1846, officials in Mexico City met in August and formed the Plan of August 4, 1846, SMLL, p. 253. In the throes of war and civil war, the central government restored the Constitution of 1824 and suspended the asambleas because they were incompatible with the fundamental codes of that venerable document, Decree of August 22, 1846, SMLL, p. 256. In New Mexico, the Asamblea remained in force and its members surrendered New Mexico to the Army of the West under General Stephen Watts Kearney.

23. Caleb Cushing, "Mexico in 1843," in The Cushing Reports: Ambassador Caleb Cushing's Confidential Diplomatic Reports to the United States Secretary of State, 1843–1844, ed. Margaret Diamond Benetz (Salisbury, N.C.: Documentary Collections, 1976), 13.

24. Ibid., 13–14.

25. Regulations for the Colonization of the Territories, November 21, 1828, SMLL, 141. The purpose of these regulations was to clarify the Decree of August 18, 1824.

26. Ibid.

27. Decree of June 13, 1843, SMLL, 77.

28. Law of March 20, 1837, SMLL, 221.

29. Charles F. Coan, A History of New Mexico, 3 vols. (Chicago: American Historical Society, 1925), 1:320–21.

30. Lansing B. Bloom, "New Mexico under Mexican Administration," Old Santa Fe 2 (July 1914–April 1915): 4.

31. Ibid., 3.

32. Ibid., 4.

33. "El Ciudadano Albino Pérez, Coronel de Caballería del Ejército permanente Jefe Político y Militar del Territorio del Nuevo México a sus conciudadanos," Santa Fe, June 26, 1835, Governors Papers, MANM, University of New Mexico microfilm.

34. Ibid.

35. Order from Albino Pérez, October 16, 1835, Ritch Papers, microfilm roll 2, frame 153, University of New Mexico.

36. Benjamin M. Read, An Illustrated History of New Mexico. ([Santa Fe: New Mexican Printing Company], 1912): 373–74.

37. Josiah Gregg, Commerce of the Prairies, or, The journal of a Santa Fè trader: During eight expeditions across the great western prairies, and a residence of nearly nine years in northern Mexico (New York: H. G. Langley, 1844), 1:130

38. Bloom, New Mexico under Mexican Administration, 13.

39. Ralph Emerson Twitchell, The Leading Facts of New Mexican History (Cedar Rapids: Torch Press, 1912), 2:57.

40. Ibid., 58.

41. Ibid., 56–57.

42. Ibid., 58.

43. Benjamin Read Papers, MANM, microfilm roll 24, frame 807.

44. Gregg, Commerce of the Prairies, 1:130.

45. Ibid.

46. Depositions and certificates testifying to the loyalty of Donaciano Vigil in the fight with the insurrectionists in August 1837, Ritch Papers, microfilm roll 24, frame 169, University of New Mexico.

47. Gregg, Commerce of the Prairies, 1:131–32.

48. Marc Simmons, Hispanic Albuquerque, 1706–1846 (Albuquerque: University of New Mexico Press, 2003), 139.

49. Ibid., 139; Gregg, Commerce of the Prairies, 1:331–32.

50. Hubert Howe Bancroft, Arizona and New Mexico, 17:318.

51. "Año de mil ochocientos," Atisbos: Journal of Chicano Research (Stanford University, Summer–Fall 1978): 182. Translated by Joseph P. Sánchez and Roberto Bacalski.

52. The Santa Fe New Mexican, June 15, 1901, p. 1.

53. Ibid.

54. Ibid.

55. Bancroft, Arizona and New Mexico, 17:320.

56. "Alos habitantes de Santa Fe y los demas pueblos de Nuevo Mexico al Oriente del Rio Grande," [1841], Daughters of the Republic of Texas Library, San Antonio, Texas. Much has been written about the purpose of the Texans in going to New Mexico. Although some writers have denied it, the commissioners had propaganda literature with them.

57. Anonymous note in Peter Gallagher, "A Journal of the Santa Fe Expedition," manuscript in the Daughters of the Republic of Texas Library, San Antonio, Texas.

58. Bancroft, Arizona and New Mexico, 17:320.

59. Gallagher, Journal, 31.

60. Ibid.

61. Bancroft, Arizona and New Mexico, 17:322.

62. A. J. Sowell, The Santa Fe Expedition (Houston: Union National Bank, 1929), 3.

63. Ibid., 3.

64. George Wilkins Kendall, Narrative of the Texan Santa Fé Expedition, 2 vols. (New York, Harper and Brothers, 1850), 1: 382.

65. Ibid., 1:383.

66. Ibid., 1:386.

67. Manuel Armijo, Proclamation, November 10, 1841, Santa Fe, Ina Sizer Cassidy Collection in Ritch Collection, no. 94, folder no. 3. New Mexico State Records Center and Archives, Santa Fe.

68. Bancroft, Arizona and New Mexico, 17:324.

69. Decree of August 18, 1824, Article 5, SMLL, 121.

70. Bowden, "Private Land Claims in the Southwest," 73.

71. Twitchell, Leading Facts, 2:196–97. See also Alan Ward Minge, "Frontier Problems in New Mexico Preceding the Mexican War, 1840–1846" (PhD diss., University of New Mexico, 1965), 306.

72. Victor Westphall, "Fraud and the Implications of Fraud in the Land Grants of New Mexico," New Mexico Historical Review 49 (July 1974): 199–200. William Keleher, The Maxwell Land Grant: A New Mexico Item (Santa Fe, N.Mex.: William Gannon, 1942); Jim Berry Pearson, The Maxwell Land Grant (Norman: University of Oklahoma Press, 1961); and Morris F. Taylor, "The Two Land Grants of Gervacio Nolan," New Mexico Historical Review 47 (April 1972), led the way in the individual treatment of land grants. Recent studies of land grants in northern New Mexico have been written by G. Emlen Hall, Four Leagues of Pecos: A Legal History of the Pecos Grant, 1800–1933 (Albuquerque: University of New Mexico Press, 1984); Anselmo Arellano, "Through Thick and Thin: Evolutionary Transitions of Las Vegas Grandes and Its Pobladores" (PhD diss., University of New Mexico, 1990); and Paul Kutsche and John Van Ness, Cañones: Values, Crisis, and Survival in a Northern New Mexico Village (Albuquerque: University of New Mexico Press, 1981). An excellent exposition of history and historiography has been written by Malcolm Ebright in Land Grants and Lawsuits in Northern New Mexico (Albuquerque: University of New Mexico Press, 1994).

73. Lawrence R. Murphy, "The Beaubien and Miranda Land Grant, 1841–1846," New Mexico Historical Review 52 (January 1967): 27–46. See also Keleher, Maxwell Land Grant (1942), and Pearson, Maxwell Land Grant (1961).

74. Taylor, "Two Land Grants of Gervacio Nolan," 151–84.

75. Herbert O. Brayer, William Blackmore: The Spanish-Mexican Land Grants of New Mexico and Colorado, 1863–1878 (Denver: Bradford-Robinson, 1949), 59–62.

76. Harold H. Dunham, "Cerán St. Vrain," in The Mountain Men, vol. 5, ed. Leroy Hafen (Glendale, Calif.: Arthur H. Clark, 1966), 310–11; Twitchell, Spanish Archives, 1:276–77.

77. Murphy, "Beaubien and Miranda," 32–33, 35; Twitchell, Spanish Archives, 1:276–77; Bowden, "Private Land Claims in the Southwest," 3:775–76.

Chapter 11

1. Article 8 of the Treaty of Guadalupe Hidalgo:

> Mexicans now established in territories previously belonging to Mexico, and which remain for the future within the limits of the United States, as defined by the present Treaty, shall be free to continue where they now reside, or to remove at any time to the Mexican Republic retaining the property which they possess in the said territories, or disposing thereof and removing the proceeds wherever they please; without their being subjected, on this account, to any contribution, tax or charge whatever.
>
> Those who shall prefer to remain in the said territories, may either retain the title and rights of Mexican citizens, or acquire those of citizens of the United States. But, they shall be under the obligation to make their election within one year from the date of the exchange of ratifications of this treaty; and those who shall remain in the said territories, after the expiration of that year, without having declared their intention to retain the character of Mexicans, shall be considered to have elected to become citizens of the United States.
>
> In the said territories, property of every kind, now belonging to Mexicans not established there, shall be inviolably respected. The present owners, the heirs of these, and all Mexicans who may hereafter acquire said property by contract, shall enjoy with respect to it, guaranties equally ample as if the same belonged to citizens of the United States.

Article 9:

> The Mexicans who, in the territories aforesaid, shall not preserve the character of citizens of the Mexican Republic, conformably with what is stipulated in the preceding article, shall be incorporated into the Union of the United States and be admitted at the proper time to be judged of by the Congress of the United States to the enjoyment of all the rights of citizens of the United States according to the principles of the Constitution; and in the mean time shall be maintained and protected in the free enjoyment of their liberty and property, and secured in the free exercise of their religion without restriction.

2. Richard Griswold del Castillo, The Treaty of Guadalupe Hidalgo: A Legacy of Conflict (Norman: University of Oklahoma Press, 1990), 78. It should be noted that the Treaty of Guadalupe Hidalgo affected Texas, already a state of the Union, only with respect to confirming the Río Grande as an international boundary. See The Handbook of Texas, 6 vols. (Austin: Texas State Historical Association, 1998), 6:559. Armando C. Alonso writes of South Texas in Tejano Legacy: Rancheros and

Settlers in South Texas, 1734–1900 (Albuquerque: University of New Mexico Press, 1998), 145, that

> at the end of the war, the older Mexican landholders on the north bank of the Río Grande often found themselves uncertain as to their rights to the lands, despite what Mexicans believed to be specific guarantees to their property and civil rights under Articles 8 and 9 of the Treaty of Guadalupe Hidalgo. The treaty itself provided no standard for validation of land grants. . . . By virtue of its prior claim to the Trans-Nueces, the state of Texas controlled the process in the newly annexed lands. Not surprisingly, some Anglos used new laws and the courts to their advantage to gain land, and occasionally resorted to devious means to subvert the Mexicans' position as dominant landholders.

3. Griswold del Castillo, Treaty of Guadalupe Hidalgo, 62.

4. Ibid., 69.

5. Robert W. Larson, New Mexico's Quest for Statehood, 1846–1912 (Albuquerque: University of New Mexico Press, 1968), 19.

6. Griswold del Castillo, Treaty of Guadalupe Hidalgo, 70.

7. George Carter v. Territory of New Mexico, 1 N.M. 317 (1859).

8. Ibid., 321.

9. Ibid., 317.

10. Ibid.

11. Ibid.

12. Ibid., 319.

13. Ibid.

14. Ibid.

15. Ibid., 320.

16. Ibid.

17. Ibid., 325, 337.

18. Ibid., 338.

19. Ibid., 339.

20. Ibid., 345.

21. Martín González de la Vara, "El traslado de familias de Nuevo México al norte de Chihuahua y la conformación de una región fronteriza, 1848–1854," Frontera Norte 6, no. 11 (January–June 1994): 15.

22. Ibid., 13.

23. Ibid., 15.

24. Hurtado v. California, 110 U.S. 516 (1884).

25. Albuquerque Land and Irrigation Co. v. Gutierrez, 10 N.M. 177, 197–98 (1900).

26. Ibid., 208.

27. Ibid., 208–209.

28. Ibid., 212–13.

29. Ibid., 253.

30. Ibid.

31. Ibid., 255.

32. Daniel Tyler, "The Spanish Colonial Legacy and the Role of Hispanic Custom in Defining New Mexico Land and Water Rights," Colonial Latin American Historical Review 4, no. 2 (Spring 1995): 165.

33. Griswold del Castillo, Treaty of Guadalupe Hidalgo, 87.

34. Ibid., 107.

35. Ibid., 88.

Chapter 12

1. Robert Wells Bradfute, The Court of Private Land Claims: The Adjudication of Spanish and Mexican Land Grant Titles, 1891–1904 (Albuquerque: University of New Mexico Press, 1975), 7.

2. Bradfute, Court of Private Land Claims, 12.

3. Bowden, "Private Land Claims in the Southwest," 249.

4. Bradfute, Court of Private Land Claims, 12.

5. Ibid., 12–13.

6. Ibid., 2–3.

7. The Town of Atrisco Grant, SG 145. These details are discussed in chapter 8.

8. Ibid.

9. Ibid.

10. Metzgar, "Atrisco Land Grant," 75.

11. Original document in the files of Mr. Ramon Herrera, a land grant heir of Atrisco.

12. Metzgar, "Atrisco Land Grant," 275.

13. An Act to Amend Section 38 of An Act of the 29th Legislative Assembly of the Territory of New Mexico, Entitled "An Act Relating to Community Land Grants, and for Other Purposes." II. B. 200 (Approved February 26, 1891). Laws of New Mexico, 1891, ch. 86, 174, University of New Mexico Law School Library, fiches 55 and 56.

14. Section 2, An Act Relating to Community Land Grants, Laws of New Mexico, 1891, ch. 86, 164.

15. Metzgar, "Atrisco Land Grant," 276.

16. Town of Atrisco v. The United States of America and the City of Albuquerque, 1892, CPLC 45.

17. Bradfute, Court of Private Land Claims, 14.

18. Ibid., 15.

19. Twitchell, Leading Facts, 2:464–65.

20. Court of Private Land Claims Act, Chap. 539, 26 Stat., 854 (1891).

21. Ibid. Regarding the date of expiration for filing petitions for land claims, sect. 12 states:

> That all claims mentioned in section six of this act which are by the provisions of this act authorized to be prosecuted shall, at the end of two years from the taking effect of this act, if no petition in respect

to the same shall have then been filed as hereinbefore provided be deemed and taken, in all courts and elsewhere, to be abandoned and shall be forever barred: Provided, That in any case where it shall come to the knowledge of the court that minors, married women, or persons non compos mentis are interested in any land claim or matter brought before the court it shall be its duty to appoint a guardian ad litem for such persons under disability and require a petition to be filed in their behalf, as in other cases, and if necessary to appoint counsel for the protection of their rights.

22. Ibid. Regarding subsoil mineral rights, sect. 13, pt. 3 states:

Third. No allowance or confirmation of any claim shall confer any right or title to any gold, silver, or quicksilver mines or minerals of the same, unless the grant claimed effected the donation or sale of such mines or minerals to the grantee, or unless such grantee had become otherwise entitled thereto in law or in equity; but all such mines and minerals shall remain the property of the United States, with the right of working the same, which fact shall be stated in all patents issued under this act. But no such mine shall be worked on any property confirmed under this act without the consent of the owner of such property until specially authorized thereto by an act of Congress here-after passed.

23. Ibid. Regarding appeal to the Supreme Court, sect. 9 states:

That the party against whom the court shall in any case decide—the United States, in case of the confirmation of a claim in whole or in part, and the claimant, in case of the rejection of a claim, in whole or in part—shall have the right of appeal to the Supreme Court of the United States, such appeal to be taken within six months from the date of such decision, and in all respects to be taken in the same man-ner and upon the same conditions except in respect of the amount in controversy, as is now provided by law for the taking of appeals from decisions of the circuit courts of the United States. On any such appeal the Supreme Court shall retry the cause, as well the issues of fact as of law, and may cause testimony to be taken in addition to that given in the court below as truth and justice may require; and on such retrial and hearing every question shall be open, and the decision of the Su-preme Court thereon shall be final and conclusive. Should no appeal be taken as aforesaid the decree of the court below shall be final and conclusive.

24. Ibid. In that regard, sect. 13, pt. 16 states:

That in township surveys hereafter to be made in the Territories of New Mexico, Arizona, and Utah, and in the States of Colorado, Nevada, and Wyoming if it shall be made to appear to the satisfaction of the deputy surveyor making such survey that any person has, through himself, his ancestor, grantors, or their lawful successors in title or possession, been in the continuous adverse actual bona fide possession, resident thereon as his home, of any tract of land or in connection therewith of other lands, all together not exceeding one hundred and sixty acres in such township for twenty years next preceding the time of making such survey, the deputy surveyor shall recognize and establish the lines of such possession and make the subdivision of the adjoining lands in accordance therewith. Such possession shall be accurately defined in the field notes of the survey and delineated on the township plat with the boundaries and area of the tract as a separate legal subdivision. The deputy surveyor shall return with his survey the name or names of all persons so found to be in possession, with a proper description of the tract in the possession of each as shown by the survey, and the proofs furnished to him of such possession.

25. Ibid., sect. 16.

26. Statistics in this paragraph are from Bowden, "Private Land Claims in the Southwest," 243–48.

27. Bowden, "Private Land Claims in the Southwest," 248. See also Chaves v. United States, CPLC, manuscript no. 57.).

28. See chapters 2–8 for the historical development of the grants within each of these themes.

29. Decree by the District Court, County of Bernalillo, Territory of New Mexico, Case no. 3278, CPLC 45.

30. Metzgar, "Atrisco Land Grant," 277.

31. Town of Atrisco v. U.S., 1892, CLPC 45.

32. The boundaries described in this petition are consistent with all previous descriptions.

[Regarding the 1692 Grant] On the North by the barranca de Juan de Perea; on the South by lands of Captain Antonio Baca; on the East by the Rio Grande, on the West by the ceja (ridge) of the Rio Puerco.

[Regarding the 1768 Grant] On the North, commencing at a point two (2) leagues south of the Town of San Fernando, in front of two large cottonwood trees standing close together,—on the South by a bent cottonwood tree, called and known as "el alamo gacho," a point three (3) leagues south of the said two large cottonwood trees before mentioned; on the West by the Rio Puerco and on the East by the ridge (ceja) of a hill called the Rio Puerco Mountain, the same being the western boundary of the first before-mentioned tract.

33. Town of Atrisco v. U.S., 1892, CPLC 45.

34. Ibid.

35. Answer of the City of Albuquerque, Town of Atrisco v. U.S., 1892, CPLC 45.

36. Ibid.

37. Ibid.

38. City of Albuquerque v. United States, no. 8, in Town of Atrisco v. U.S., 1892, CPLC 45.

39. Town of Atrisco v. U.S., 1892, CPLC 45.

40. "Comes now the Atlantic and Pacific Railroad Company," Town of Atrisco v. U.S., 1892, CPLC 45.

41. "Comes now the United States by its attorney," Town of Atrisco v. U.S., 1892, CPLC 45.

42. Ibid.

43. Statement signed by Eusebio Chacón, Town of Atrisco v. U.S., 1892, CPLC 45.

44. Deraignment of Title of plaintiff, Town of Atrisco v. U.S., 1892, CPLC 45. The document reads:

> The incorporators of the Town of Atrisco are the lineal descendants and heirs of the original grantees to the land included in the Grant made on the twenty-eighth day of October A.D. 1692, and to the land included in the Grant made on the twenty-eighth day of April A.D. 1768, by the Government and Kingdom of Spain to the inhabitants of the Town or Community of Atrisco, the names of the said incorporators include all the owners, occupants and residents of the land described in said two grants, including the following:
>
> Antonio Jose Chaves, one of the incorporators of the Town of Atrisco, is the son and heir of Antonio Chaves and of Manuelita García de Chaves. Antonio Chaves was the son of and heir of Pablo Chaves. Pablo Chaves was a brother and heir of Efigenia Chaves. Efigenia Chaves was one of the original grantees of the Atrisco Grant. Manuelita García de Chaves was the daughter and heir of Tomas García. Tomas García was one of the original grantees of the Atrisco Grant.
>
> Juan Baca, one of the incorporators of the Town of Atrisco, is the son and heir of Jose Baca and Maria Antonia García de Baca. Maria Antonia García de Baca was the daughter and heir of Tomas García. Tomas García was one of the original grantees.
>
> Juan Sanchez, one of the incorporators of the Town of Atrisco, is a son and heir of Ramon Sanchez. Ramon Sanchez was the son and heir of Rafael Sanchez. Rafael Sanchez was the son and heir of Pedro Sanchez. Pedro Sanchez was one of the original grantees of the Atrisco Grant.
>
> Jose de la Luz Sanchez, one of the incorporators of the Town of Atrisco and one of the Trustees of said Town, is the son and heir of Diego Antonio Sanchez. Diego Antonio Sanchez was the son and heir of Antonio Jose Sanchez. Antonio Jose Sanchez was the son of Jose Sanchez. Jose Sanchez was one of the original grantees of the Atrisco Grant.

45. Decision signed by Chief Justice Joseph R. Reed, September 4, 1894, Town

of Atrisco v. U.S., 1892, CPLC 45.

46. Decision signed by Chief Justice Joseph R. Reed, September 4, 1894, Town of Atrisco v. U.S., SG 145, New Mexico State Records Center and Archives, Santa Fe. See also Decision signed by Chief Justice Joseph R. Reed, September 4, 1994, Town of Atrisco v. U.S., 1892, CPLC 45.

47. Decision signed by Chief Justice Joseph R. Reed, September 4, 1894, Town of Atrisco v. U.S., 1892, CPLC 45.

48. "Comes now the United States," 1897, Town of Atrisco v. U.S., 1892, CPLC 45.

49. Metzgar, "Atrisco Land Grant," 279.

50. Ibid., 279–80.

51. Order by Chief Justice Joseph R. Reed, April 17, 1898, Santa Fe, New Mexico, Town of Atrisco v. U.S., 1892, CPLC 45.

52. Metzgar, "Atrisco Land Grant," 280.

Chapter 13

1. José María Romero, administrator of the estate of Trinidad R. de Jaramillo, v. Manuel Antonio Jaramillo, et al., in the District Court for the County of Bernalillo, Territory of New Mexico (1901), Case no. 5977, New Mexico State Records Center and Archives, Santa Fe.

2. Ibid.

3. Ibid.

4. Policarpio Armijo y Jaramillo was one of the signers of the commission to drive squatters out of Tajique in February 1884.

5. Romero v. Jaramillo.

6. José María Romero v. Manuel Antonio Jaramillo, et al. (1901), County Judgments Docket, Second Judicial District Court, New Mexico State Records Center and Archives.

7. Romero v. Jaramillo (1901), Signed statement by E. W. Dobson, June 3, 1901.

8. José María Romero, Administrator, versus Manuel Antonio Jaramillo, et al. (1901), Summons, filed on November 29, 1901.

9. Romero v. Jaramillo, Exhibit C, Transcript of Judgment Docket.

10. Ibid.

11. Ibid.

12. Ibid.

13. Ibid.

14. Ibid.

15. Ibid.

16. Statement by Jesús Armijo y Jaramillo notarized by B. S. Rodey, July 18, 1896, Transcript of Judgment, Romero v. Jaramillo.

17. Demurrer, Romero v. Jaramillo (1901).

18. Romero v. Jaramillo (1901), Complaint, Article 11, In the District Court

of the Second Judicial District of the Territory of New Mexico, within and for the County of Bernalillo.

19. Romero v. Jaramillo (1901), Territory of New Mexico, County of Bernalillo, In the District Court, signed by W. E. Dame, Clerk of the District Court of the Second Judicial District of the Territory of New Mexico, January 16, 1903.

20. Romero v. Jaramillo, Final Judgment and Decree, Article 6.

21. Ibid.

22. Romero v. Jaramillo, Final Judgment and Decree, Territorial Supreme Court, March 28, 1903.

Epilogue

1. Metzgar, "Atrisco Land Grant," 281.

2. Ibid.

3. "List of Ditches in Rio Grande Valley, New Mexico," in W. W. Follett, Civil Engineer of El Paso, Senate Documents, vol. 21, no. 229, 55th Congress, 2nd Session, pp. 47–177, 1896. Aside from Ranchos de Atrisco, the Upper Atrisco, with 42 acequias on that portion of the stream, used 1,620 acre-feet of water in 1894; 2,160 acre-feet of water in 1895; and 1,080 acre-feet of water in 1896. Similarly, the Middle Atrisco, with 43 acequias on that portion of the stream, used 900 acre-feet of water in 1894; 1,200 acre-feet of water in 1895; and 600 acre-feet of water in 1896. The Lower Atrisco, with 44 acequias on that portion of the stream, used 2,940 acre-feet of water in 1894; 3,920 acre-feet of water in 1895; and 1,960 acre-feet of water in 1896.

4. Metzgar, "Atrisco Land Grant," 281.

5. Ibid., 282.

6. Ibid., 282–83.

7. Ibid., 283.

8. Ibid.

9. Ibid.

10. Ibid., 286.

11. Alfredo Armijo v. Town of Atrisco, 56 N.M. 2, 6. (1952)

12. Ibid., 8.

13. Jake Armijo, Benjamin Benavidez, David J. Armijo, Trinidad Lovato, Ufella Gomes, Marcelino Saavedra, Manuel García, Tranquillino Barela, Roman Salas, Samuel García, Carlos Gomes, Rumaldo García, Filemon Chavez, B. W. Sloan, Arturo Gonzales, Max Griego, in their own behalf and in behalf of others similarly situated, Petitioners-Appellants, v. Town of Atrisco, a corporation, Respondent-Appellees, Case no. 6145, 62 N.M. 440, 446 (1957).

14. Jake Armijo, et al., v. Town of Atrisco, 62 N.M. 440, 445 (1957).

15. Ibid., 448.

16. Metzgar, "Atrisco Land Grant," 289.

17. See Joseph P. Sánchez, "Plan de Pitic de 1789."

18. See Joseph P. Sánchez, "Plan de Pitic de 1789."

19. Christi Chisholm, "A Place by the Water," Alibi (Albuquerque), December 15–21, 2005.

20. "Board Asked to Sit on Mesa Plan," Albuquerque Journal, West Side Journal supplement, August 31, 2006.

21. Jerome A. Padilla, quoted in Albuquerque Journal, March 15, 2006.

22. "Westland Purchase Vote Is Monday," Albuquerque Journal, West Side Journal supplement, November 2, 2006; "Judge Rejects Suit Against Westland Sale," Albuquerque Journal, West Side Journal supplement, November 3, 2006.

23. "Westland Acquisition Would Impact City," Albuquerque Journal, West Side Journal supplement, October 11, 2006.

24. Ibid.

25. Ibid.

26. "Land Grant Questions Addressed," Albuquerque Journal, West Side Journal supplement, July 5, 2006.

27. "Westland Acquisition Would Impact City," Albuquerque Journal, West Side Journal supplement, October 11, 2006.

28. Response by Rory McClannahan, reporter, in "Land Grant Questions Addressed," Albuquerque Journal, West Side Journal supplement, July 5, 2006.

29. "Shareholder's Votes on Westland's Fate Due Today," Albuquerque Journal, November 6, 2006.

30. "Board Asked to Sit on Mesa Plan," Albuquerque Journal, West Side Journal supplement, August 31, 2006. A subsequent article reiterates that "Westland had put together the Zacate Master Plan for 14,000 acres south of Interstate 40 at the request of Bernalillo County. The plan had been given to the county for consideration in 2005. . . . The plan had been scheduled to be considered by the commission in August, but Westland asked for several deferrals because the company was in the midst of a takeover bid, which eventually led [to] the SunCal deal in December." "SunCal May Toss Zacate Project," Albuquerque Journal, West Side Journal supplement, January 6, 2007.

31. "Board Asked to Sit on Mesa Plan," Albuquerque Journal, West Side Journal supplement, August 31, 2006; "SunCal May Toss Zacate Project," Albuquerque Journal, West Side Journal supplement, January 6, 2007.

32. "Land Grant Questions Addressed," Albuquerque Journal, West Side Journal supplement, July 5, 2006.

33. "SunCal May Toss Zacate Project," Albuquerque Journal, West Side Journal supplement, January 6, 2007.

34. "Shareholder Making Bid for Westland," Albuquerque Journal, West Side Journal supplement, October 24, 2006.

34. Ibid.

36. "Judge Rejects Suit Against Westland Sale," Albuquerque Journal, West Side Journal supplement, November 3, 2006.

37. "Sale of Westland Appears Likely," Albuquerque Journal, November 7, 2006.

38. "Westland Shareholders Approve Sale," Albuquerque Journal, West Side

Journal supplement, November 22, 2006.

39. Ibid.

40. "Westland Deal Nearly Done," Albuquerque Journal, West Side Journal supplement, December 9, 2006.

41. "Sale of Westland Appears Likely," Albuquerque Journal, November 7, 2006.

42. "Westland Deal Nearly Done," Albuquerque Journal, West Side Journal supplement, December 9, 2006.

43. Ibid.

Bibliography

Books and Articles

Adams, Eleanor B., ed. *Bishop Tamarón's Visitation of New Mexico, 1760.* Albuquerque: Historical Society of New Mexico, 1954.

Alonso, Armando. *Tejano Legacy: Rancheros and Settlers in South Texas, 1734–1900.* Albuquerque: University of New Mexico Press, 1998.

Bancroft, Hubert Howe. *History of Arizona and New Mexico, 1530–1888.* Vol. 17. San Francisco: History Company, 1889.

Baxter, John O. *Las Carneradas: Sheep Trade in New Mexico, 1700–1800.* Albuquerque: University of New Mexico Press, 1987.

Bloom, Lansing B. "New Mexico under Mexican Administration," *Old Santa Fe* 2 (July 1914–April 1915): 4.

Bolton, Herbert E. *Coronado: Knight of Pueblos and Plains.* Albuquerque: University of New Mexico Press, 1949.

———. *Spanish Exploration in the Southwest, 1542–1706.* New York: Barnes and Noble, 1952.

Bradfute, Robert Wells. *The Court of Private Land Claims: The Adjudication of Spanish and Mexican Land Grant Titles, 1891–1904.* Albuquerque: University of New Mexico Press, 1975.

Brayer, Herbert O. *William Blackmore: The Spanish-Mexican Land Grants of New Mexico and Colorado, 1863–1878.* Denver: Bradford-Robinson, 1949.

Carroll, H. Bailey, and J. Villasana Haggard, eds. and trans. *Three New Mexico Chronicles: The* Exposición *of Don Pedro Bautista Pino, 1812; the* Ojeada *of Lic. Antonio Barreiro, 1832; and the additions of Don José Agustín de Escudero, 1849.* Albuquerque: Quivira Society, 1942.

Casado-Fuente, Ovidio. *Don Francisco Cuerbo y Valdés: Gobernador de Nuevo México, fundador de la Ciudad de Alburquerque.* Oviedo, Spain: Principado de Asturias, Instituto de Estudios Asturianos, 1983.

Cather, Willa. *Death Comes for the Archbishop.* New York: Vintage Books, [1927]1971.

Chávez, Fray Angélico. "Don Fernando Durán y Chávez," *El Palacio* (Santa Fe, N.Mex.) 55, no. 4 (April 1948): 103–21.

———. *Origins of New Mexico Families in the Spanish Colonial Period.* Santa Fe, N.Mex.: William Gannon, 1975.

Cushing, Caleb. "Mexico in 1843." In *The Cushing Reports: Ambassador Caleb Cushing's Confidential Diplomatic Reports to the United States Secretary of State, 1843–1844,* edited by Margaret Diamond Benetz. Salisbury, N.C.: Documentary Collections, 1976.

Dunham, Harold H. "Cerán St. Vrain." In *The Mountain Men and the Fur Trade of the Far West*, 5. Edited by Leroy Hafen. Glendale, Calif.: Arthur H. Clark, 1966.

Dusenberry, William H. *The Mexican Mesta: The Administration of Ranching in Colonial Mexico*. Urbana: University of Illinois Press, 1963.

Ebright, Malcolm. *Land Grants and Lawsuits in Northern New Mexico*. Albuquerque: University of New Mexico Press, 1994.

Engstrand, Iris H. W. "A Note on the Plan of Pitic," *Colonial Latin American Historical Review* 3, no. 1 (Winter 1994): 73–78.

Espinosa, Gilberto, and Tibo J. Chavez. *El Rio Abajo*. Belen, N.Mex.: Bishop Publishing, n.d.

Gerhard, Peter. *A Guide to the Historical Geography of New Spain: A Revised Edition*. Norman: University of Oklahoma Press, 1993.

González de la Vara, Martín. "El traslado de familias de Nuevo México al norte de Chihuahua y la conformación de una región fronteriza, 1848–1854." *Frontera Norte* 6 (January–June 1994): 9–21.

Greenleaf, Richard E. "Atrisco and Las Ciruelas." *New Mexico Historical Review* 42 (January 1967): 5–25.

Griswold del Castillo, Richard. *The Treaty of Guadalupe Hidalgo: A Legacy of Conflict*. Norman: University of Oklahoma Press, 1990.

Hackett, Charles Wilson, ed. *Historical Documents Relating to New Mexico, Nueva Vizcaya, and Approaches Thereto, to 1773*. 3 vols. Washington, D.C.: Carnegie Institution of Washington, 1937.

———, ed. *Revolt of the Pueblo Indians of New Mexico, and Otermín's Attempted Reconquest, 1680–1682*. Translated by Charmion Clair Shelby. 2 vols. Albuquerque: University of New Mexico Press, 1942.

Hall, G. Emlen. *Four Leagues of Pecos: A Legal History of the Pecos Grant, 1800–1933*. Albuquerque: University of New Mexico Press, 1984.

Hammond, George P., and Agapito Rey, trans. *Narratives of the Coronado Expedition, 1540–1542*. Albuquerque: University of New Mexico Press, 1940.

———. *The Rediscovery of New Mexico, 1580–1594*. Albuquerque: University of New Mexico Press, 1966.

The Handbook of Texas. 6 vols. Austin: Texas State Historical Association, 1996.

Hordes, Stanley M. *To the End of the Earth: A History of the Crypto-Jews of New Mexico*. New York: Columbia University Press, 2005.

Karttunen, Frances. *An Analytical Dictionary of Nahuatl*. Norman: University of Oklahoma Press, 1983.

Keleher, William A. *The Maxwell Land Grant: A New Mexico Item*. Santa Fe, N.Mex.: William Gannon, 1942.

Kendall, George Wilkins. *Narrative of the Texan Santa Fé Expedition*. 2 vols. New York: Harper and Brothers, 1850.

Kutsche, Paul, and John Van Ness. *Cañones: Values, Crisis, and Survival in a Northern New Mexico Village*. Albuquerque: University of New Mexico Press, 1981.

Larson, Robert W. *New Mexico's Quest for Statehood, 1846–1912*. Albuquerque: University of New Mexico Press, 1968.

Metzgar, Joseph V. "The Atrisco Land Grant, 1692–1977." *New Mexico Historical Review* 52 (October 1977): 269–96.

Murphy, Lawrence R. "The Beaubien and Miranda Land Grant, 1841–1846." *New Mexico Historical Review* 52 (January 1967): 27–46.

Noble, David Grant, ed. *Santa Fe: History of an Ancient City*. Santa Fe, N.Mex.: School of American Research, 1989, rev. ed. 2008.

"Noticias que da Juan Candelaria vecino de esta villa de San Francisco Xavier de Albuquerque de edad de 84 años; nació el año de 1692." *New Mexico Historical Review* 4 (1929): 274–97.

Olmstead, Virginia Langham, transcriber. *Spanish and Mexican Censuses of New Mexico: 1750–1830*. Albuquerque: New Mexico Genealogical Society, 1981.

Pacheco, Joaquín F., Francisco de Cárdenas, and Luis Torres de Mendoza, eds. *Colección de documentos inéditos relativos al descubrimiento, conquista y organización de las antiguas posesiones españolas de América y Oceanía*. 42 vols. Madrid: M. B. de Quirós, 1864–1884.

Parish, William J. *The Charles Ilfeld Company: A Study of the Rise and Decline of Mercantile Capitalism in New Mexico*. Cambridge, Mass.: Harvard University Press, 1961.

Pearson, Jim Berry. *The Maxwell Land Grant*. Norman: University of Oklahoma Press, 1961.

Pino, Pedro Baptista. *The Exposition on the Province of New Mexico by Don Pedro Baptista Pino*. Translated and edited by Adrian Bustamante and Marc Simmons. Santa Fe: Rancho de las Golondrinas, and Albuquerque: University of New Mexico Press, 1995.

Read, Benjamin M. *An Illustrated History of New Mexico*. [Santa Fe: New Mexican Printing Company], 1912.

Sánchez, Jane C. "The Plan of Pitic: Galindo Navarro's Letter to Teodoro de Croix, Comandante General de las Provincias Internas." *Colonial Latin American Historical Review* 3 (Winter 1994): 79–89.

Sánchez, Joseph P. "Año Desgraciado, 1837: The Overthrow of New Mexico's Jefe Político Albino Pérez." *Atisbos: Journal of Chicano Research* (Stanford University, Summer–Fall 1978): 180–91.

———. *Don Fernando Duran y Chaves's Land and Legacy*. Albuquerque: National Park Service, Department of the Interior, 1999.

———. *Explorers, Traders, and Slavers: Forging the Old Spanish Trail, 1678–1859*. Salt Lake City: University of Utah Press, 1997.

———. "The Peralta-Ordóñez Affair and the Founding of Santa Fe." In *Santa Fe: History of an Ancient City*, edited by David Grant Noble. Santa Fe, N.Mex.: School of American Research, 1989.

———. "El Plan de Pitic de 1789 y las nuevas poblaciones proyectadas en las provincias internas de la Nueva España." *Colonial Latin American Historical Review* 2, no. 4 (Fall 1993): 449–67.

———. *The Río Abajo Frontier, 1540–1692: A History of Early Colonial New Mexico*. Albuquerque: Albuquerque Museum, 1987.

————. "Twelve Days in August: The Pueblo Revolt in Santa Fe." In *Santa Fe: History of an Ancient City*, edited by David Grant Noble. Santa Fe, N.Mex.: School of American Research, 1989.

Sánchez, Joseph P., and Janet Lecompte. "When Santa Fe Was a Mexican Town." In *Santa Fe: History of an Ancient City*, edited by David Grant Noble. Santa Fe, N.Mex.: School of American Research, rev. ed. 2008.

Sánchez, Fr. William. "Descendents of Francisco Muñoz." *Legacy* (January 14, 2007).

Simmons, Marc. *Hispanic Albuquerque, 1706–1846*. Albuquerque: University of New Mexico Press, 2003.

————. *The Little Lion of the Southwest: A Life of Manuel Antonio Chaves*. Chicago: Swallow Press, 1973.

————. *Spanish Government in New Mexico*. Albuquerque: University of New Mexico Press, 1968.

Sánchez, Fr. William. "Descendents of Francisco Muñoz." *Legacy*(January 14, 2007.

Sowell, A. J. *The Santa Fe Expedition*. Houston: Union National Bank, 1929.

Tate, Bill. *Guadalupe Hidalgo Treaty of Peace 1848 and the Gadsden Treaty with Mexico 1853*. Española, N.Mex.: Rio Grande Sun Press, 1969.

Taylor, Morris F. "The Two Land Grants of Gervacio Nolan." *New Mexico Historical Review* 47 (April 1972): 151–84.

Twitchell, Ralph Emerson. *The Leading Facts of New Mexican History*. 2 vols. Cedar Rapids: Torch Press, 1912.

————, ed. *The Spanish Archives of New Mexico*. 2 vols. Cedar Rapids: Torch Press, 1914.

Tyler, Daniel. "The Spanish Colonial Legacy and the Role of Hispanic Custom in Defining New Mexico Land and Water Rights." *Colonial Latin American Historical Review* 4, no. 2 (Spring 1995): 49–165.

U.S. General Accounting Office (GAO). Report to Congressional Requesters. *Treaty of Guadalpe Hidalgo: Findings and Possible Options Regarding Longstanding Community Land Grant Claims in New Mexico. El Tratado de Guadalupe Hidalgo: Hallazgos y opciones posibles con respecto a los reclamos de larga duración de mercedes de tierras comunitarias en Nuevo México*. Translated by Joseph P. Sánchez, Jerry Gurulé, and Mario Milliones. GAO-04-60 (June 2004).

Warner, Ted J., ed., and Fray Angélico Chávez, trans. *The Domínguez-Escalante Journal: Their Expedition through Colorado, Utah, Arizona, and New Mexico in 1776*. Salt Lake City: University of Utah Press, 1995.

Weber, David J., ed. "An Unforgettable Day: Facundo Melgares on Independence." *New Mexico Historical Review* 48 (1973): 27–44.

Westphall, Victor. "Fraud and the Implications of Fraud in the Land Grants of New

Mexico." *New Mexico Historical Review* 49 (July 1974): 189–218.

Dissertations and Theses

Arellano, Anselmo. "Through Thick and Thin: Evolutionary Transitions of *Las Vegas Grandes* and Its *Pobladores*." PhD diss., University of New Mexico, 1990.

Bowden, J. J. "Private Land Claims in the Southwest." 6 vols. LLM thesis, Southern Methodist University, 1969.

Minge, Allen Ward. "Frontier Problems in New Mexico Preceding the Mexican War, 1840–1846." PhD diss., University of New Mexico, 1965.

Palladini, Eric Louis. "Don Fernando's Legacy: A Microhistory of Atrisco, New Mexico, 1692–1821." Master's thesis, Tulane University, 1990.

Tyler, Daniel. "New Mexico in the 1820's: The First Administration of Manuel Armijo." PhD diss., University of New Mexico, 1970.

Index

www.ingramcontent.com/pod-product-compliance
Lightning Source LLC
Chambersburg PA
CBHW020855270326
41928CB00006B/713

* 9 7 8 0 8 0 6 1 9 4 0 8 0 *